The Pursuit of Signs

The Pursuit of Signs

Semiotics, Literature, Deconstruction

Jonathan Culler

Professor of English
Cornell University

Routledge & Kegan Paul
London and Henley

First published in 1981
by Routledge & Kegan Paul Ltd
39 Store Street, London WC1E 7DD and
Broadway House, Newtown Road,
Henley-on-Thames, Oxon RG9 1EN
Set in 10 on 12 pt Palatino by
Rowland Phototypesetting Ltd
Bury St Edmunds, Suffolk, England
and printed in the United States of America by
Vail-Ballou Press, Inc., Binghamton, New York

British Library Cataloguing in Publication Data

Culler, Jonathan

The pursuit of signs.
1. Semiotics and literature
I. Title
801   PN98.S46

ISBN 0-7100-0757-4
ISBN 0-7100-0758-2 Pbk

Contents

Preface   vii
Acknowledgments   xiii

Part One
1 Beyond Interpretation   3
2 In Pursuit of Signs   18

Part Two
3 Semiotics as a Theory of Reading   47
4 Riffaterre and the Semiotics of Poetry   80
5 Presupposition and Intertextuality   100
6 Stanley Fish and the Righting of the Reader   119

Part Three
7 Apostrophe   135
8 The Mirror Stage   155
9 Story and Discourse in the Analysis of Narrative   169
10 The Turns of Metaphor   188
11 Literary Theory in the Graduate Program   210

References   227
Index   239

Preface

One important feature of literary criticism in recent years has been the growth of interest in signs and their modes of signification. In the early 1960s Roland Barthes informed readers who were interested in the latest intellectual fashion that the way to recognize a structuralist was by a certain vocabulary of signification: look for *signifiant* and *signifié* or *syntagmatic* and *paradigmatic*; by these signs shall ye know them. This may or may not have been a sure test at the time, but today, doubtless because of the proselytizing activity of structuralists themselves, this vocabulary has grown common. *Signifier* and *signified* are no longer reliable signs of a particular theoretical commitment. They appear in a range of critical and interpretive writings and even in works of literary history. The activity of criticism has become bound up with the sign and the debates of literary theory bear upon the possibility of mastering it.

Criticism is the pursuit of signs, in that critics, whatever their persuasion, are incited by the prospect of grasping, comprehending, capturing in their prose, evasive signifying structures. Criticism occurs because the signs of literature are never simply given as such but must be pursued, and different modes of criticism can be distinguished by the accounts they give of this pursuit. Semiotics, which defines itself as the science of signs, posits a zoological pursuit: the semiotician wants to discover what are the species of signs, how they differ from one another, how they function in their native habitat, how they interact with other species. Confronted with a plethora of texts that communicate various meanings to their readers, the analyst does not pursue a meaning; he seeks to identify signs and describe their functioning. For other critics, this general and classificatory project is of minor interest. Like hunters pursuing a particular beast that will make a splendid trophy, they have a more precise goal. A sign sequence is there to be interpreted; one pursues it to capture its meaning.

This book investigates the problems and projects of a semiotics of literature, particularly those that have figured in current theoretical debate. Semiotics has in general claimed that the study of literature ought to be above all an investigation of the ways and means of literary signification. Sometimes theorists argue that the possibility of interpreting individual works depends upon mastery of the systems and procedures that semiotics seeks to elucidate: critics cannot hope to work out compelling interpretations of a novel unless they have a thorough understanding of the nature and conventions of narrative, the relations between story and discourse, and possibilities of thematic structure. At other times semioticians emphasize that the interpretations of readers and critics are themselves part of the material they study: to investigate literary signification is to analyze how works communicate to readers. In both cases, however, the task of semiotics is to describe the system of literary signification that is drawn upon by readers and critics in their encounters with literary works. The goal is a complete description of this system, just as the goal of linguistics is a complete description of the sets of rules and conventions that constitute a language and enable linguistic communication to take place.

Such general and ambitious projects provoke disputes: disagreements within semiotics about how to proceed; disagreements with other theorists about the possibility of such an enterprise. This book is concerned with both. Part One offers two overviews, of recent criticism and of semiotics, outlining two major questions treated in the following sections. The first is the role or status of interpretation. In reading reviews of critical and theoretical works one is struck by how frequently they are submitted to one and the same test: does this discussion enable us to produce new interpretations of literary works? If so, let us debate their validity. If not, consign it to the flames, for the proof of a theoretical discourse lies in the interpretations it yields when 'applied.' This notion that the production of new interpretations is the task of literary study, the *raison d'être* of all writing about literature, is now such a fundamental assumption of Anglo-American criticism that it has a decisive impact on all developments in contemporary criticism.

The second question is the relation of semiotics to deconstruction, which also arises from a reflection on signs but whose ambitions are different. Deconstruction is, as Barbara Johnson has put it, 'a careful teasing out of warring forces of signification within the text.'[1] Skeptical of the possibility of mastering meaning with a comprehensive system or discipline, it investigates what the most powerful and interesting texts have to tell us about signification and shows how they undo the logics of signification on which they rely.

After these overviews, Part Two takes up the problems of literary semiotics in more detail, assessing various ways of approaching literary signification and the uses of certain concepts such as 'horizon of expectations' and 'intertextuality.' A major development in recent criticism has been the focus on the reader, both in theories of literary signification and in criticism that describes the meaning of the work as the experience it provokes in the reader. As a method of interpretation reader-response criticism poses numerous questions but from my perspective the most important concerns its relation to poetics and semiotics, which can be conceived as theories of reading. Throughout this section I argue for a distinction between interpretive criticism and poetics which seems to me the only way of avoiding a confusion that has surrounded both structuralism and literary semiotics.

Part Three could be placed under the aegis of deconstruction since its concern is the implications for semiotics of the aspects of literary meaning that deconstruction has brought to the fore. Elsewhere, in *On Deconstruction: Literary Theory in the 1970s*, I confront deconstruction directly, undertaking extended exposition of Derrida's arguments and a survey of deconstruction in literary criticism. Here I am concerned not with philosophical arguments, nor with the relation between speech and writing, but with how certain problematic moments in texts would fit into a semiotics and what effect they would have on a semiotics that tried to encompass them. For example, Chapter 7 'Apostrophe' began as a semiotic investigation of a striking but puzzling feature of the ode and of lyrics generally, the invocation of or address to absent beings and various non-human entities: souls, skylarks, sofas. Apostrophes have interesting linguistic properties; the question is, how do these linguistic signs function in the second-order system of the lyric? In principle one might hope to isolate a number of different signifying functions and the features by which they could be discriminated. The immediate effect or impact of apostrophes is embarrassment, and with this as a point of departure one can identify a series of poetic possibilities. The results indicate, however, a certain structural reversibility of figures which would make impossible a semiotics committed to a one-to-one mapping of signifiers to signifieds.

Deconstruction enters the later chapters somewhat more explicitly. 'The Mirror Stage' (Chapter 8) investigates how deconstruction might lead one to reconsider certain classical positions, such as those enunciated in *The Mirror and the Lamp*, revealing a complexity hitherto masked. The next chapters illustrate the impact on traditional semiotic subjects—'analyse du récit' and the analysis of metaphor—of the self-deconstructive moments in literary works described by critics like Paul de Man; and the final chapter considers the relation of these theoretical debates and issues to university curricula. What these essays show, I believe, is that deconstruction has not 'refuted' structuralism and semiotics, as some 'post-structuralists' would have it. If deconstructive readings give us reasons to believe that a complete and non-contradictory science of signs is impossible, that does not mean that the enterprise should be abandoned, any more than Gödel's proof of the incompleteness of metamathematics leads mathematicians to abandon their metamathematic investigations. One might even say that the paradoxes which deconstructive readings identify as important insights into the nature of literary language are for semiotics the result of basic methodological distinctions—between *langue* and *parole*, system and event, synchronic and diachronic, signifier and signified, metaphor and metonymy—which are still essential to the analytical project even though they break down at certain points or yield two perspectives that cannot be synthesized.

Semiotics is a metalinguistic enterprise. It attempts to describe the evasive, ambiguous, paradoxical language of literature in a sober, unambiguous metalanguage. But with the proliferation of critical metalanguages in recent years, it has become clear that critical and theoretical discourse shares many properties with the language it attempts to describe. The discourse which attempts to analyze metaphor does not itself escape metaphor. There is a metalinguistic function—language can discuss language—but there is no metalanguage, only more language piled upon language. Deconstruction has been particularly acute in showing the uncanny involvement of theories in the domains they claim to describe, in showing how critics become engaged in a displaced reenactment of a text's scenario.

Criticism is thus a pursuit of signs in a second sense: a pastime or activity that is in and of the sign. The fact that signs are not just the objects of the critic's quest but also the agents and even grounds of that quest does not mean that the critic must deem himself a poet or seize every opportunity to pun. On the contrary, one can continue the pursuit of signs, the attempt to grasp, master, formulate, define, even though one knows that one is caught up in a signifying process that one cannot fully control—a process at work even at the moments when one produces one's best formulation, one's most productive insight.

Much of the material in this book has appeared elsewhere in a different form. I have revised extensively in order to eliminate what now seem to me mistakes and to give the book focus and continuity, but one result of this process of composition is the difficulty of thanking the people who have helped in its gestation: all those who asked questions or offered an objection after lectures or who commented, succinctly or extensively, on published papers. Since one of the subjects of this book is the dependency of any discourse on innumerable other discourses, most of them anonymous, I will simply thank the intertextuality of current critical debate for its essential assistance, singling out only Cynthia Chase, whose critical comments on all the essays provoked rewriting and rethinking. I am also grateful to the Guggenheim Foundation for a Fellowship during which the project was completed.

Acknowledgments

Portions of Chapter 1 are reprinted by permission from *Comparative Literature*, vol. 28 (1976) pp. 244–56. Chapter 2 is reprinted by permission of *Daedalus*, Journal of the American Academy of Arts and Sciences, Fall 1977, *Discoveries and Interpretations: Studies in Contemporary Scholarship*, vol. II. Portions of Chapter 3 are taken from *The Reader in the Text*, ed. Susan Suleiman and Inge Crosman, copyright © 1980 by Princeton University Press. Reprinted by permission. Material in Chapter 4 was published in *Semiotic Themes* (University of Kansas Humanistic Studies, 53), ed. Richard T. De George, Lawrence: University of Kansas Publications, 1981. A different version of Chapter 5 appeared in *Modern Language Notes* 91 (1976), pp. 1380–96. Reprinted by permission of The Johns Hopkins University. Earlier versions of Chapters 6 and 7 were published in *Diacritics* (Spring 1975 and Winter 1977). Chapter 8 was written for *High Romantic Argument: Essays for M. H. Abrams*, ed. Lawrence Lipking, copyright © 1981 by Cornell University Press, 1981. Chapter 9 is a revised version of 'Fabula and Sjuzhet in the Analysis of Narrative: Some American Discussions,' from *Poetics Today* 1:3 (1980). Chapter 10 is a modified version of a paper written for a Festschrift for Stephen Ullmann, ed. T. E. Hope, to be published by Basil Blackwell. Chapter 11 first appeared in the *ADE Bulletin*, vol. 62 (September–November 1979). I am grateful to editors and publishers for permission to use this material.

PART ONE

1

Beyond Interpretation

In the years since World War II, the New Criticism has been challenged, even vilified, but it has seldom been effectively ignored. The inability if not reluctance of its opponents simply to evade its legacy testifies to the dominant position it has come to occupy in American and British universities. Despite the many attacks on it, despite the lack of an organized and systematic defense, it seems not unfair to speak of the hegemony of New Criticism in this period and of the determining influence it has exercised on our ways of writing about and teaching literature. Whatever critical affiliations we may proclaim, we are all New Critics, in that it requires a strenuous effort to escape notions of the autonomy of the literary work, the importance of demonstrating its unity, and the requirement of 'close reading.'

In many ways the influence of the New Criticism has been beneficent, especially on the teaching of literature. Those old enough to have experienced the transition, its emergence from an earlier mode of literary study, speak of the sense of release, the new excitement breathed into literary education by the assumption that even the meanest student who lacked the scholarly information of his betters could make valid comments on the language and structure of the text. No longer was discussion and evaluation of a work something which had to wait upon acquisition of a respectable store of literary, historical, and biographical information. No longer was the right to comment something earned by months in a library. Even the beginning student of literature was now confronted with poems, asked to read them closely, and required to discuss and evaluate their use of language and thematic organization. To make the experience of the text itself central to literary education and to relegate the accumulation of information about the text to an ancillary status was a move which gave the study of literature a new focus and justification, as well as promoting a more precise and relevant understanding of literary works.

But what is good for literary education is not necessarily good for the study of literature in general, and those very aspects of the New Criticism which ensured its success in schools and universities determined its eventual limitations as a program for literary criticism. Commitment to the autonomy of the literary text, a fundamental article of faith with positive consequences for the teaching of literature, led to a commitment to interpretation as the proper activity of criticism. If the work is an autonomous whole, then it can and should be studied in and for itself, without reference to possible external contexts, whether biographical, historical, psychoanalytic, or sociological. Distinguishing what was external from what was internal, rejecting historical and causal explanation in favor of internal analysis, the New Criticism left readers and critics with only one recourse. They must interpret the poem; they must show how its various parts contribute to a thematic unity, for this thematic unity justifies the work's status as autonomous artifact. When a poem is read in and for itself critics must fall back upon the one constant of their situation: there is a poem being read by a human being. Whatever is external to the poem, the fact that it addresses a human being means that what it says about human life is internal to it. The critic's task is to show how the interaction of the poem's parts produces a complex and ontologically privileged statement about human experience.

Though they may occasionally attempt to disguise the fact, the basic concepts of the New Critics and their followers derive from this thematic and interpretive orientation. The poem is not simply a series of sentences; it is spoken by a *persona*, who expresses an *attitude* to be defined, speaking in a particular *tone* which puts the attitude in one of various possible modes or degrees of commitment. Since the poem is an autonomous whole its value must lie within it, in richness of attitude, in complexity of judgment, in delicate balance of values.

Hence one finds in poems *ambivalence, ambiguity, tension, irony, paradox*. These are all thematic operators which permit one to translate formal features of the language into meanings so that the poem may be unified as a complex thematic structure expressing an attitude toward the world. And in place of a theory of reading which would specify how order was to be achieved, the New Criticism deployed a common humanism or, as R. S. Crane calls it, a 'set of reduction terms' toward which analysis of ambivalence, tension, irony, and paradox was to move: 'life and death, good and evil, love and hate, harmony and strife, order and disorder, eternity and time, reality and appearance, truth and falsity . . . emotion and reason, simplicity and complexity, nature and art.'[1] A repertoire of contrasting attitudes and values relevant to the human situation served as a target language in the process of thematic translation. To analyze a poem was to show how all its parts contributed to a complex statement about human problems.

In short, it would be possible to demonstrate that, given its premises, the New Criticism was necessarily an interpretive criticism. But in fact this is scarcely necessary since the most important and insidious legacy of the New Criticism is the widespread and unquestioning acceptance of the notion that the critic's job is to interpret literary works. Fulfillment of the interpretive task has come to be the touchstone by which other kinds of critical writing are judged, and reviewers inevitably ask of any work of literary theory, linguistic analysis, or historical scholarship, whether it actually assists us in our understanding of particular works. In this critical climate it is therefore important, if only as a means of loosening the grip which interpretation has on critical consciousness, to take up a tendentious position and to maintain that, while the experience of literature may be an experience of interpreting works, in fact the interpretation of individual works is only tangentially related to the understanding of literature. To engage in the study of literature is not to produce yet another interpretation of *King Lear* but to advance one's understanding of the conventions and operations of an institution, a mode of discourse.

There are many tasks that confront criticism, many things we need to advance our understanding of literature, but one thing we do not need is more interpretations of literary works. It is not at all difficult to list in a general way critical projects which would be of compelling interest if carried through to some measure of completion; and such a list is in itself the best illustration of the potential fecundity of other ways of writing about literature. We have no convincing account of the role or function of literature in society or social consciousness. We have only fragmentary or anecdotal histories of literature as an institution: we need a fuller exploration of its historical relation to the other forms of discourse through which the world is organized and human activities are given meaning. We need a more sophisticated and apposite account of the role of literature in the psychological economies of both writers and readers; and in particular we ought to understand much more than we do about the effects of *fictional* discourse. As Frank Kermode emphasized in his seminal work, *The Sense of an Ending*, criticism has made almost no progress toward a comprehensive theory of fictions, and we still operate with rudimentary notions of 'dramatic illusion' and 'identification' whose crudity proclaims their unacceptability. What is the status and what is the role of fictions, or, to pose the same kind of problem in another way, what are the relations (the historical, the psychic, the social relationships) between the real and the fictive? What are the ways of moving between life and art? What operations or figures articulate this movement? Have we in fact progressed beyond Freud's simple distinction between the figures of condensation and displacement? Finally, or perhaps in sum, we need a typology of discourse and a theory of the relations (both mimetic and nonmimetic) between literature and the other modes of discourse which make up the text of intersubjective experience.

The fact that we are so far from possessing these things in what is, after all, an age of criticism—an age where unparalleled industry and intelligence have been invested in writing about literature—is in part due to the preeminent role accorded to interpretation. Indeed, one of the best ways of talking about the failures of contemporary criticism is to look at the fate which has befallen three very intelligent and promising attempts to break away from the legacy of the New Criticism. In each case the failure to combat the notion of interpretation itself, or rather the conscious or unconscious persistence of the notion that a critical approach must justify itself by its interpretive results, has emasculated a highly promising mode of investigation.

My first case, in many ways the most significant, is that of Northrop Frye's *Anatomy of Criticism*. Frye's polemical introduction is, of course, a powerful indictment of contemporary criticism and an argument for a systematic poetics: criticism is in a state of 'naïve induction,' trying to study individual works of literature without a proper conceptual framework. It must recognize that literature is not a simple aggregate of discrete works but a conceptual space which can be coherently organized; and it must, if it is to become a discipline, make a 'leap to a new ground from which it can discover what the organizing or containing forms of its conceptual framework are.'[2] Working on this new ground involves assuming the possibility of 'a coherent and comprehensive theory of literature, logically and scientifically organized, some of which the student unconsciously learns as he goes on, but the main principles of which are as yet unknown to us.'[3]

This is certainly a direct attack on the atomism of the New Criticism and the assumption that one should approach each individual work with as few preconceptions as possible in order to experience directly the words on the page, but Frye does not realize the importance of attacking interpretation itself. He hovers on the edge of the problem, characterizing as 'one of the many slovenly illiteracies that the absence of systematic criticism has allowed to grow up' the notion that 'the critic should confine himself to "getting out" of a poem exactly what the poet may vaguely be assumed to have been aware of "putting in"'; but the function of this argument in his overall enterprise is anything but clear. It is wrongly assumed, he continues, that the critic needs no conceptual framework and that his job is simply 'to take a poem into which a poet has diligently stuffed a specific number of beauties or effects, and complacently to extract them one by one, like his prototype Little Jack Horner.'[4]

One might take this sentence as a general attack on interpretation, especially interpretation of a complacent and fundamentally tautological kind, but in fact, as the earlier sentence makes clear, Frye's real target is interpretation of an intentionalist kind. Joining the New Critics in rejecting criticism which is guilty of the intentional fallacy, Frye has picked the wrong enemy and opened the door to a trivialization of his enterprise. The systematic poetics for which he calls and to which he makes a substantial contribution can thus be seen as a prelude to interpretation. Approaching the text with a conceptual framework—the theories of Modes, Symbols, Myths, and Genres as outlined in the *Anatomy*—the critic can interpret the work not by pulling out what the poet was aware of putting in but by extracting the elements of the various modes, genres, symbols, and myths which may have been put in without the author's explicit knowledge. In this case, interpretation would still be the test of a critical method, and the value of Frye's approach would be that it enabled one to perceive meanings which hitherto had been obscure.

Certainly this is not the justification Frye would wish to give his project. His repeated assertions that criticism must seek a comprehensive view of what it is doing, that it must try to attain an understanding of the fundamental principles which make it a discipline and mode of knowledge, show that he has other goals in mind. But his failure to question interpretation as a goal creates a fundamental ambiguity about the status of his categories and schemas. In identifying Spring, Summer, Autumn, and Winter as the four mythic categories, what exactly is Frye claiming? He might be suggesting that these categories form a general conceptual map which we have assimilated through our experience of literature and which lead us to interpret literature as we do. In other words, he might be claiming that in order to account for the meanings and effects of literary works one must bring to light these fundamental distinctions which are constantly at work in our reading of literature. Alternatively, he might be claiming that he has discovered categories of experience basic to the human psyche and that in order to discover the true or deepest meaning of literary works we must apply to them these categories, as hermeneutic devices.

Though the difference between these alternatives may seem slight, it is in fact crucial to the project of a poetics. In the second case one is claiming to have discovered distinctions which serve as a method of interpretation: which enable one to produce new and better readings of literary works. In the first case one is not offering a method of interpretation but is claiming to explain why we interpret literary works as we do. In the context of the polemical introduction and the suggestion that we should try to make explicit the implicit theory of literature which students unconsciously acquire in their literary education, the first interpretation would certainly be preferable; but in terms of the traditional tasks and preoccupations of criticism, which Frye has not thought to reject, the second interpretation is more likely to prevail.

In fact, this is exactly what has happened. Though it began as a plea for a systematic poetics, Frye's work has done less to promote work in poetics than to stimulate a mode of interpretation which has come to be known as 'myth-criticism' or archetypal criticism. The assumption that the critic's task is to interpret individual works remains unchanged, only now, on the theory that the deepest meanings of a work are to be sought in the archetypal symbols or patterns which it deploys, Frye's categories are used as a set of labeling devices. Frye failed to recognize that the enemy of poetics is not just atomism but the interpretive project to which atomism ministers, and this led not only to deflection of systematic energy but to the promotion of a rather anodyne mode of interpretation.

The second example of a potentially powerful theoretical mode that had adopted the project of interpreting works is psychoanalytic criticism. In the 1960s the best works of psychoanalytic criticism avoided the questions concerning the status and effects of fiction which might have been elucidated by a psychoanalytic approach and concentrated on interpretation, as if they could only prove themselves by demonstrating their interpretive prowess. In *The Sins of the Fathers: Hawthorne's Psychological Themes* Frederick Crews demonstrates the appropriateness of a psychoanalytic method for making sense of many powerful and puzzling elements in Hawthorne's work. Oddities of plot, character, and fantasy become more interesting and their force more intelligible when they are analyzed as representations of the consequences of unresolved Oedipal conflicts: the works 'rest on fantasy, but on the shared fantasy of mankind, and this makes for a more interesting fiction than would any illusionistic slice of life.'[5]

The Sins of the Fathers is admirable, except in its implication that the goal of the psychoanalytic critic is to identify and interpret what the subtitle calls 'psychological themes.' If critics devote themselves to identifying in literary works the forces and elements described by psychoanalytic theory, if they make psychoanalysis a source of themes, they restrict the impact of potentially valuable theoretical developments, such as the insights that have emerged from recent French rereadings of Freud. This body of work provides, among other things, an account of processes of textual transference by which critics find themselves uncannily repeating a displaced version of the narrative they are supposed to be comprehending—just as the psychoanalyst, through the process of transference and counter-transference, finds himself caught up in the reenactment of the analysand's drama.[6] Contemporary psychoanalytic theory might have much to teach us about the logic of our interaction with texts but it is impoverished when it is treated as a repository of themes—themes to be identified when interpreting literary works. Leo Bersani's perceptive and original *Baudelaire and Freud* slides into this perspective in treating *Les Fleurs du Mal* as a drama of the struggle between what Lacan calls the Symbolic and the Imaginary.[7] In Lacan these are two modes of representation. Interpretive criticism makes them two psychic conditions, one good and the other bad, and translates events of the narrative into a struggle between them, thus producing something like an updated version of the hunt for Oedipus complexes and phallic symbols.

My third case is the 'Affective Stylistics' of Stanley Fish, which begins with a determined attempt to break away from the assumptions and procedures of the New Criticism but which, again, fails to identify interpretation as the real enemy and so compromises the theoretical insights on which it is based. Wimsatt and Beardsley had argued that one must not confuse the poem and its effects ('what it *is* and what it *does*'), lest 'the poem itself, as an object of specifically critical judgment . . . disappear.'[8] This is precisely what should happen, replies Fish, for meaning lies not in the object but in the event or experience of reading. To ask about the meaning of a word or sentence is to ask what it *does* in the work, and to specify what it does one must analyze 'the developing responses of the reader in relation to the words as they succeed one another in time.'[9]

This is a fruitful reorientation, for reasons discussed in Chapter 6 below. Above all, it makes clear the need for a poetics, for if the meaning of works lies in the successive effects of their elements on readers, then one needs a powerful theory that will acount for these effects by analyzing the norms, conventions, and mental operations on which they depend. A theory focussed on the reader and reading ought to undertake to make explicit the implicit knowledge that readers deploy in responding as they do.

But Fish fails to take this step because he assumes that the task of criticism is to interpret individual works, and he proposes to do this—for *Paradise Lost* and then for a series of 'self-consuming' seventeenth-century artifacts—by describing the reader's experience of hazarding judgments and then finding them proved wrong. In fact, this interpretive orientation has placed him in a rather tight corner: to claim simultaneously that one is describing the experience of the reader and that one is producing valuable new interpretations is a difficult act to sustain, and despite Fish's skill and energy he will not sustain it for long.[10] The future lies, rather, in the theoretical project that he flees.

These three cases, though very different in the content of their proposals and results, suggest a gloomy prognosis: the principle of interpretation is so strong an unexamined postulate of American criticism that it subsumes and neutralizes the most forceful and intelligent acts of revolt. However, the increasing influence of European criticism is making available a greater variety of ways of writing about literature, and if we can refrain from redirecting them to the restricted task of interpretation, American criticism will be much the richer.

At its most basic the lesson of contemporary European criticism is this: the New Criticism's dream of a self-contained encounter between innocent reader and autonomous text is a bizarre fiction. To read is always to read in relation to other texts, in relation to the codes that are the products of these texts and go to make up a culture. And thus, while the New Criticism could conceive of no other possibility than interpreting the text, there are other projects of greater importance which involve analysis of the conditions of meaning. If works were indeed autonomous artifacts, there might be nothing to do but to interpret each of them, but since they participate in a variety of systems—the conventions of literary genres, the logic of story and the teleologies of emplotment, the condensations and displacements of desire, the various discourses of knowledge that are found in a culture— critics can move through texts towards an understanding of the systems and semiotic processes which make them possible.

Criticism informed by these principles may take many guises. A semiotics of literature would attempt to describe in systematic fashion the modes of signification of literary discourse and the interpretive operations embodied in the institution of literature. Alternatively, Fredric Jameson proposes to work towards a dialectical criticism which would not attempt to resolve difficulties but would take as its object of enquiry a work's resistance to interpretation. In defining the nature of a work's opacity one would attempt to discover its historical grounds: 'Thus our thought no longer takes official problems at face value but walks behind the screen to assess the very origin of the subject–object relationship in the first place.'[11] The product or result of dialectical criticism is not an interpretation of the work but a broader historical account of why interpretation should be necessary and what is signified by the need for particular types of interpretation.

Jameson's enterprise would lead, he says, 'to a dialectical rhetoric in which the various mental operations are understood not absolutely, but as moments and figures, tropes, syntactical paradigms of our relationship to the real itself, as, altering irrevocably in time, it nonetheless obeys a logic that like the logic of a language can never be fully distinguished from its object.'[12] A Marxist criticism conceived in this spirit would demonstrate that the relationship between a literary work and a social and historical reality is one not of reflected content but of a play of forms. Social reality includes paradigms of organization, figures of intelligibility; and the interplay between a literary work and its historical ground lies in the way its formal devices exploit, transform, and supplement a culture's ways of producing meaning.

Another version of this historical project is the *Rezeptions-ästhetik* proposed by Hans Robert Jauss. Emphasizing that the meaning of a work depends upon the horizon of expectations against which it is received and which poses the questions to which the work comes to function as an answer, Jauss has inaugurated the vast and complex enterprise of describing these horizons, which are of course the product of the discourses of a culture. *Rezeptionsästhetik* is not a way of interpreting works but an attempt to understand their changing intelligibility by identifying the codes and interpretive assumptions that give them meaning for different audiences at different periods.[13]

These two examples suggest that one source of energy for criticism in the coming years may be the reinvention of literary history. The historical perspective enables one to recognize the transience of any interpretation, which will always be succeeded by other interpretations, and to take as object of reflection the series of interpretive acts by which traditions are constituted and meaning produced. This new historical orientation seems the common factor in the work of three otherwise very different critics, Geoffrey Hartman, Harold Bloom, and Paul de Man. Drawing sustenance from a historically conceived romantic poetry rather than from an ahistorical Metaphysical or Modernist verse, invoking as the stimulus of repeated quest and failure the impossible calling of high Romanticism, they treat literature and reading as a repeated historical error or deformation. 'History,' writes Hartman, 'is the wake of a mobile mind falling in and out of love with the things it detaches by its attachment.'[14] This becomes the temporal scheme of Harold Bloom's *The Anxiety of Influence*: each poet must slay his poetic father; he must displace his precursors by a revisionary misreading which creates the historical space in which his own poetry takes place. The hidden order of literary history is based on a negative and dialectical principle, which also orders the relationship between reader and text: the reader, like the new poet, is a latecomer bound to misconstrue the text so as to serve the meanings required by his own moment in literary history. That the greatest insights are produced in the process of necessary and determinate misreadings is the claim of another theorist of deformation, Paul de Man, for whom interpretation is always in fact covert literary history and inevitable error, since it takes for granted historical categorizations and obscures its own historical status.[15]

These critics certainly do not oppose interpretation; indeed, they publicly indulge in it, but by defining it as necessary error they lead us to enquire about its nature and status and thus to consider central questions about the nature of literary language. The effect of their writings has been to broaden the possibilities of literary investigation, but since they do not question the assumption that interpretation is the purpose of criticism they are immediately assimilated to the project of interpretation, at the cost of some confusion.

Consider the case of Harold Bloom. He proposes a theory of how poems come into being. Few critics would claim that an account of a poem's genesis is an account of its meaning, but since we assume that the task of critics is to interpret poems, we leap to the conclusion that when Bloom writes about a poem he is telling us its meaning. Even when he warns us that poems do not have meanings at all or that 'the meaning of a poem can only be a poem, but *another poem*, a *poem not itself*,'[16] we ignore his statement and take what he says about a poem and its intertextual, tropological genesis as an interpretation, even though it is not another poem—after which we are affronted that his 'interpretation' should be so extravagant, so different from what the poem appears to say. The assumption that critics *must* interpret is so powerful that we will not allow Bloom's writing to be anything else, and one suspects that Bloom himself is influenced by this assumption, against the explicit claims of his own theory.

Or consider *deconstruction*. Although Derrida's writings all involve close engagement with various texts, they seldom involve interpretations as traditionally conceived. There is no deference to the integrity of the text, no search for a unifying purpose that would assign each part its appropriate role. Derrida characteristically concentrates on elements which others find marginal, seeking not to elucidate what a text says but to reveal an uncanny logic that operates in and across texts, whatever they say. His treatment of Rousseau in *Of Grammatology* is part of an investigation of the place of writing in Western discussions of language, a disclosure of the process which has preserved an idealized model of speech by attributing certain problematical features of language to writing and then setting writing aside as secondary and derivative. Derrida notes that terms Rousseau uses to describe writing, the noun *supplément* and the verb *suppléer*, appear in discussions of other phenomena such as education and masturbation, and in following up these references in fictional, autobiographical, and expository texts, he describes what he calls the 'logic of supplementarity', a general operation which we can now see at work as a source of energy in a wide variety of texts.[17] Is this an interpretation of Rousseau? It omits most of the contents of every text it mentions and fails to identify a thematic unity or a distinctive meaning for any of Rousseau's writings. Derrida is working, rather, to describe a general process through which texts undo the philosophical system to which they adhere by revealing its rhetorical nature.

But when deconstruction comes to America a shift takes place, subtly inaugurated in Paul de Man's critique of Derrida in *Blindness and Insight*. De Man argues that Rousseau's text already carries out the deconstructive operations which Derrida claims to perform on it, so that Derrida is in fact elucidating Rousseau, though he pretends to be doing something else because it makes, as de Man puts it, a better story.[18] This displacement has since been transformed into a central methodological principle by J. Hillis Miller, who argues not just that a text already contains the operation of self-deconstruction, in which two contradictory principles or lines of argument confront one another, but that this undecidability 'is always thematized in the text itself in the form of metalinguistic statements.'[19] In other words, the text does not just contain or perform a self-deconstruction but is *about* self-deconstruction, so that a deconstructive reading is an interpretation of the text, an analysis of what it says or means. 'Great works of literature,' Miller insists, 'have anticipated explicitly any deconstruction the critic can achieve,' so that energetic deference and interpretive elucidation are the appropriate critical stances. Thus is deconstruction tamed by the critical assumption and made into a version of interpretation.

In the hands of its best practitioners, such as Paul de Man and Barbara Johnson, deconstruction is an interpretive mode of unusual power and subtlety.[20] In other hands there is always the danger that it will become a process of interpretation which seeks to identify particular themes, making undecidability, or the problem of writing, or the relationship between performative and constative, privileged themes of literary works. It seems to me that just because it easily becomes a method of interpretation, deconstruction has succeeded in America in a way that Marxism and structuralism have not. Marxism is committed to the immense and difficult project of working out the complicated processes of mediation between base and superstructure. When enlisted to interpret a particular work it is bound to seem, as we say, 'vulgar.' Structuralism is also committed to large-scale projects, such as elaborating a grammar of plot structure or the possible relations between story and discourse, and has thus seemed irrelevant except in so far as its concepts and categories can be 'applied' in the activity of interpretation. The possibility of pursuing these larger projects depends on our ability to resist the assumption that interpretation is the task of criticism.

Of course, in one sense all projects involve interpretation: selecting facts that require explanation is already an act of interpretation, as is positing descriptive categories and organizing them into theories. But this is no reason to take as the only valid form of critical writing the highly specialized exercise of developing for one work after another an interpretation sufficiently grounded in tradition to seem valid and sufficiently new to be worth proposing. This exercise has a strategic place in the production of literary tradition, but that does not mean that it should dominate literary studies. Readers will continue to read and interpret literary works, and interpretation will continue in the classroom, since it is through interpretation that teachers attempt to transmit cultural values, but critics should explore ways of moving beyond interpretation. E. D. Hirsch, for many years a leading champion of interpretation, has reached the conclusion that criticism should no longer devote itself to the goal of producing ever more interpretations: 'A far better solution to the problem of academic publishing would be to abandon the idea that has dominated scholarly writing for the past forty years: that interpretation is the only truly legitimate activity for a professor of literature. There are other things to do, to think about, to write about.'[21] The essays that follow explore some of these possibilities.

2

In Pursuit of Signs

It is a commonplace of historiography that decisive events are difficult to perceive, except retrospectively. It is the future which will promote incidents of our own time to the status of events and which will enable those events to take their places in the causal sequences we are pleased to call 'history.' Much the same can be said of events in the history of scholarship. Generally, it is not until years afterward, perhaps not until an influential movement has run its course or changed its direction, that one can identify as crucial the events which led to its foundation or determined its development. And therefore the observer of contemporary scholarship who wishes to make projects, articles, and alliances into the stuff of history is compelled to imagine a future from whose proleptic vantage point he can construct causal sequences and narrate the 'real history' of his own time.

This kind of temporal projection, however fanciful it may seem, is the condition of understanding: unavoidable though problematic, like interpretation itself. A statement about the forces at work in the present always implies a future, and method requires only that we proceed with some awareness of the tendentiousness of our procedure. But if our subject is not the progress of a national economy or the fortunes of a political party, if our subject is method itself—method as manifested in some of the varieties of contemporary scholarship—then the observer's difficulties are compounded. He may labor to imagine a future toward which present scholarly activities will lead, as cause leads to effect. But more important than the attempt to decide which causal sequences, among the many imaginable, correctly define the present is another question: what kind of causation is at work in the movement of ideas? Our understanding of the intellectual activity of earlier centuries does not usually take the form of causal reconstruction; characteristically, our discussion of an age focuses on a few commanding projects which both sum up and transcend the activities of many predecessors and contemporaries. Imagining causal sequences has not seemed, nor does it now seem, the most appropriate way of undertaking definition and assessment of scholarly activity. One does better to look for symbolic rather than causal relationships, for events which signify the configurations of contemporary scholarship. Such events may seem the very opposite of the hidden causes which clever and determined historians are supposed to seek, since organizers and participants may unabashedly declare the historic importance of their activities; but their very self-consciousness about the symbolic function of the event is itself part of the general state of consciousness that the event claims to record and promote.

Such an event was the First Congress of the International Association for Semiotic Studies, held in Milan in 1974. Even if none of the participants learned anything or altered in consequence the nature or direction of his research, the presence of about 650 committed or bemused scholars at a congress of this sort made it an event and testified to a new articulation of scholarly activity. If 650 people attend conferences on semiotics, that does not necessarily cause mutations in the world of scholarship, but it is a fact of symbolic importance. Semiotics, the science of signs, becomes something to be reckoned with, even for those who reject it as a Gallic or a technological obfuscation. And of course when a discipline establishes an organization with committees, officers, publications, when it distributes titles and responsibilities to its adherents, it imposes itself on the scholarly world in symbolic fashion. The proliferation of offices and committees probably inhibits scholarship more than it promotes it, but it does give a discipline an effective presence in the symbolic system of academic research.

The establishment of a new discipline within the system of academic research is not a frequent event. Generally new arrivals explicitly identify themselves as subdivisions of old disciplines and simply undertake to organize more rationally and to pursue more vigorously an existing line of research. The emergence of a discipline like semiotics, however, cannot be guaranteed to leave other disciplines unaffected. Not only would they lose momentum if those who previously called themselves linguists, anthropologists, sociologists, literary critics, philosophers, and so forth, were to identify themselves as semioticians, but the nature of these other disciplines would alter as they lost various kinds of specificity. What might previously have been secondary features of a discipline, what might have seemed simple consequences of its interest in particular objects, might become defining characteristics as semiotics offers another approach to phenomena whose domain previously sufficed to identify a species of scholarly research. Disciplines of *les sciences humaines*—to avoid the English phrasing with its futile attempt to distinguish the humanities from the social sciences—are not autonomous activities but elements of a system with gaps, redundancies, special relationships and indeterminacies. The emergence of a new and aggressive discipline involves a complex readjustment of boundaries and points of focus; no discipline can assume immunity from the effects of this process.

A discussion of the nature and role of semiotics, whose emergence is, at various levels, an event in the world of contemporary scholarship, cannot therefore be simply an account of the methods and content of this particular discipline. If one reflects on the significance of semiotics, one must consider the way in which research and writing in the humanities and social sciences are affected by the presence of a new articulation of knowledge: new objects, questions, or criteria. First of all, as a discipline makes a place for itself it makes a past for itself, claiming certain scholars as precursors, interpreting their work in a new light, identifying and redefining forces previously at work in older disciplines and now come into their own as semiotics. To proclaim the advent of semiotics as an event in contemporary scholarship is simultaneously to identify those who will be honored as

The establishment of a new discipline within the system of academic research is not a frequent event. Generally new arrivals explicitly identify themselves as subdivisions of old disciplines and simply undertake to organize more rationally and to pursue more vigorously an existing line of research. The emergence of a discipline like semiotics, however, cannot be guaranteed to leave other disciplines unaffected. Not only would they lose momentum if those who previously called themselves linguists, anthropologists, sociologists, literary critics, philosophers, and so forth, were to identify themselves as semioticians, but the nature of these other disciplines would alter as they lost various kinds of specificity. What might previously have been secondary features of a discipline, what might have seemed simple consequences of its interest in particular objects, might become defining characteristics as semiotics offers another approach to phenomena whose domain previously sufficed to identify a species of scholarly research. Disciplines of *les sciences humaines*—to avoid the English phrasing with its futile attempt to distinguish the humanities from the social sciences—are not autonomous activities but elements of a system with gaps, redundancies, special relationships and indeterminacies. The emergence of a new and aggressive discipline involves a complex readjustment of boundaries and points of focus; no discipline can assume immunity from the effects of this process.

A discussion of the nature and role of semiotics, whose emergence is, at various levels, an event in the world of contemporary scholarship, cannot therefore be simply an account of the methods and content of this particular discipline. If one reflects on the significance of semiotics, one must consider the way in which research and writing in the humanities and social sciences are affected by the presence of a new articulation of knowledge: new objects, questions, or criteria. First of all, as a discipline makes a place for itself it makes a past for itself, claiming certain scholars as precursors, interpreting their work in a new light, identifying and redefining forces previously at work in older disciplines and now come into their own as semiotics. To proclaim the advent of semiotics as an event in contemporary scholarship is simultaneously to identify those who will be honored as

leading champion of interpretation, has reached the conclusion that criticism should no longer devote itself to the goal of producing ever more interpretations: 'A far better solution to the problem of academic publishing would be to abandon the idea that has dominated scholarly writing for the past forty years: that interpretation is the only truly legitimate activity for a professor of literature. There are other things to do, to think about, to write about.'[21] The essays that follow explore some of these possibilities.

2

In Pursuit of Signs

It is a commonplace of historiography that decisive events are difficult to perceive, except retrospectively. It is the future which will promote incidents of our own time to the status of events and which will enable those events to take their places in the causal sequences we are pleased to call 'history.' Much the same can be said of events in the history of scholarship. Generally, it is not until years afterward, perhaps not until an influential movement has run its course or changed its direction, that one can identify as crucial the events which led to its foundation or determined its development. And therefore the observer of contemporary scholarship who wishes to make projects, articles, and alliances into the stuff of history is compelled to imagine a future from whose proleptic vantage point he can construct causal sequences and narrate the 'real history' of his own time.

This kind of temporal projection, however fanciful it may seem, is the condition of understanding: unavoidable though problematic, like interpretation itself. A statement about the forces at work in the present always implies a future, and method requires only that we proceed with some awareness of the tendentiousness of our procedure. But if our subject is not the progress of a national economy or the fortunes of a political party, if our subject is method itself—method as manifested in some of the varieties of contemporary scholarship—then the observer's difficulties are compounded. He may labor to imagine a future toward which present scholarly activities will lead, as cause leads

to effect. But more important than the attempt to decide which causal sequences, among the many imaginable, correctly define the present is another question: what kind of causation is at work in the movement of ideas? Our understanding of the intellectual activity of earlier centuries does not usually take the form of causal reconstruction; characteristically, our discussion of an age focuses on a few commanding projects which both sum up and transcend the activities of many predecessors and contemporaries. Imagining causal sequences has not seemed, n[o] does it now seem, the most appropriate way of undertaki[ng] definition and assessment of scholarly activity. One does be[t] to look for symbolic rather than causal relationships, for ev[] which signify the configurations of contemporary scholar[s] Such events may seem the very opposite of the hidden [] which clever and determined historians are supposed t[o] since organizers and participants may unabashedly decl[] historic importance of their activities; but their ve[] consciousness about the symbolic function of the even[t] part of the general state of consciousness that the even[t] record and promote.

Such an event was the First Congress of the I[n] Association for Semiotic Studies, held in Milan in [] none of the participants learned anything or alt[] sequence the nature or direction of his research[] of about 650 committed or bemused scholars at[] this sort made it an event and testified to a new[] scholarly activity. If 650 people attend conferen[ce] that does not necessarily cause mutations in the[] ship, but it is a fact of symbolic importance. Sem[] of signs, becomes something to be reckoned w[] who reject it as a Gallic or a technological [] course when a discipline establishes an org[] mittees, officers, publications, when it dis[] sponsibilities to its adherents, it imposes[] world in symbolic fashion. The proliferat[] mittees probably inhibits scholarship m[] but it does give a discipline an effective [] system of academic research.

pioneers and to delineate the failures of various disciplines to deal with the problems that semiotics confronts.

Second, a new discipline has broad implications for contemporary scholarship by the questions it asks and the kinds of answer it seeks. Although it does not set standards for other disciplines, by arguing explicitly for its methods and purposes it does bring to the fore criteria and preoccupations which become relevant to the discussion of other disciplines. More specifically, anthropologists, literary critics, linguists, and others are affected in that they must decide whether to move toward a semiotic viewpoint, to oppose it, or to argue that they have always been doing what now masquerades under a new name.

Finally, a new discipline projects a future. By announcing ambitious programs, which it can do with a more sincere fervor than long-established disciplines which have had a chance to fulfill their promises, semiotics calls upon other disciplines to justify themselves by offering their own visions of the tasks to be accomplished and compels them, in some measure, to take a position on the issues to which it proposes to dedicate itself. Offering a program, it leads opponents or skeptics to say whether its goals are worthwhile and to argue about the scope and validity of the methods with which it proposes to attack these problems. And so in centering my discussion on the pursuit of signs I am engaged less in an explicit evaluation of semiotics as a discipline than in a consideration of the way that reflection on signs is affecting contemporary scholarship in the humanities and social sciences. The emergence of a new discipline, as I have said, creates a past, articulates a present, and projects a future, but to discuss these three activities in turn, as I shall do, is not to attempt anything like a history of semiology: in each case, whether the ostensible topic be the past, present, or future, the real subject is the implications of thinking about signs, the prospects and difficulties which this perspective discloses.

Reflection on signs and meaning is, of course, nothing new. Philosophers and students of language have of necessity always discussed signs in one way or another, and the advent of semiotics has helped to reveal, for example, that what had previously been sneered at as medieval scholasticism was in many respects a subtle and highly developed theory of signs. But, with this exception, until recently the discussion of signs was always ancillary to some other enterprise, usually a discussion of language or of psychology. There had been no attempt to bring together the whole range of phenomena, linguistic and non-linguistic, which could be considered as signs—no attempt to make the problem of the sign and its varieties the center of intellectual enquiry. Now that people are attempting to do this and have given the name of *semiotics* or *semiology* to their pursuit, one effect is to cast into prominence, as predecessors to be honored, two men who in the early years of the century envisaged a comprehensive science of signs: the American philosopher Charles Sanders Peirce and the Swiss linguist Ferdinand de Saussure.

They are an ill-sorted couple. Saussure was a successful and respectable professor who had doubts about the foundations of linguistics as then practiced and therefore wrote practically nothing, but he did argue, in lectures that have come down to us through students' notes, that since language was a system of signs linguistics ought to be part of a larger science of signs, 'a science which would study the life of signs within society. . . . We call it *semiology* from the Greek *semeion* ("sign"). It would teach us what signs consist of, what laws govern them. Since it does not yet exist we cannot say what it will be, but it has a right to existence; its place is insured in advance.'[1]

These suggestions were not taken up immediately, and only later, when various disciplines had taken structural linguistics as a methodological model and become versions of structuralism, did it become evident that the semiology Saussure postulated had begun to develop. At this point he became a powerful influence, partly because the program he had outlined for semiotics was easy to grasp: linguistics would serve as example and its basic concepts be applied to other domains of social and cultural life. The semiotician is attempting to make explicit the system (*langue*) which underlies and makes possible meaningful events (*parole*). He is concerned with the system as functioning totality (*synchronic* analysis), not with the historical provenance of its various elements (*diachronic* analysis), and he must describe two kinds of relations: contrasts or oppositions between signs (*paradigmatic* relations) and possibilities of combination through which signs create larger units (*syntagmatic* relations).

Peirce is a very different case. A wayward philosophical genius, denied tenure by the Johns Hopkins University at Baltimore, he devoted himself wholeheartedly to 'semeiotic', as he called it, which would be the science of sciences, since 'the entire universe is perfused with signs if it is not composed entirely of signs.'[2] If the universe consists entirely of signs (and he argued, for example, that man was a sign), then the question immediately arises, what are the species of signs, the important distinctions? Peirce's voluminous writings on semiotics, which for a long time remained unreadable and unpublished, are full of taxonomic speculations which grow increasingly more complicated. There are, he decided, ten trichotomies by which signs can be classified (only one of which, distinguishing icon, index, and symbol, has been influential), yielding a possible 59,049 classes of sign. Fortunately, there are redundancies and dependencies, so that 'they will only come to sixty-six' classes, but even this has been too much for all but the most masochistic theorists. The breadth and complexity of Peirce's scheme, not to speak of the swarm of neologisms spawned to characterize the sixty-six types of sign, have discouraged others from entering his system and exploring his insights.

We have two approaches to semiotics here. By conceiving semiotics on the model of linguistics, Saussure gave it a practical program, at the cost of begging important questions about the similarities between linguistic and non-linguistic signs—questions which would eventually lead to a critique of his model. But by attempting to construct an autonomous semiotics, Peirce condemned himself to taxonomic speculations that denied him any influence until semiotics was so well developed that his obsession seemed appropriate. While Saussure identified a handful of communicative practices that might benefit from a semiotic approach, and thus provided a point of departure, Peirce's insistence that everything is a sign did little to help found a discipline,

though today his claims seem an appropriate if radical consequence of a semiotic perspective.

The offerings of Saussure and Peirce are thus in various ways
complementary. Moreover, they occasionally reach the same
conclusion though beginning with different assumptions.
Saussure, taking the linguistic sign as the norm, argues that all
signs are arbitrary, involving a purely conventional association of
conventionally delimited signifiers and signifieds; and he ex-
tends this principle to domains such as etiquette, arguing that
however natural or motivated signs may seem to those who use
them, they are always determined by social rule, semiotic
convention. Peirce, on the contrary, begins with a distinction
between arbitrary signs, which he calls 'symbols,' and two sorts
of motivated signs, indices and icons; but in his work on the latter
he reaches a conclusion similar to Saussure's. Whether we are
dealing with maps, paintings, or diagrams, 'every material image
is largely conventional in its mode of representation.'[3] We can
only claim that a map actually resembles what it represents if we
take for granted and pass over in silence numerous complicated
conventions. Icons seem to be based on natural resemblance, but
in fact they are determined by semiotic convention. Despite their
different points of departure, Saussure and Peirce agree that the
task of semiotics is to describe those conventions that underlie
even the most 'natural' modes of behavior and representation.

The creation and adoption of fathers is a traditional intellectual
activity, and Saussure and Peirce were certainly worthy choices,
but one suspects that semiotics could well have defined itself
without them, as the logical outcome of an intellectual reorientation that had been under way for some time. In 1945 the philosopher Ernst Cassirer wrote that 'in the whole history of science
there is perhaps no more fascinating chapter than the rise of the
new science of linguistics. In its importance it may very well be
compared to the new science of Galileo which in the seventeenth
century changed our whole concept of the physical world.'[4] For
Cassirer what was revolutionary in linguistics was the primacy
granted to relations and systems of relations. Noises that we
make have no significance by themselves; they become elements
of a language only by virtue of the systematic differences among

them, and these elements signify only through their relations with one another in the complex symbolic system we call a 'language'. But if linguistics simply told us this about language it could scarcely have the impact which Cassirer's hyperbolic comparison claimed for it.

To be comparable with Galileo's new science, linguistics would have to change the way in which we think of the universe, or at least of the social and cultural universe. For this to happen, it would have to become a model for thinking about social and cultural activities in general. In short, now that semiology exists it is easy to see that Cassirer's statement implicitly predicts what semiotics explicitly does: that we come to think of our social and cultural world as a series of sign systems, comparable with languages. What we live among and relate to are not physical objects and events; they are objects and events with meaning: not just complicated wooden constructions but chairs and tables; not just physical gestures but acts of courtesy or hostility. As Peirce says, it is not that we have objects on the one hand and thoughts or meanings on the other; it is, rather, that we have signs everywhere, 'some more mental and spontaneous, others more material and regular.'[5]

If we are to understand our social and cultural world, we must think not of independent objects but of symbolic structures, systems of relations which, by enabling objects and actions to have meaning, create a human universe. Several major works of the period between the two world wars—Cassirer's *The Philosophy of Symbolic Forms*, Alfred North Whitehead's *Symbolism: Its Meaning and Effects*, and Susanne K. Langer's *Philosophy in a New Key*—forcefully asserted the primacy of the symbolic dimension in human experience. Today the configuration of scholarship allows us to see that semiotics, which seeks to describe the underlying systems of distinctions and conventions that enable objects and activities to have meaning, is the systematic fulfillment of a reorientation which they began to describe.

But we can also argue, organizing the history of our modernity from the perspective of the sign, that the crucial insights which semiotics develops lie further back, in the work of Marx, Durkheim, and Freud, who insisted on the primacy of social facts. Human reality cannot be described as a set of physical events, and in focusing on social facts, which are always of a symbolic order, Marx, Freud, and Durkheim dramatically showed that individual experience is made possible by the symbolic systems of collectivities, whether these systems be social ideologies, languages, or structures of the unconscious.

The important question here—as I have said—is not whether one can construct a causal chain of true precursors, or which authors and works should be included in the genealogy of semiotics. The point is that semiotics enables us to perceive in recent intellectual activity a general tendency, variously stated and of differing degrees of explicitness, to stress the role of symbolic systems in human experience and thus to think in terms not of autonomous objects but of systems of relations. Semiotics, in its own historical perspective, becomes the attempt to exploit these insights systematically by identifying and investigating a variety of sign systems; but it is only the insights generated in the emergence of semiotics in recent years that enable one to discover these insights in predecessors.

The case of Claude Lévi-Strauss, who more than anyone else is responsible for the development of structuralism in fields outside linguistics, illustrates nicely both the major principles of structuralist-semiotic thought and the curious ways in which such insights may emerge. Lévi-Strauss began not with a reading of Saussure, an acquaintance with linguistics, or a desire to investigate the symbolic codes of a society; he began hiking over hills and exploring their geological configurations. His eloquent chapter on 'The Making of an Anthropologist' in *Tristes Tropiques* cites as the paradigm of the intellectual quest the moment when, to the geological eye, apparent chaos becomes intelligible; 'space and time become one. . . . I feel myself to be steeped in a more dense intelligibility, within which centuries and distances answer each other and speak with one and the same voice.'[6] In interpreting terrain the geologist may imagine a history, but 'unlike the history of the historians, that of the geologist is similar to that of the psychoanalyst, in that it tries to project in time—rather in the manner of a *tableau vivant*—certain basic characteristics of the physical or mental universe.' To geology and Freud,

Lévi-Strauss adds a third master, Marx (who 'established that social science is no more founded on the basis of events than physics is founded on sense data'). 'All three demonstrate that understanding consists in reducing one type of reality to another; that the true reality is never the most obvious; and that the nature of truth is already indicated by the care it takes to remain elusive.'[7]

One would expect someone with an interest in geological signs to take historical reconstruction as his goal and to assume that the sign relation was one of effect to cause. Someone interested in psychoanalysis might investigate symptoms as signs of prior causes and seek to reconstruct a history of traumatic events. Or again, a Marxist might see his task as interpreting social phenomena as signs of the events of economic history which caused them. In all three cases, that is to say, there is a temptation to think of interpretation as involving historical reconstruction. Lévi-Strauss's initial insight, without which much of the scholarship of our time might have been different, was the realization that the three cases were not versions of a single reality called 'history' and based on causation. Each discipline employs a temporal projection of a very different sort to describe what is essentially a structure in a system. The eons of the geologist translate the interrelation of strata he sees before him. The economic trends of a century are for the Marxist a projection of the contradictions he finds in a social system. And what the psychoanalyst projects as events of an infantile period may be purely psychic occurrences of very vague temporality which form an unconscious structure. Lévi-Strauss saw that the various temporal projections concealed a common act of understanding which reduced phenomena to structures of a system, to a model, or *tableau vivant* as he calls it. From the unlikely starting-point of geology he had developed what was to be a basic principle of structuralist analysis: to understand phenomena is to reconstruct the system of which they are manifestations.

This insight is consolidated in a famous article of 1945 entitled 'Structural Analysis in Linguistics and Anthropology' in which Lévi-Strauss argues that anthropologists might learn more directly from linguistics what he had discovered in more oblique fashion. Linguistics, and particularly phonology, which was the most striking early success of structural linguistics, 'ought to play the same renovating role for the social sciences that nuclear physics, for example, played for the exact sciences.' In reducing the apparent chaos of speech sounds to an order, phonology moved 'from the study of conscious linguistic phenomena to that of their unconscious infrastructure.'[8] A speaker of a language is not consciously aware of the phonological system of his language, but an unconscious system of distinctions and oppositions must be postulated to account for the fact that he interprets two physically different sound sequences as instances of the same word, yet in other cases distinguishes among sequences which are acoustically very similar. Phonology reconstructs an underlying system, and in so doing it focuses not on terms or individual elements but on relations. Sounds of a language are not defined by some essential properties but by a series of functional distinctions. I can pronounce *cat* in various ways so long as I maintain a distinction between *cat* and *bat, cut, cad,* etc. The example of linguistics, Lévi-Strauss argues, teaches the anthropologist that he should try to understand phenomena by considering them as manifestations of an underlying system of relations. To describe that system would be to identify the oppositions which combine to differentiate the phenomena in question.

Lévi-Strauss's studies of marriage rules in *The Elementary Structures of Kinship*, his work on *Totemism*, his discussion of various logics in *The Savage Mind*, and his monumental four-volume study of North and South American mythology, all follow, in various ways, this procedure. The marriage practices of various societies are reduced to systems of rules, and these systems are themselves described as variant realizations of a limited set of elementary oppositions. *The Savage Mind* and *Totemism* argue that anthropologists have often failed to understand the thought and behavior of their subjects because they have attempted atomistic and functionalist explanations, taking phenomena one by one rather than treating them as part of an underlying system with a logic of its own. If a particular clan has the bear as its totem, one need not indulge in far-fetched religious, historical, or economic explanations. 'To say that clan A is "descended" from the bear and clan B is "descended" from the eagle is only a concrete and abbreviated way of stating the relationship between A and B as analogous to the relationship between the two species.'[9] Bear and eagle are logical operators, concrete signs, and to understand them is to analyze their place in a system of signs.

The study of myth is Lévi-Strauss's most ambitious project, because the myths he investigates appear totally bizarre and inexplicable, full of the most unaccountable incidents, characters, metamorphoses. As he explains in the preface to his first volume, *Le Cru et le cuit,* 'if it were possible to show that the apparent arbitrariness of myths, the supposed freedom of inspiration, the seemingly uncontrolled process of invention, implied the existence of laws operating at a deeper level, then the conclusion would be inescapable . . . if the human mind is determined even in its creation of myths, *a fortiori* it is determined in other spheres as well.'[10] The chaos of myths is a challenge to the mind nurtured on geology, Marx, and Freud, and the quest for an underlying system which would order their multifarious forms involves treating them as manifestations of a 'language' whose fundamental units and oppositions he must identify.

In isolating fundamental oppositions, such as raw–cooked, day–night, sun–moon, and many of more exotic and unexpected sorts, Lévi-Strauss is describing codes: sets of categories drawn from a single area of experience and related to one another in ways that make them useful logical tools for expressing other relations. His method shows that within the most bizarre incidents can be found categories which, because of their relations to other categories within codes, have an expressive function. The general implication of this method, which has become a fundamental principle of structural and semiotic analysis, is that elements of a text do not have intrinsic meaning as autonomous entities but derive their significance from oppositions which are in turn related to other oppositions in a process of theoretically infinite semiosis. If a text compares a woman with the moon, that predication has no inherent meaning; significance depends on the opposition between sun and moon, either or both of which may have other correlations within the text itself, within other related texts, and within the general symbolic codes of a culture. The relational nature of signs produces a potentially infinite process of signification.

There is still much debate about precisely what Lévi-Strauss has achieved in his analysis of myths. Anyone who reads his discussions of these incomprehensible tales can see that he has discovered an underlying logic, though it is not clear whether one could ever in principle or in practice show that it is *the* logic of myths. What is crucial for contemporary scholarship, however, is another methodological issue which his work has raised and which can reorganize one's conception of research in *les sciences humaines*.

In speaking of understanding as a process of reducing one type of reality to another, Lévi-Strauss explicitly avoids the model of causal explanation. The type of explanation which he offers in his analysis may on occasion be projected in time and treated as a causal analysis, but that is never its central or defining feature. Structural explanation, as it seems best to call it, relates objects or actions to an underlying system of categories and distinctions which make them what they are. In this perspective, to explain phenomena is not to discover temporal antecedents and link them in a causal chain but to specify the place and function of the phenomena in a system.

This is one of the more important lessons that linguistics has offered other disciplines of the humanities and social sciences: that without opposing the notion of causal explanation, they can shift from a historical to an ahistorical perspective and attempt to describe systems rather than trace the antecedents of individual events. The distinction between what linguistics calls *synchronic* description—the analysis of a system without respect to time—and *diachronic* analysis—the attempt to construct a historical evolution—has become a major criterion in characterizing research. Increasingly, even in fields where scholarship was previously presumed to mean historical research, attention has turned to synchronic analyses. To understand social and cultural phenomena, whether they be congressional committees, neckties, or cross-country skiing, is not to trace their historical evolution but to grasp their place and function in various systems of activity and to identify the distinctions which give them significance. The single most important way of characterizing a piece of research may be to ask whether it is synchronic or diachronic in character, and it is the structuralist perspective which has given this question such prominence.

Lévi-Strauss's frequent references to linguistics, and his announcement in his inaugural lecture at the Collège de France in 1961 that he saw anthropology as part of semiology, cast him in the role of a scholar engaged in the pursuit of signs, but the role and status of signs in his work is a problem of some complexity. Lévi-Strauss always deals with symbolic systems and attempts to reconstruct the codes which constitute these systems: but whereas a linguist analyzing a language asks what are the rules and conventions which enable sequences of sounds to have the meanings they do for members of a culture, Lévi-Strauss does not ask what are the codes that account for the meanings that myths have within a particular culture. Though he does often draw upon ethnographic information in isolating functional oppositions, he is constructing a transcultural logic of myth. He is not interested in elements of myths as signs within a particular native culture. Myths are always and primarily signs of the logic of myth itself. 'I do not aim,' he says, 'to show how men think in myths, but how myths think in men, unbeknownst to them.'[11]

Lévi-Strauss's paradoxical formulation poses a question which, as we shall see below, is central to the semiotic perspective: what is it that enables one to say that language speaks, myth thinks, signs signify? But in neglecting the opportunity to study myths as signs within a particular culture, Lévi-Strauss is bypassing the central activity of semiotics as it has recently taken shape. Treating as signs objects or actions which have meaning within a culture, semiotics attempts to identify the rules and conventions which, consciously or unconsciously assimilated by members of that culture, make possible the meanings which the phenomena have. Information about meaning—whether particular actions are considered polite or impolite, whether a musical sequence seems resolved or unresolved, whether an object connotes luxury or penury—is therefore crucial, since what the analyst wishes to do is to isolate those distinctions which are responsible for differences of meaning.

For example, a semiologist, sociologist, or ethnologist (the way that semiotics displaces traditional disciplinary boundaries becomes obvious here) who sets out to study clothing in a culture would ignore many features of garments which were of great importance to the wearer but which did not carry social significance. To wear bright garments rather than dark may be a meaningful gesture, but to opt for brown rather than gray might not. Length of skirts might be a matter of purely personal preference, whereas choice of materials would be rigidly codified. In attempting to reconstruct the system of distinctions and rules of combination which members of a culture display in choosing their own garments and in interpreting those of others as indications of a particular life-style, social role, or attitude, the semiotician would be identifying the distinctions by which garments become signs.

Whatever area he is working in, someone adopting the semiotic perspective attempts to make explicit the implicit knowledge which enables people within a given society to understand one another's behavior. Often, of course, this implicit knowledge is a deeply rooted set of cultural norms and conventions which operate subconsciously and which members of a culture might angrily deny. In these cases, the description of a semiotic system becomes an act of demystification, of exposure. The pleasure of revealing the culturally determined nature of behavior has doubtless been the impetus behind much semiotic analysis, but one would be mystified by the demystification itself if one thought that the description of semiotic systems made the individual more free or that the semiotic analysis was in any way inspired by the prospect of liberating man. On the contrary, structuralist and semiotic thinking has been repeatedly labeled 'antihumanistic,' and Michel Foucault has provided a target for such attacks in maintaining that 'man is only a recent invention, a figure not yet two centuries old, a simple fold in our knowledge' which will soon disappear.[12]

What does the pursuit of signs have to do with the disappearance of man? A whole tradition of thought treats man as essentially a thinking being, a conscious subject who endows objects around him with meaning. Indeed, we often think of the meaning of an expression as what the subject or speaker 'has in mind.' But as meaning is explained in terms of systems of signs— systems which the subject does not control—the subject is deprived of his role as source of meaning. I know a language, certainly, but since I need a linguist to tell me what it is that I know, the status and the nature of the 'I' which knows is called into question: 'The goal of the human sciences,' says Lévi-Strauss, 'is not to constitute man but to dissolve him.'[13] Although they begin by making man an object of knowledge, these disciplines find, as their work advances, that the self is dissolved as its various functions are ascribed to impersonal systems which operate through it.

'The researches of psychoanalysis, of linguistics, of anthropology have "decentered" the subject in relation to the laws of its desire, the forms of its language, the rules of its actions, or the play of its mythical and imaginative discourse,' writes Foucault.[14] The distinction between man and the world is a variable one that depends on the configurations of knowledge at a given time, and the various disciplines engaged in semiotic analysis have treated as systems of conventions so much of what used to be the property of the thinking subject that any notion of man founded thereon becomes problematic. As the self is broken down into component systems, deprived of its status as source and master of meaning, it comes to seem more and more like a construct: a result of systems of convention. Even the idea of personal identity emerges through the discourse of a culture: the 'I' is not something given but comes to exist as that which is addressed by and relates to others. In short, as Jean-Marie Benoist puts it in his account of *La Révolution structurale*, what theoretical investigation discovered was not man but signs. No longer man-centered, 'contemporary research could conceive of itself as a semiotics: semiotics of the unconscious for Lacan, semiotics of the codes of kinship and myth for Lévi-Strauss, semiotics of the relations and contradictions in society for Althusser, semiotics of literature for Barthes and Genette, and a semiotics of historical discourse and documents, of which Foucault provides the discourse on method.'[15] In each case, explanation involves the description of systems of signs, not the tracing of an event to a mind which would be allowed to count as its source.

If the 'dissolution' of man into a series of systems is the ultimate effect of a structuralist and semiotic perspective, if everything which is meaningful within human cultures can be treated as a sign, then, as Benoist's list already suggests, semiotics embraces a vast domain: it moves in, imperialistically, on the territory of most disciplines of the humanities and social sciences. Any sphere of human activity, from music to cooking to politics, can be an object of semiotic study; and it is precisely because any signifying activity calls for semiotic investigation that the emergence of semiotics may bring about a major reorganization of scholarly research. If the study of music as a sign system is assimilated to semiotics, the other aspects of musicology will form a discipline which must define itself in a new way.

Whatever configurations the future holds, semiotics at the moment brings together a whole series of projects which study signs but which it does not know how to classify. Umberto Eco's recent *A Theory of Semiotics* offers a list of current concerns which is amusing in its very disorder: Zoosemiotics, Olfactory signs, Tactile communication, Codes of taste, Paralinguistics, Medical semiotics, Kinesics and proxemics, Musical codes, Formalized languages, Written language, Unknown alphabets and secret codes, Natural languages, Visual communication, Systems of objects, Plot structure, Text theory, Cultural codes, Aesthetic texts, Mass communication, Rhetoric.[16]

As this list makes abundantly clear, one of the major tasks that semiotics must face is to organize itself. This is in fact its primary concern, since it involves determining what are the principal varieties of sign and how they relate to one another. But this is a question which will be confronted by other disciplines as well as they react to the imperialistic claims of semiotics. If they welcome assimilation to or association with semiotics they will try to determine how significance takes place in the sphere of human activity that concerns them and how these processes relate to others studied by semiotics; but if they resist the claims of semiotics they will also engage in debate about the processes of signification that concern them. The result of these various efforts will doubtless be a demonstration of the inadequacy of the categories and distinctions which semiotics has so far proposed for classifying signs. As Julia Kristeva has written:

> semiotics cannot develop except as a critique of semiotics. At every moment in its development semiotics must theorize its object, its own method, and the relationship between them; it therefore theorizes itself and becomes, by thus turning back on itself, the theory of its own scientific practice. . . . It is a direction for research, always open, a theoretical enterprise which turns back upon itself, a perpetual self-criticism.[17]

The best way to illustrate the complex and self-reflexive progress of a semiotic enterprise is to consider what semiotics has done and promised to do for the study of the most complex of sign systems, *literature*. Literature is the most interesting case of semiosis for a variety of reasons. Though it is clearly a form of communication, it is cut off from the immediate pragmatic purposes which simplify other sign situations. The potential complexities of signifying processes work freely in literature. Moreover, the difficulty of saying precisely what is communicated is here accompanied by the fact that signification is indubitably taking place. One cannot argue, as one might when dealing with physical objects or events of various kinds, that the phenomena in question are meaningless. Literature forces one to face the problem of the indeterminacy of meaning, which is a central if paradoxical property of semiotic systems. Finally, unlike so many other systems which are devoted to ends external to themselves and their own processes, literature is itself a continual exploration of and reflection upon signification in all its forms: an interpretation of experience; a commentary on the validity of various ways of interpreting experience; an exploration of the creative, revelatory, and deceptive powers of language; a critique of the codes and interpretive processes manifested in our languages and in previous literature. In so far as literature turns back on itself and examines, parodies, or treats ironically its own signifying procedures, it becomes the most complex account of signification we possess.

Literary criticism, as a result of the semiotic perspective, has devoted much time to showing that this is so. In interpreting a novel like Flaubert's *Madame Bovary*, for example, one would show how irony, which is itself a process of signification, works to undermine other types of signification: both Emma's reading of her own experience and the reader's attempt to make events and descriptive details fit into 'novelistic' signifying patterns. One can show that the novel, like all discourse which takes the initial step of calling itself fictive and thereby poses inescapably the problem of its signifying status, is ultimately 'about' signs and meaning. Or again, in interpreting a poem like Blake's 'London', one would argue that though in one sense it is a vision of urban misery, it narrates, at a literal level, acts of interpretation, a reading of signs; and the rhetorical figures which the poem uses to narrate the vision ('the hapless soldier's sigh/Runs in blood down palace walls' and 'the youthful harlot's curse/. . . blights with plagues the marriage hearse'), because they are so very unusual, pose the question of the status of the interpretive acts here recounted. If we imagine a speaker walking through London streets reacting in this way to sighs and curses, then we have an account of a signifying process gone wrong, an obsessional imagination; in order to accept and make sense of the interpretations which the poem offers we must treat as fictions the interpretive acts which the poem describes. In leading the reader to choose an interpretive strategy, the poem explores the paradoxical qualities of fictional discourse and the undecidable nature of figurative language. (See Chapter 3 below.)

Other literary works, of course, are much more violently explicit in their dealings with signs and signification, transgressing in their own several ways all the linguistic and discursive conventions one can think of. As explorations both of the power of language to create thought and of the limits of discourse, works of this sort constitute a radical contribution to a theory of signs and signification, for they show the impossibility of treating signification as a purely code-like phenomenon. When they appear in literature, as they do, new lexical items will be given some kind of meaning by readers (consider Joyce's 'Stay us wherefore in our search for tighteousness' or Carroll's 'brillig') and syntactic combinations one would have thought impossible will be interpreted (Cummings's 'Anyone lived in a pretty how town/ with up so floating many bells down'). Criticism attuned to semiotics interprets works as semiotic explorations.

But if literary works make it clear that one cannot set limits to the signifying process and define once and for all the appropriate system of conventions, they also provide conclusive evidence for the existence of a semiotic system which makes literature possible. Just as violations of etiquette testify to the existence of conventions which make it possible to be polite or impolite, so the flouting of linguistic and literary conventions by which literary works bring about a renewal of perception testifies to the importance of a system of conventions as the basis of literary signification. Precisely because literary works so often attempt to achieve their effects by parodying or treating ironically previous conventions, by ending in unexpected ways or using details in ways which will surprise readers, it is important, for any account of literature, to try to define the underlying systems of convention, to characterize literature as an institution.

One must distinguish between the kind of interpretive criticism discussed earlier, which interprets individual works as statements about signification, and this semiotics of literature, which does not interpret works but tries to discover the conventions which make meaning possible. Here the goal is to develop a poetics which would stand to literature as linguistics stands to language. Just as the task of linguists is not to tell us what individual sentences mean but to explain according to what rules their elements combine and contrast to produce the meanings sentences have for speakers of a language, so the semiotician attempts to discover the nature of the codes which make literary communication possible.

This project, whether explicitly defined as it was by Tzvetan Todorov, or elegantly and obliquely pursued as it was by Roland Barthes and Gérard Genette, inspired a great deal of highly original critical and theoretical discussion of literature in France

in the 1960s, but it is no longer exclusively or even primarily a
French concern. Work on plot structure, the goal of which is a
grammar of plots, has been carried out in many countries. Work
on narrative codes or techniques can assimilate recent French
discussions like Genette's 'Discours du récit'[18] to research done
earlier in a different intellectual context in Germany and the
United States. Indeed, today the semiotics of literature is very
much an American and European phenomenon organized into
loose groups of varying persuasions but not into national
schools. It is governed by the assumption that a systematic theory
of discourse if not of literature (for one of the effects of semiotics is
to question the distinction between literary and nonliterary discourse) is possible, though there may be little agreement about
precisely what 'languages' (information theory, semantics,
systems theory, psychoanalysis) will be most useful in establishing the categories and identifying the codes of the discursive
systems at work in texts. A major point on which there would be
agreement, however, is that literary works are to be considered
not as autonomous entities, 'organic wholes,' but as intertextual
constructs: sequences which have meaning in relation to other
texts which they take up, cite, parody, refute, or generally transform. A text can be read only in relation to other texts, and it is
made possible by the codes which animate the discursive space of
a culture. The work is a product not of a biographically defined
individual about whom information could be accumulated, but of
writing itself. To write a poem the author had to take on the
character of poet, and it is that semiotic function of poet or writer
rather than the biographical function of author which is relevant
to discussion of the text.

Literary study experienced what Barthes called 'the death of
the author' but almost simultaneously it discovered the reader,
for in an account of the semiotics of literature someone like the
reader is needed to serve as center. The reader becomes the name
of the place where the various codes can be located: a virtual site.
Semiotics attempts to make explicit the implicit knowledge which
enables signs to have meaning, so it needs the reader not as a
person but as a function: the repository of the codes which
account for the intelligibility of the text. Because literary works do

have meaning for readers, semiotics undertakes to describe the systems of convention responsible for those meanings.

This is a coherent and necessary program: since communication does take place we must discover how it occurs if we wish to understand ourselves as social and cultural beings. But literature itself, in its continual pressure on and violation of codes, reveals a paradox inherent in the semiotic project and in the philosophic orientation of which it is the culmination. To account for the signification of, shall we say, a metaphor is to show how the relationship between its form and its meaning is already virtually present in the systems of language and rhetoric. The metaphor itself becomes not a radical or inaugural act but a manifestation of a preexistent connection. Yet the value of the metaphor, the value of our experience of the metaphor, lies in its innovatory, inaugural force. Indeed, our whole notion of literature makes it not a transcription of preexisting thoughts but a series of radical and inaugural acts: acts of imposition which create meaning. The very conventions to which we appeal in explaining literary meanings are products: products which, it would seem, must have acts as their source.

This second perspective deconstructs the first; it seems to bring about a reversal, explaining meaning not by prior conventions but by acts of imposition. However, the first perspective also deconstructs the second in its turn, for acts of imposition are themselves made possible by the situations in which they occur, and meanings cannot be imposed unless they are understood, unless the conventions which make possible understanding are already in place. The semiotics of literature thus gives rise to a 'deconstructive movement' in which each pole of an opposition can be used to show that the other is in error but in which the undecidable dialectic gives rise to no synthesis because the antinomy is inherent in the very structure of our language, in the possibilities of our conceptual framework.

What happens in literary semiotics is but one version of a general situation which is gradually coming to be recognized as an inescapable feature of our ways of thinking about texts and signification. Semiotics is the instrument of this revelation because it is the logical culmination of what Jacques Derrida calls the 'logo-centrism' of Western culture: the rationality which treats mean-ings as concepts or logical representations that it is the function of signs to express. We speak, for example, of various ways of saying 'the same thing.'

Semiotics begins as a critique of the logocentric assumption that concepts exist prior to and independently of their expres-sion. In analyzing signification Saussure and his later followers insist that forms and concepts do not exist independently of one another but that the sign consists of the union of a signifier and signified. Moreover—and this is the important point—both signifiers and signifieds are purely relational entities, products of a system of differences. To speak of the concept of 'brown,' for example, is, according to semiotics, a way of referring to a com-plex network of oppositions which articulates the spectrum of colors on the one hand and the spectrum of sound on the other. The meaning of *brown* is not a representation in my mind at the moment of utterance but a space in a complex network of dif-ferences.[19]

Semiotics thus takes up the problem of the *sign*, on which logocentric notions of signification have been based, and gives it a relational or differential interpretation which seems to not only make possible a new type of explanation—structural explanation in terms of underlying systems of relation—but also to displace logocentrism. However, as Derrida has shown, in a series of works which are the most brilliant products of a semiotics whose limits they describe and attempt to transcend, semiotics does not escape logocentrism: though the source of meanings is no longer a consciousness in which they exist prior to their expression, their source becomes a system of differences which semiotics treats as the necessary condition of any act of signification.[20] This is a marked advance, a far more adequate account of signification than that which it originally set out to criticize, but it ultimately encounters the same formal difficulty: instead of depending on the prior existence of a system of concepts, expression now depends on the prior existence of a system of signs.

One deconstructs this perspective by arguing that the dif-ferences ultimately responsible for meaning did not simply fall from heaven but are themselves products. Acts of signification are necessary to create signifying differences. But this perspective gives rise to no discipline; it is not a position that can be maintained because if one tries to discuss acts of signification one immediately is led to describe the oppositions which enable an act to signify; one inevitably finds oneself back in the semiotic perspective, describing a system. This irresolvable dialectic, the solidarity of these contradictory perspectives, Derrida captures with the term *différance*, which is both a difference and a differing, designating a passive difference always already in place as the ground of signification and an act of differing which produces the differences it presupposes. To spell *différance* with an *a* instead of an *e* is of course to press against the limits of a logocentric language, but the concept it produces can be understood only in our language, in which, of course, it is a contradiction. More generally, escape from logocentrism is impossible because the language we use to criticize or to formulate alternatives works according to the principles being contested.

The paradoxes and undecidables which this perspective discloses as the unavoidable bases of language and thought are more familiar and more easily exemplified in the realm of literature than elsewhere. The very notion of rhetorical figures, which have now become a major object of critical attention, captures a fundamental paradox.[21] A rhetorical figure is a situation in which language means something other than what it says, a violation of the code. But lest that violation introduce a radical undecidability to linguistic situations, leading us to wonder how we could ever know whether language means what it appears to be saying, these violations are codified, as a repertoire of highly artificial and conventional devices which writers can draw on to produce meaning. What looks at first like an inaugural creative act, a violation of the code, is accounted for by the formulation of a code on which its meaning is said to depend. Nor is this last move an unfortunate error which might have been avoided. The very notion of rhetorical effects—the possibility of metaphorical signification, for example—requires there to be a distinction between literal meaning and metaphorical meaning and hence the beginnings of a rhetorical code.

Thus, even the study of reputedly deviant forms of signification leads one back to the same problematic. Undertaking a rigorous investigation of signs and signification, semiotics produces a discipline which, ultimately, reveals the fundamental contradictions of the signifying process as we understand it. Semiotics leads, necessarily, to a critique of semiotics, to a perspective which shows the errors of its ways. But that perspective is never a viable alternative. It is not a position from which one could undertake an alternative analysis of signs and systems of signs, for the notion of analysis, of explanation, of production of models are all part of the semiotic perspective, and to undertake any of them is immediately to revert to that perspective. The alternative, then, is not a discipline, not another mode of analysis, but acts of writing, acts of displacement, play which violates language and rationality. Though these acts can themselves be analyzed and understood, discussed in terms of codes which make them meaningful, they are in their moment, as examples of the play of signifiers, challenges to a perspective whose limitations they expose.

Given this structure, one can think of semiotics and the future it projects in two ways. First, it offers a discipline which can bring together in a comparative perspective a whole range of phenomena which do respond to treatment by a common method. Proposing structural explanation in place of historical and causal reconstruction, making explicit the interdependence of social phenomena on one another by analyzing them in terms of systems of relations, and demonstrating the extent to which what we call 'man' is the juncture of a series of interpersonal systems which operate through him, semiotics offers both methodological claims which will be debated even by those who reject them, and a program which in its ambitious scope will provide a place for numerous analytical projects. The fact that the pursuit of semiotics leads to an awareness of its limits, to an awareness that signification can never be mastered by a coherent and comprehensive theory, should not be a reason for spurning its analytical programs as if there were some more valid or comprehensive perspective on signification.

But, on the other hand, in so far as it leads to the limits of its own theory, semiotics gives rise to a kind of interpretive activity, a Derridean *double science*, a deconstructive mode of reading which works both within and against it. Deconstruction enjoys announcing the impossibility of the semiotic activity it inhabits as it undertakes the task it has set itself: reading the major texts of Western literature and philosophy as sites on the boundaries of logocentrism and showing, in the most subtle interpretations that scholarship has yet produced, how these texts are already riven by the contradictions and indeterminacies that seem inherent in the exercise of language.[22] The tense interplay between the opposed yet inseparable activities of semiotics and deconstruction is already a major source of energy in literary studies, and it would be rash indeed to predict when or how its dominance will end.

PART TWO

3

Semiotics as a Theory of Reading

The fact that people engaged in the study of literature are willing to read works of criticism tells us something important about the nature of our discipline. Few people, one imagines, take up a critical article because it is the most pleasant or entertaining way to spend an hour; they do so, they would say, because they hope to hear worthwhile arguments and proposals. Our assumptions that significant things will be said in critical writings may be an expectation more frequently defeated than fulfilled, but its presence, indeed its extraordinary persistence in the face of defeat, suggests that we see literary criticism as a discipline that aims at knowledge.

Of course, it may be difficult to explain how our discipline does move toward knowledge. Ever since literary studies turned from erudition to interpretation it has been easy to question the notion of a cumulative discipline. Acts of interpretation do not necessarily seem to bring us closer to a goal such as a more accurate understanding of all the major works of European literature. Indeed, the cynic might say that criticism does not move toward better interpretations and fuller understanding so much as toward what Schoenberg achieved in his *Erwartung*: a chromatic plenitude, a playing of all possible notes in all possible registers, a saturation of musical space.

One strategy popular in these circumstances is to legislate against the proliferation of interpretations by proposing a theory declaring that each work has *a* meaning and that the critic's quest for knowledge is an attempt to discover that meaning. If the

47

meaning of a work is what its author meant by it, or what it would have meant to an ideal audience of its day, or what accounts for its every detail without violating the historical norms of the genre, then the critic knows what he is attempting to discover. But such theories do not persuade readers and critics to restrict themselves to interpretations of the preferred kind, and the very existence of competing theories of the meaning of works encourages and reproduces the proliferation each theory was designed to cure. To make the goal of literary studies knowledge of the meaning of each individual literary work involves the futile attempt to impose a particular standard and a single goal upon the activity of reading.

The question then becomes: what sort of knowledge is possible? Instead of taking the proliferation of interpretations as an obstacle to knowledge, can one attempt to make it an object of knowledge, asking how it is that literary works have the meaning they do for readers? The institution of literature involves interpretive practices, techniques for making sense of literary works, which it ought to be possible to describe. Instead of attempting to legislate solutions to interpretive disagreements, one might attempt to analyze the interpretive operations that produce these disagreements—discord which is part of the literary activity of our culture. Such a program falls under the aegis of semiotics, which seeks to identify the conventions and operations by which any signifying practice (such as literature) produces its observable effects of meaning.

A signal virtue of semiotics (and perhaps in these early days its principal virtue) is the methodological clarity it can introduce into literary studies by explicit identification of assumptions and goals. Semiotic investigation is possible only when one is dealing with a mode of signification or communication. One must be able to identify effects of signification—the meanings objects and events have for participants and observers. Then one can attempt to construct models of signifying processes to account for these effects. A semiotics of literature is thus based on two assumptions, both of which can be questioned: first, that literature should be treated as a mode of signification and communication, in that a proper description of a literary work must refer to the meanings it has for readers; second, that one can identify the effects of signification one wants to account for.

Objections to the first assumption insist on the importance of attempting to separate the work itself from interpretations of it: interpretations vary in unpredictable ways; they are determined by factors external to the work and should not be seen either as part of it or as reliable guides to it. Instead of adopting the semiotic perspective and treating interpretations as the completion of a work, this argument would run, one should seek ways of analyzing the work as an objective artifact. Debates on this point have now become familiar, and there is little reason to believe that either side will discover a decisive argument.

But even if one accepts the first assumption, that literature is a mode of communication, one might still be skeptical of the possibility of identifying and collecting effects of signification. Any technique for ascertaining the meanings works have for readers, one might argue, will produce massive distortions, either because the questions asked will provoke reflections that did not belong to the 'original' response, or else because the procedure will collect only certain kinds of responses and interpretations. One cannot deny that works do have an impact on readers and do produce effects of signification, but these effects, one can argue, are not a content that could be grasped, catalogued, and studied.

These are reasonable grounds for disputing the assumptions of semiotics. When confronted with such objections, the semiotician must choose between two strategies. He may disagree, asserting that literature is a form of communication and that what it communicates cannot be ignored even if one wishes to. Or else he may grant the objections and modestly claim the reduced role that remains. Even if interpretations and responses do not belong to the structure of the work, they are an important cultural activity that should be studied; and even if responses are not objects that can be collected and analyzed, there are still numerous records of responses and interpretations that semiotics can use. Since communication does take place, since interpretations are recorded, one can study literary signification by attempting to describe the conventions and semiotic operations responsible for these interpretations.

In the end, the semiotician's choice of strategy will affect the claims he makes for his conclusions but may not greatly alter the structure of his enterprise. Whether he claims that an account of interpretive operations bears upon the very essence of literature, or whether he presents his work as the study of an important cultural activity closely related to literature, his data are the judgments and interpretations of readers and his conclusions are an attempt to account for them.

Such a semiotics would be a theory of reading and its object would not be literary works themselves but their intelligibility: the ways in which they make sense, the ways in which readers have made sense of them. Indeed, the semiotic program may be better expressed by the concepts of 'sense' and 'making sense' than by the concept of 'meaning,' for while 'meaning' suggests a property of a text (a text 'has' meaning), and thus encourages one to distinguish an intrinsic (though perhaps ungraspable) meaning from the interpretations of readers, 'sense' links the qualities of a test to the operations one performs upon it. A text can make sense and someone can make sense of a text. If a text which at first did not make sense comes to make sense, it is because someone has made sense of it. 'Making sense' suggests that to investigate literary signification one must analyze interpretive operations.

The most common objection to a semiotics of reading, especially one that invokes the example of linguistics and speaks of its project as an attempt to describe 'literary competence,' is that it wrongly assumes agreement among readers or posits as a norm a 'competent' reading which other readers ought to accept. It is crucial to insist that a semiotics of reading leaves entirely open the question of how much readers agree or disagree in their interpretations of literature. It attempts to account for facts about interpretation, whatever one takes those facts to be. It is interested in the range of readings for a given work, whether one takes that range to be wide or narrow. Where there seems to be agreement among readers—that *King Lear* has tragic impact—this is an important fact about interpretation; where disagreement seems clearly focussed—is Marvell's 'Horatian Ode' a celebration or an ironic critique of Cromwell?—that is of interest; when there is a much wider spread of interpretations, as in readings of Wordsworth's 'A Slumber did my Spirit Seal,' that also needs to be accounted for. In general, divergence of readings is more interesting than convergence, though of course it must be defined in relation to convergence. In any event, since facts of interpretation constitute the point of departure and the data to be explained, a semiotic discussion will simply be judged irrelevant if it starts from a blatantly unrepresentative range of interpretations.

One could, of course, scrap the term 'literary competence' to avoid the appearance of presuming agreement among readers on the existence of a normative, 'competent' interpretation, but this would involve a loss, since 'competence' does indicate that one is dealing with an ability involving norms. Not only does interpretation employ repeatable operations, but in one's attempt to interpret a text one is always implicitly appealing to norms. When one wonders whether a particular line of thought will work out, whether one will succeed in elucidating an obscure passage, one posits norms of successful interpretations, adequate clarity, sufficient coherence. These norms may remain vague and they may vary greatly from one situation to another and from one interpretive community to another, but the process of interpretation is incomprehensible without them, and one is usefully reminded of this by the allusion to norms implicit in the concept of 'literary competence.'

The study of reading can proceed in various ways. One's focus can be synchronic or diachronic; one can concentrate on readings of a particular work or readings of numerous works by a particular group of readers; one can draw data from diverse sources to focus on a particular problem or distinction, or one can seek out comparable interpretations for the easier identification of convergences and differences. These are all ways of organizing information that comes from actual readers, be they famous critics, or colleagues and students, or oneself. In comparing and interpreting this information one will, of course, construct models of interpretive processes which, as models, will be idealizations, but notions of an ideal reader or a superreader ought to be avoided. To speak of an ideal reader is to forget that reading has a history. There is no reason to believe that the perfect master of today's favorite interpretive techniques is the ideal reader, and it is not clear how the study of reading would benefit from positing a transhistorical ideal. Reading is historical, even though it need not be studied historically.

However, there is a danger here. One should not assume that because one is interested in real rather than in ideal readers one ought to rush into the libraries armed with questionnaires. Norman Holland's *Five Readers Reading* shows how easily well-intentioned empirical research can miscarry. Interested in how far the range of responses to a work might be due to the personalities of readers, Holland took five undergraduates who could read, gave them personality tests to determine their five personalities, and then discussed with them several stories they had read, asking them 'how they felt' about particular characters, events, and situations, or asking them to imagine how a particular character might have acted in different circumstances. 'By so informal a procedure,' he reports, 'I was hoping to get out free associations to the stories.'[1] ('Get out,' one might add, does not mean 'eliminate' but 'elicit.') Holland discovered a significant correlation between his readers' free associations to the stories and their personalities, as determined by free association tests.

The example is instructive in its demonstration of the way in which dubious principles make potentially relevant experiments irrelevant. Holland was working from the assumptions of American ego psychology, which endows each individual with a distinctive 'identity theme' that is present in all his behavior and makes his life an organic unity. (It would not be wrong to detect here a vulgarized and sentimentalized version of the New Criticism, with organic unity transferred from the work of art to the entire 'text' of a person's life.) The literary work, Holland argues, does not have meaning in itself, but is given meaning by the reader, who projects onto it his unique identity theme. To illustrate this hypothesis, Holland needed to ask questions that would fail to set in motion public interpretive processes and would thereby give distinctive identity themes a chance to manifest themselves. Instead of asking students to organize and synthesize according to their usual procedures of interpretation, he asked them to free-associate. But even then he did not get today's favorite interpretive techniques is the ideal reader, and it is not clear how the study of reading would benefit from positing a transhistorical ideal. Reading is historical, even though it need not be studied historically.

However, there is a danger here. One should not assume that because one is interested in real rather than in ideal readers one ought to rush into the libraries armed with questionnaires. Norman Holland's *Five Readers Reading* shows how easily well-intentioned empirical research can miscarry. Interested in how far the range of responses to a work might be due to the personalities of readers, Holland took five undergraduates who could read, gave them personality tests to determine their five personalities, and then discussed with them several stories they had read, asking them 'how they felt' about particular characters, events, and situations, or asking them to imagine how a particular character might have acted in different circumstances. 'By so informal a procedure,' he reports, 'I was hoping to get out free associations to the stories.'[1] ('Get out,' one might add, does not mean 'eliminate' but 'elicit.') Holland discovered a significant correlation between his readers' free associations to the stories and their personalities, as determined by free association tests.

The example is instructive in its demonstration of the way in which dubious principles make potentially relevant experiments irrelevant. Holland was working from the assumptions of American ego psychology, which endows each individual with a distinctive 'identity theme' that is present in all his behavior and makes his life an organic unity. (It would not be wrong to detect here a vulgarized and sentimentalized version of the New Criticism, with organic unity transferred from the work of art to the entire 'text' of a person's life.) The literary work, Holland argues, does not have meaning in itself, but is given meaning by the reader, who projects onto it his unique identity theme. To illustrate this hypothesis, Holland needed to ask questions that would fail to set in motion public interpretive processes and would thereby give distinctive identity themes a chance to manifest themselves. Instead of asking students to organize and synthesize according to their usual procedures of interpretation, he asked them to free-associate. But even then he did not get

meanings it has for readers; second, that one can identify the effects of signification one wants to account for.

Objections to the first assumption insist on the importance of attempting to separate the work itself from interpretations of it: interpretations vary in unpredictable ways; they are determined by factors external to the work and should not be seen either as part of it or as reliable guides to it. Instead of adopting the semiotic perspective and treating interpretations as the completion of a work, this argument would run, one should seek ways of analyzing the work as an objective artifact. Debates on this point have now become familiar, and there is little reason to believe that either side will discover a decisive argument.

But even if one accepts the first assumption, that literature is a mode of communication, one might still be skeptical of the possibility of identifying and collecting effects of signification. Any technique for ascertaining the meanings works have for readers, one might argue, will produce massive distortions, either because the questions asked will provoke reflections that did not belong to the 'original' response, or else because the procedure will collect only certain kinds of responses and interpretations. One cannot deny that works do have an impact on readers and do produce effects of signification, but these effects, one can argue, are not a content that could be grasped, catalogued, and studied.

These are reasonable grounds for disputing the assumptions of semiotics. When confronted with such objections, the semiotician must choose between two strategies. He may disagree, asserting that literature is a form of communication and that what it communicates cannot be ignored even if one wishes to. Or else he may grant the objections and modestly claim the reduced role that remains. Even if interpretations and responses do not belong to the structure of the work, they are an important cultural activity that should be studied; and even if responses are not objects that can be collected and analyzed, there are still numerous records of responses and interpretations that semiotics can use. Since communication does take place, since interpretations are recorded, one can study literary signification by attempting to describe the conventions and semiotic operations responsible for these interpretations.

In the end, the semiotician's choice of strategy will affect the claims he makes for his conclusions but may not greatly alter the structure of his enterprise. Whether he claims that an account of interpretive operations bears upon the very essence of literature, or whether he presents his work as the study of an important cultural activity closely related to literature, his data are the judgments and interpretations of readers and his conclusions are an attempt to account for them.

Such a semiotics would be a theory of reading and its object would not be literary works themselves but their intelligibility: the ways in which they make sense, the ways in which readers have made sense of them. Indeed, the semiotic program may be better expressed by the concepts of 'sense' and 'making sense' than by the concept of 'meaning,' for while 'meaning' suggests a property of a text (a text 'has' meaning), and thus encourages one to distinguish an intrinsic (though perhaps ungraspable) meaning from the interpretations of readers, 'sense' links the qualities of a test to the operations one performs upon it. A text can make sense and someone can make sense of a text. If a text which at first did not make sense comes to make sense, it is because someone has made sense of it. 'Making sense' suggests that to investigate literary signification one must analyze interpretive operations.

The most common objection to a semiotics of reading, especially one that invokes the example of linguistics and speaks of its project as an attempt to describe 'literary competence,' is that it wrongly assumes agreement among readers or posits as a norm a 'competent' reading which other readers ought to accept. It is crucial to insist that a semiotics of reading leaves entirely open the question of how much readers agree or disagree in their interpretations of literature. It attempts to account for facts about interpretation, whatever one takes those facts to be. It is interested in the range of readings for a given work, whether one takes that range to be wide or narrow. Where there seems to be agreement among readers—that *King Lear* has tragic impact— this is an important fact about interpretation; where disagreement seems clearly focussed—is Marvell's 'Horatian Ode' a celebration or an ironic critique of Cromwell?—that is of interest; when there is a much wider spread of interpretations, as in

readings of Wordsworth's 'A Slumber did my Spirit Seal,' that also needs to be accounted for. In general, divergence of readings is more interesting than convergence, though of course it must be defined in relation to convergence. In any event, since facts of interpretation constitute the point of departure and the data to be explained, a semiotic discussion will simply be judged irrelevant if it starts from a blatantly unrepresentative range of interpretations.

One could, of course, scrap the term 'literary competence' to avoid the appearance of presuming agreement among readers on the existence of a normative, 'competent' interpretation, but this would involve a loss, since 'competence' does indicate that one is dealing with an ability involving norms. Not only does interpretation employ repeatable operations, but in one's attempt to interpret a text one is always implicitly appealing to norms. When one wonders whether a particular line of thought will work out, whether one will succeed in elucidating an obscure passage, one posits norms of successful interpretations, adequate clarity, sufficient coherence. These norms may remain vague and they may vary greatly from one situation to another and from one interpretive community to another, but the process of interpretation incomprehensible without them, and one is usefully reminded this by the allusion to norms implicit in the concept of 'literary competence.'

The study of reading can proceed in various ways. One can be synchronic or diachronic; one can concentrate on readings of a particular work or readings of numerous works by a particular group of readers; one can draw data from diverse sources, focus on a particular problem or distinction, or one can seek comparable interpretations for the easier identification of convergences and differences. These are all ways of organizing information that comes from actual readers, be they famous critics or colleagues and students, or oneself. In comparing and interpreting this information one will, of course, construct interpretive processes which, as models, will be useful, but notions of an ideal reader or a superreader are to be avoided. To speak of an ideal reader is to forget that reading has a history. There is no reason to believe that the quite the results he desired, for their free associations revealed above all the clichés of the various subcultures and cultural discourses that work to constitute the consciousness of American college students. *Five Readers Reading* might be interpreted as confirmation of the axiom that modern research has established: that the individuality of the individual cannot function as a principle of explanation, for it is itself a complex cultural construct, a heterogeneous product rather than a unified cause. More interesting than the clichés of his readers' differences are the factors that make their perceptions and associations converge. When, for example, they agree that a particular episode bears suggestions of a primal scene, we can observe, as Frederick Crews notes, 'three students doing what comes naturally in their predicament, i.e. humoring the teacher.'[2]

If one were interested not in free associations but in the synthesizing operations of interpretive understanding, one would have to ask different questions. But in fact there is little need to concern oneself with the design of experiments, for several reasons. First, there already exist more than enough interpretations with which to begin. By consulting the interpretations which literary history records for any major work, one discovers a spectrum of interpretive possibilities of greater interest and diversity than a survey of undergraduates could provide. These considered reactions of readers are more than adequate as a point of departure for a semiotics of reading. Moreover, even if one were to work primarily from one's own interpretations in an attempt to formulate one's own literary competence, the processes of writing and formulation would themselves accentuate everything that is public and generalizable in the reading process. In attempting to make explicit the assumptions, conventions, and interpretive operations at work in one's own responses, one casts them in a generalizable form and exposes them to judgment, both one's own and others'. In any case, since one's notions of how to read and of what is involved in interpretation are acquired in commerce with others, there is every likelihood that an explicit formulation of one's own interpretive operations would have considerable general validity. The possibility that it might not is no reason for refusing the attempt.

A semiotics of reading that seeks to avoid Holland's errors thus remains relatively unrestricted and can adopt any of numerous approaches. One possibility, for example, is Hans Robert Jauss's *Rezeptionsästhetik*. Arguing that 'if literary history is to be rejuvenated, the prejudices of historical objectivity must be removed and the traditional approach to literature replaced by an esthetics of reception and impact,' Jauss underlines the importance of reception studies for any account of literary signification.[3] A work does not have an inherent meaning: it does not speak, as it were, it only answers. Karl Popper, one of Jauss's theoretical sources, observes that 'in every moment of our pre-scientific or scientific development we possess something which I usually refer to as a "horizon of expectations". . . . In every case the horizon of expectations plays the role of a frame of reference, without which experiences, observations, etc. would have no meaning.'[4]

The meaning of a work is its answers to the questions posed by a horizon of expectations. To understand the interaction between a work and the reading public we must reconstruct this horizon, which at a given moment is the result of three principal factors: previous understanding of the genre in question, the form and theme of earlier works assumed to be known, and the distinction between poetic and practical language, which will be differently situated in different periods. Jauss insists on the possibility of describing reception precisely and explicitly in relation to this 'objectively formulatable reference system of expectations.'

> The psychical process of the reception of a text on the primary horizon of esthetic experience is by no means only a random succession of merely subjective impressions but the carrying out of certain directions in a process of directed perception which can be comprehended from the motivations that constitute it and the signals which set it off, and which can be described linguistically.[5]

Indeed, it is only possible to pose the question of the subjectivity of a response or of differences in readers' tastes once one has identified the 'transsubjective horizon of understanding' of a particular period.

Though he presents *Rezeptionsästhetik* as a partial method that does not exhaust the historical aspects of literature, Jauss outlines a program that includes not only the study of responses to individual works and the reconstruction of the horizons of expectations responsible for those responses but also the investigation of how the interaction of expectations and innovatory works leads to changes in canons and esthetic norms. Finally, *Rezeptionsästhetik* should help to elucidate the social impact of literature: in Jauss's view, it is through this dialectic of question and answer, problem and solution, that works of art have a historical effect.

This is an immense program, and Jauss, with his expertise in a range of periods and literatures, has been working on it in various ways, analyzing medieval genre theory or studying different aspects of the reception of French and German works from the seventeenth to the twentieth century. For example, he has investigated how the 'horizon of expectations' in France of the 1850s led to very different receptions for two novels about adultery: Flaubert's *Madame Bovary*, which was prosecuted on a morals charge, and Feydeau's *Fanny*, which had a huge popular success.[6]

In a different sort of comparison, of Racine's *Iphigénie en Aulide* and Goethe's *Iphigenie auf Tauris*, he attempts to show how 'the historical classicism of the age of Goethe turns into an aesthetic classicism, which allows the forgetting of the change of horizon of aesthetic experience that had also originally been required by Goethe's *Iphigenie*. In other words, the original negativity of the work is transformed into the guaranteedness of what has become familiar ("die Verbürgtheit des nunmehr Vertrauten").'[7] Goethe's play was in part a response to certain problems that, according to an eighteenth-century perspective, Racine had left unsolved; in relation to the horizon of expectations of Goethe's day, *Iphigenie auf Tauris* was powerful and innovatory, but it contributed to the establishment of a classicism which gave it something of the status of a monument—which is what it has become for later generations.

A third investigation focuses not on the reception of a particular work and the way a change of horizon transforms a work but on one portion of the horizon of expectations in the France of 1857, the year of Baudelaire's *Les Fleurs du Mal*. 'Le Crépuscule du soir' in the section 'Tableaux parisiens' concludes its invocation of the Parisian night and the prostitutes, gamblers, thieves, and mortally ill who are awake in it with the lines:

> Encore la plupart n'ont-ils jamais connu
> La douceur du foyer et n'ont jamais vécu!

> [Most, indeed, have never known
> the sweetness of the hearth and have never truly lived!]

This cliché of 'the circle of happiness at the hearth' is 'a social ideal of sacral origin' that 'keeps recurring in the lyrics of the year [1857] as an independent, implicit, or explicit theme,' and Jauss sets out to investigate the nature and role of this topos in the horizon of expectations: 'The lyric theme, with its variations, presents experience, rules of conduct and norms of common knowledge in the forms of a social paradigm.'[8] There is what he calls 'the basic situation pattern' with the privileged role of the mother and a 'nurturing' model of social interaction, the 'normative basic pattern' or maxims and values associated with this scene and its actors, and finally the ideological function of this pattern of images. The association of happiness with the return to a maternal fireside after a day's virtuous labor is both a nostalgic projection onto the rest of life of a certain world of childhood and also an attempt to transform a particular aspect of middle-class behavior into a natural or universal model of happiness. By working out the models of experience that underlie and are referred to by the lyric poetry of this year, Jauss hopes to capture the disruptive force of Baudelaire's lyrics, which by explicitly speaking of those who are excluded from a certain pattern of bourgeois domesticity reveal the ideological nature of the assumptions that exclude them from happiness.

Jauss's program for the study of reception is ambitious and valuable, but three questions arise about its orientations. First, despite his disclaimers, Jauss's formulations frequently suggest that the reason for undertaking the reconstruction of horizons is to discover the original meaning of a particular work and thus to provide an historically authorized interpretation. For example, his work on Goethe's *Iphigenie* seems in part aimed at showing that it was truly an original and interesting play: 'As an implicit answer and thus above all as a moment of the social process, the meaning of Racine's or Goethe's *Iphigenie* can be ascertained only from the receptive consciousness [of the time] through objectively verifiable stages of reflection.'[9] Though the theory suggests there is no original meaning since meaning is a function of an ongoing process of question and answer, the very process of historical research, with its emphasis on the recovery of something that has been covered over by time, may tempt the investigator to believe that he is in fact en route to discovering the work's true meaning.

Second, perhaps because of the attraction of an original meaning, Jauss often seems to work from the text itself rather than from information about responses, emphasizing what is new in the themes and techniques of a work. If he began instead with information about responses, he might encounter greater diversity and chaos; he might find that works are often the object of fierce disputes rather than answers to questions posed by a homogeneous horizon of expectations. Of course, in many cases we may lack detailed responses from readers of earlier periods, but a *Rezeptionsästhetik* ought at least to exploit as thoroughly as possible any richness and diversity that is available, rather than positing a unified horizon in the hope of discovering the true meaning of a work in its own age.

Finally, when Jauss does write in detail about a horizon of expectations, as in his article on 'La Douceur du foyer,' he concentrates on beliefs and commonplaces rather than on interpretive operations. Once again, this may be due to a lack of detailed information about interpretations, but one should bear in mind that a reader's response is not simply a process of comparing the statements of a work with his own beliefs or the beliefs of his time. As we shall see in the readings of Blake's 'London' discussed at the end of this chapter, critics who doubtless share a general horizon of expectations, including notions of urban misery and the imperfections of social institutions, nevertheless reach strikingly different interpretations of the poem (some maintaining that the institution of marriage creates prostitutes, others that an exploitative social system which includes prostitutes blights marriage). Though critics' beliefs about sex, marriage, and social institutions may have some role to play, it is easier and more plausible to explain these varying responses as the result of different interpretive operations and the application of different conventions than as the product of different beliefs. If *Rezeptionsästhetik* concentrates on beliefs alone, it will oversimplify the process of response.

Nevertheless, this project has considerable promise and could teach us a great deal about literature and signification. A focus on response can direct attention to crucial and neglected topics. Recently, for example, Jauss has begun to investigate the nature of esthetic experience: is there such a thing as esthetic emotion? what is the nature of esthetic pleasure and what is its bearing on response?[10] An account of reading should not neglect such questions, and *Rezeptionsästhetik* may help to answer them.

A second possibility for a semiotics of reading is founded not on the analysis of particular reading publics but on basic distinctions that readers seem able or inclined to make. Thus Tzvetan Todorov, in his *Introduction à la littérature fantastique*, defines the fantastic as a literary genre based on particular operations of reading. A work becomes an instance of the fantastic when readers hesitate between naturalistic and supernatural explanations. If in the end the work leads them to opt for the former, it falls into the class of the 'strange,' where the most improbable events turn out to have a naturalistic explanation. If a supernatural explanation is offered, then the work falls into a different class, the marvellous. It is only when readers are left suspended between the two modes of explanation that they are in the realm of the fantastic.[11]

This approach to genre theory creates a certain indeterminacy that might be held against it. It is not clear whether membership of a genre is determined by properties of the work which induce certain reactions on the part of readers—properties such as the presence or absence of naturalistic explanations—or whether genre is determined by the reaction of the reader, who might, for example, have missed a naturalistic explanation subtly outlined in the text. In fact, this indeterminacy may be a virtue rather than a disadvantage: it captures an important aspect of texts and reading. On the one hand, the responses of readers are not random but are significantly determined by the constituents of texts, yet on the other hand the interpretive orientation of a response is what gives certain elements significance within a work. If we were to opt solely for the determination of genre by structural features, then we should be obliged to say that *The Turn of the Screw*, for example, truly belongs to a particular genre but that readers and critics have some difficulties discovering its genre. However, if we allow response to be a determinant of genre, then we can say, in what seems a better description of the encounters with this story, that different interpretations are different generic interpretations. Those who read it as a ghost story are led to favor certain details and minimize the importance of others; those who opt for naturalistic, psychological explanations see these details differently, and those who, like Todorov, place it in the realm of the fantastic, stress the impossibility or inappropriateness of choosing between these options. The responses of readers and critics are not simply idiosyncratic; specifiable features of *The Turn of the Screw* make it subject to such debate, and a certain number of basic generic orientations (the attempt to provide naturalistic explanation, the assumption of supernatural explanation, or the refusal to choose between them) determine to a large extent the identification and organization of textual details into a story. There seem good reasons to insist on the constitutive force of generic conventions and their links with the most general reading strategies.

Such an approach is promising and could be extended further. If, for example, one wished to produce an account not of the fantastic but of fantasy in literature, one might look to operations of reading and start with basic facts about reading, such as readers' abilities to distinguish between a realistic novel (*Middlemarch*) and visionary fantasies (Blake's prophetic books). A theory of fantasy in literature would be an attempt to reconstruct the norms and categories which guide the distinctions readers make and the effects they experience.

Thus, if we began with the hypothesis that fantasy in literature was closely related to the deployment of figurative language, we would find that evidence from the practice of reading led us to reject this view. 'Look, the dawn in russet mantle clad/ Walks o'er the dew of yon high eastward hill' may seem fantasy by comparison with 'the sun is rising.' Our models of *vraisemblance* mark the former as strange, encourage us to imagine the dawn in this way and to appreciate the wonder implied by recourse to these metaphors; but the operation of 'seeing-as,' on which the understanding of metaphor seems to depend, is one of our major strategies for avoiding fantasy, for making the strange natural. Donne's phrase 'her pure and eloquent blood spoke in her cheeks' could be read literally if it appeared in a text where a certain kind of fantasy was the norm, but when we read 'spoke' as a metaphor the fantasy is preserved only, if at all, as a brief assertion of poetic intensity. André Breton's assertion, 'This summer the roses are blue' is fantasy if read literally, as a statement invoking a fantastic world. If we were able to read it as a figure, the interpretive operations and literary effects would be quite different, and it is this decisive difference in reading strategies that an account of fantasy would need to stress.

These examples suggest that fantasy is best thought of in terms of the worlds to which readers relate sentences in interpreting them. To identify the modes of fantasy might be to grasp the different figures that relate these worlds to our own. In Jakobsonian terms, the most elementary are metaphor and metonymy: a metaphorical world is separate but analogous, a member of a paradigm of conceivable worlds, while a metonymical world is contiguous with or part of our own, unexplored but governed by the same laws.

This basic distinction is easy to observe in our interpretations of novels. *The Lord of the Rings* counts as fantasy because it is read literally, as description of a metaphorical world. We must accept the powers of Sauron, Saruman, Gandalf, and the ring itself if we are to understand their actions. We must judge the elves by their own standards; we must preserve the distance between this world and ours if we are to feel the book's elegiac power. But we know that we should miss a good deal in *Women in Love* and gain a perversely vacuous experience if we referred it to a world other than our own. The importance of this distinction is confirmed by the fact that the ambiguity of novels is often the result of a hesitation between strategies. If we read Flaubert's *Salammbô* as about a real Carthage, a distant part of our own world, then we may find the characters credulous and confused—Salammbô becomes an antique Emma Bovary—and may interpret the mythological elements ironically in the attempt to reach an appropriate thematic synthesis. But if Flaubert's Carthage is a mythical world, recreated to be set against our own as an unreal alternative, then the powers of its solar and lunar deities provide a principle of intelligibility that calls for something more than ironic dismissal. The ambiguity of the novel results from the impossibility of carrying out these two different interpretive strategies.[12]

Fantasy is linked with the production and identification of metaphorical worlds. 'The admission of the marvellous,' wrote Walter Scott, 'expressly resembles a sort of entry-money paid at the door of a lecture room.'[13] For example, the premise of *Frankenstein* is 'to the highest degree extravagant'; 'we grant the extraordinary postulates which the author demands as the foundation of his narrative only on condition of his deducing the consequences with logical precision.'[14] And indeed, given the premise, the monster's actions and thoughts are 'most natural to his unnatural condition and origin.' Fantasy is the strange or unnatural that the reader accepts as another nature, whose laws may be set forth in a coherence of detail to rival a Balzacian universe. In Mervyn Peake's *Titus Groan* a series of tomes lists the actions Lord Groan must perform at every moment of the day—a telling representation of the artificial logic and verisimilitude of fantasy.

Distinctions between metaphorical and metonymical worlds, or between reading a proposition as literally true in a metaphorical world and metaphorically true in a literal world, are of course basic to reading and criticism, but if one were investigating the notion of fantasy in literature by considering operations of reading one would come upon another possibility. It is always open to readers to consider both metaphorical and metonymical worlds as products of an obsessional fantasy: instead of accepting these worlds and their logics of action as the bases for interpreting events in these worlds, they can in their reading focus on the ways in which these worlds are produced and the possible reasons for their production. From this perspective, Balzac's fervor to create an intelligible world, and his proliferation of theories—phrenology, magnetism, and various social, historical and biological determinisms—to produce a verisimilitude, is an obsessional fantasy not unlike the production of the fantastic world of *The Lord of the Rings*. In both cases, the identification of a fantastical project is a way for the reader to reflect upon what this fantasy enables author and readers to assert. One might, for example, read *The Lord of the Rings* as an indication that our ordinary sense of the world prevents us from making certain kinds of moral statements which are possible only in a universe where fantasy protects them from irony. And *La Comédie humaine*, for example, might be interpreted as an attempt to preserve, through a monstrous fantasy, possibilities of explanation and understanding in a period which, as Flaubert's competing vision suggests, had put in doubt the validity of traditional narrative schemes. When critics propose such interpretations, they are identifying a certain kind of fantasy as the principle by which novels are constructed.

An investigation of notions and distinctions of this sort as applied in reading would give us not a semiotics that places texts definitively in taxonomic categories—this is a fantasy, this is not—but rather a description of interpretive possibilities. By identifying the conventions of reading that underlie various interpretations and by linking notions such as 'fantasy' with particular processes of reading, this project emphasizes, for example, not that Balzac's novels are ambiguously situated between realism and fantasy, but that different interpretations of Balzac (or of *The Lord of the Rings*) result from the application of certain concepts and procedures of reading at different levels. What is realism at one level is fantasy at another. Instead of focusing, like an esthetics of reception, on the practice of a particular group of readers, this approach appeals to distinctions that are thought to underlie and make possible a range of interpretive possibilities. Readers who do not accept these possibilities will reject the analyses as without interest, just as readers who do not accept Todorov's use of his examples will reject his generic distinctions. It is in this respect that such theories are subject to test.

Another possibility for a semiotics of reading is to investigate interpretations of a single work, attempting to spell out the assumptions and interpretive operations that lead from text to interpretation. Traditionally, surveys of critical opinion are organized diachronically, describing the historical evolution of an author's reputation, or synchronically, identifying points of discord and the reasons for them. Roughly the same alternatives are open here, though a semiotics of reading should get at differences in interpretive conventions and procedures rather than describing differences of opinion.

A historical study might enable one to identify, for example, changes in the ordering of interpretive codes from one period to another. A study by Ivor Indyk of interpretations of *Tom Jones* seeks to explain different readings in terms of four different hierarchies of codes. The earliest opinions emphasize plot, or what Barthes calls the 'proaeretic code,' and transcoding operations move towards this code: characters are interpreted as constituents of the plot. Later interpretations seem to be based on an inversion of this hierarchy of codes: incident is interpreted as a revelation of character. Most twentieth-century interpretations, however, cannot be accounted for by this hierarchy; they appear to be made possible by a different assumption: that the constituents of the novel must ultimately be interpreted in terms of a unifying vision of the world, so that *dianoia* or the thematic code has the supreme integrative function. However, there is yet one further reordering of codes that generates a different sort of interpretation: when it is assumed that works of art should account for themselves and that this is the uppermost level of structure, a code of irony and self-reflexivity becomes the integrative device, and the ultimate meaning of episodes and formulations is what they tell us about literary discourse and the novel itself.[15]

Such diachronic investigations can be extremely interesting and should benefit from similar work in historiography, such as Hayden White's description of historical interpretation as a tropological process in which the dominant trope changes from one period to the next. [16] However, projects of this kind court two dangers, of which semioticians should be aware. First, the attempt to describe changes in interpretive conventions commits one, in effect, to oversimplification. If one's work of meta-interpretation is to seem successful, one must identify a series of different historical classes—each of which is homogenous, in that interpretations within the same class employ roughly the same conventions—and one must describe these classes in ways that make them comparable so that they can form an intelligible historical series.

Thus my own attempt to identify in literature of the late eighteenth and early nineteenth centuries a shift from one tropological and interpretive strategy to another now seems to me a very dubious enterprise. [17] The fact that certain Romantic discussions of figuration condemn allegory as a figure of discontinuity and celebrate the continuity of the symbol, in which the form is itself an instance of what it signifies, suggests the possibility of identifying in the literature of Romanticism, as well as in other areas of thought—from landscape-gardening to political philosophy—a preferred mode of figuration and signification based on *synecdoche*, the relation between part and whole. This could then be contrasted with a discontinuous, allegorical mode of signification, apparent in writings of Baudelaire and Flaubert that insist on the discrepancy between form and meaning or treat meaning as a dubious imposition. Though it is possible to find numerous examples to establish a contrast of this kind, the process of interpreting such examples depends on a simple and questionable historical scheme that opposes an ambitious and deluded Romanticism, committed to an organic theory of imagination and to the possibility of continuity between form and meaning, with an ironic, self-conscious Modernism that arises by questioning these assumptions. By interpreting Wordsworth as a non-ironic Romantic and Baudelaire as an ironic Modernist one can produce a contrast between two modes of figuration, but it is equally possible, as a host of recent studies have shown, to read Wordsworth or Rousseau as one had earlier read Baudelaire and Flaubert, thus reversing the simple historical scheme of Romantic

blindness and Modernist insight.[18] By the new scheme Wordsworth and Rousseau become examples of a Romantic insight
fated to be misread so as to permit the emergence of Modernism.
The identification of historical sequences, while an inevitable and
indispensable aspect of literary study is not just open to oversimplification; it is itself an act of oversimplification.

Moreover, Hayden White's example suggests that models of
narrative coherence have a great deal to do with the structure of
the historical sequences the analyst discovers. A sequence will
preferably have two to four terms; more will make it less concise
and intelligible. White's sequence consists of four tropes, metaphor, metonymy, synecdoche, and irony: naïve, metaphoric
history is succeeded by the metonymic constitution of the
historical object, then by synecdochic interpretation, and finally,
in the most sophisticated stage, by ironic and self-conscious
history. But this order is also the traditional order of tropes in
Renaissance rhetoric, and White discovers the same order in
Marx's tendency to divide all historical phenomena into four
stages.[19] One begins to suspect that there is a powerful tropological model at work here, a logical or epistemological system
whose momentum is its own, not the movement of history. As
Hans Kellner has shown, analyzing a range of examples of this
series from Goethe's *Faust* to White's *Metahistory*, the tropes
become 'moments' of tropology itself, which is seen not so much
as a set of forms or categories but as a system, indeed *the* system,
by which the mind comes to grasp the world conceptually in
language. The order in which the tropes present themselves in
this system is strictly and logically entailed. That is, to speak of
the 'four master tropes' as a tropology necessarily invokes the
sequence of the series, which thus represents a narrative curriculum with its own propulsive forces.[20] Historical schemes,
however useful and interesting, are always open to deconstruction as the product of narrative exigencies (see Chapter 9
below).[21]

A safer option, at least more able to resist oversimplification
because of its avoidance of narrative, is the synchronic study of
interpretations of a work, which may either focus on the readings
of a particular period or else work with a range of interpretations

without regard to time. Susan Horton's *Interpreting Interpreting*: *Interpreting Dickens' 'Dombey'*, despite its pleonastic title, is an astute account of the interpretive strategies that have enabled critics to produce their differing accounts of *Dombey and Son*. Focusing on critics' endless capacity to build explanations for the facts of a literary text, particularly those facts that initially seem in some way odd and thus significant, Horton describes an 'interpretive ladder' with various levels at which critics take up details and use them in interpretation.[22] Interpretation in her account is a process of contextualizing, but since contexts are never fixed or given, since they are always produced in and by further or prior interpretation, we have, as she says, a hermeneutic circle that can never be completely described. 'What has not been sufficiently noted and what is responsible for those apparently infinite and infinitely variable interpretations of our texts, including *Dombey and Son*, is that everything else in that hermeneutic circle, and not just the reader, is in motion at the same time.'[23] In fact, in her enthusiasm for variability, Horton overstates her case, for what her analyses demonstrate is not that everything is simultaneously in movement, but on the contrary that any element can be put in movement by holding another element firm, and that therefore while any act of interpretation must posit something as given, this given is not a fixed center around which all interpretations turn but rather a product of other interpretations which take something else as given.

Such studies of interpretation can also take as their point of departure a particular textual problem, as in Stephen Mailloux's investigation of critics' ways of coming to terms with the 'maimed' text of *The Red Badge of Courage*, which was for a long time the only text available. In the published text many passages from Crane's manuscript, including one entire chapter, were deleted, creating numerous puzzles. 'If the Appleton text is illogical and inconsistent,' Mailloux asks, 'how have "*Red Badge*" critics been able to make any sense of it, let alone call it an American classic?'[24] His answer shows the force of conventional narrative expectations, especially those linked with a genre that has become prominent. By the late nineteenth century the realistic war novel had become an identifiable genre, opposed to the narrative celebration of heroic deeds in battle. Contemporary critics compared Crane's novel with Tolstoy's *Sebastopol* and Zola's *La Débâcle* and others have continued to read it according to the conventional narrative pattern in which an untried civilian, exposed to the horrors of war, loses his innocence and registers a gain of some sort. The difficulty of deciding how to name this gain is some indication that the structure is derived as much from generic expectations as from clear indications of the text itself. Critics bring into play a variety of oppositions (innocence/ experience, ignorance/self-knowledge, cowardice/bravery) to explain what Crane's hero, Henry, is supposed to have achieved.

Mailloux is less convincing in his discussion of other conventions, because of a tendency to divide critics into two groups: those who misread because they had only a 'maimed text' and not the 'real' text, and those who nevertheless manage to interpret correctly without having seen the real text. Indeed, the danger of focusing on interpretations of a single work is that one will slide from the attempt to describe interpretive conventions to an attempt to convince one's readers that a particular interpretation is right or that all other interpretations are only incomplete contributions to one's own synoptic view. To discuss other interpretations in an attempt to arrive at one's own is, of course, a thoroughly traditional and respectable enterprise, but it is based on different assumptions from those that govern a semiotics of reading. We all assume that we can in principle adjudicate between readings; to be an experienced reader of literature is precisely to feel oneself in a position to appreciate, evaluate, synthesize, and reject others' readings. A semiotics of reading, however, is an attempt to work from a different assumption: that these various readings are the product of interpretive conventions that can be described. This project is disrupted whenever one slips back into the position of judge.

Such slippage may have interesting effects. In *Surprised by Sin* Stanley Fish produces an attractive reading of *Paradise Lost* by arguing that other critics quarrel over ambiguities that are meant to be experienced rather than resolved; they attempt to explain away discrepancies that are meant to confound the reader.[25] But when investigations of the conventions of reading turn to interpretation, their assertions invariably put in question the status of interpretive conventions, which come to be characterized as various forms of error. They can, of course, be evaluated in this way, but that is a different perspective which should be distinguished from the program of a semiotics of reading.

To illustrate more fully the operations such a project might identify and to demonstrate in more detail the conventionality of interpretive procedures, one might take as example a poem that has been frequently interpreted but which has not been thought so difficult as to require spectacular interpretive techniques. Blake's 'London' is a useful and interesting example in that critics have disagreed about its force and meaning while agreeing on its power:

> I wander thro' each charter'd street
> Near where the charter'd Thames does flow,
> And mark in every face I meet
> Marks of weakness, marks of woe.
>
> In every cry of every Man,
> In every Infant's cry of fear,
> In every voice, in every ban,
> The mind-forg'd manacles I hear.
>
> How the Chimney-sweeper's cry
> Every black' ning Church appalls;
> And the hapless Soldier's sigh
> Runs in blood down Palace walls.
>
> But most thro' midnight streets I hear
> How the youthful Harlot's curse
> Blasts the new-born Infant's tear
> And blights with plagues the Marriage hearse.[26]

What the various interpretations of this poem demonstrate most emphatically is the importance of the convention of *unity*. If a returning tourist were to tell us what he had seen and heard while wandering through the streets of London, we might be appalled (or delighted) but we would feel no overwhelming compulsion to transform these heterogeneous experiences into a unified vision. Readers of poems, however, do. The first task of the commentator, it seems, is to bring under some general heading the particulars that the poem lists and describes. S. Foster Damon speaks of the poem as 'concentrated wrath directed against the corruption of civilization by the power of Reason, whose "mind-forged manacles" have restricted every joy into a terrible agony.'[27] For Geoffrey Keynes, 'Blake is writing of a mental state symbolized by the social injustices seen every day in London.'[28] For Mark Schorer the poem is unified as the contemplation of 'unrelieved misery.'[29] In general the interpretations of the poem show, as one would expect, that the reading process involves the attempt to bring together the various sights and sounds according to one of our models of unity. The model most frequently used here is that of the synecdochic series, where a list of particulars are interpreted as instances of a general class to which they all belong. Critics name this class in different ways— social problems of eighteenth-century urban life, evils produced by the artificial impositions of Reason, generalized human suffering—and their interpretations explain, where it is not obvious, how each of the sights and sounds fits into the class so named.

The other model of unity that appears in interpretations of the poem is what one might call the *pattern of aletheic reversal*: first a false or inadequate vision, then its true or adequate counterpart. By this model, more common in interpretations of other works, one unifies the poem by identifying a shift. Here it comes with the third stanza: there is, writes Heather Glen, 'a release from the repetitiveness of the preceding stanzas. The abstracting sameness of "every . . . every . . . every," the dimly realized cries and voices, give way to specifically realized human situations.'[30]

Interpretations of Blake's 'London' are more frequently based on the former model of unity, though the latter offers a dramatic structure that students of literature have frequently deemed superior. Whichever model is used, however, the interpreter calls upon further conventions—such as the superiority of the particular to the general—to fit the language of the poem to the structure proposed. The reader must perform imaginative transformations on the various things seen and heard so as to relate them to one another in a way that fits the model. The poem's statements become figural notations that require interpretation.

The complexity of the interpretive process is clearest in the operations performed on the last two stanzas. The fact that every critic finds the third stanza a vision of misery and oppression testifies once again to the power of the convention of unity, but the different paths to this conclusion are fascinating.

The chimney sweep, of course, is for our culture the very type of the oppressed innocent, but his cry is said to 'appall' the church. How can one explain the fact that no critic accepts this statement at face value, that each finds a way around it? If the literal statement is inadmissible, this is for reasons that have nothing to do with language or thought in general but only with conventions of literary structure; and one can only explain why 'appall' is interpreted as it is by guessing what are the conventions at work here. First, we seem to have no model of unity that would permit at this point a note of institutional outrage that is neither carried on in the fourth stanza nor explicitly denied or explained. Either of those developments might give us a new structure, but in their absence the convention of unity rules out a literal reading of 'appalled.' Secondly, the parallelism between

	sweeper	cry	church
and			
	soldier	sigh	palace

brings into play the convention that parallelism of expression creates parallelism of thought: the structure brings together church and palace in such a way that their roles must be either opposed (which, as I suggested, would be ruled out by the demands of unity at this point) or equivalent. The conventions thus give the reader a goal that governs his interpretation of the third stanza: find a common relationship between institution and individual in the two cases.

Given this goal, the results are predictable: the Church will be an oppressor of the sweep as the Palace is an oppressor of the soldier. 'Without a church which sustains social injustice by promises of Heaven,' writes E. D. Hirsch, 'there would be no chimney sweeps.'[31] Or, as Keynes has it, 'the chimneysweeper's "weep, weep" is called up to illustrate social evils condoned by the Church.'[32] Critics all tend towards this conclusion, which the conventions of interpretive coherence require, but the interpretive moves by which they fit details of the language to this structure are surprising in their variety. D. G. Gillham, for example, is alone in his initial interpretation of 'appalls': 'The Church is horrified,' he writes, 'at the evil of the sweeper's condition.' But recognizing the inappropriateness of this reading to the larger structure, he swiftly tells us a story about churches that neutralizes 'appalls' and gets us back to the conclusion that unity demands: 'the Church is horrified . . . but it is helpless to do much about it—no vigorous remedy may be undertaken because institutions are, by nature, conservative.'[33] The inherent conservatism of the sympathetic institution thus puts it in effect on the side of the oppressors.

More ingenious and attractive is the solution of Bernard Blackstone:

> There it is, the accusation: you, minister of religion, are responsible for the torture of the child against whose exploitation you raise not a word of protest. The compression of the thought is brilliant: the very walls of the church are *appalled* by a misery to which the hearts of the clergy are quite apathetic.[34]

Exploiting the ambiguity of *church*, this critic reads the line in relation to a topos of which it can be seen as a transformation: when the very stone is moved, then the misery is extreme. But since the parallelism still requires an oppressor, that role is assigned to the other signified of *church*, the clergy.

Another way of transforming 'appalls' is to call it *ironic*. This is a major interpretive operation, a powerful tool for making what seems deviant accord with various structural demands and conventions. Thus Hazard Adams treats 'appalls' as an ironic indication of the church's hypocritical attitude: 'The church is once again a symbol of complacency and blindness. It is "appalled" at the conditions it observes, but its histrionic reaction is clearly hypocritical.'[35] As this example shows, one must think of irony not just as a technique available to authors but as a trope or interpretive operation available to readers whenever they encounter problems which it might help to solve.

However, a more common strategy in this particular case is based on a special convention that allows puns or lexical decomposition in cases where they contribute to coherence and do not displace a satisfactory literal reading. In *The Visionary Company*, Harold Bloom argues that the cry 'appalls' in the sense that 'it makes the church pale and so exposes the church as a whited sepulchre.'[36] Other critics, while striving toward the same interpretive conclusion, disagree about the figural route: 'appall' means to cast a pall over or so to blacken rather than whiten, 'blackening with the guilt of its indifference far more than with soot,' argues Martin Price.[37] To appall is here to darken, writes Thomas Edwards, stressing that 'the church itself is not horrified.'[38] This reading, which plays with the metaphorical soot of guilt, is doubtless reinforced by the fact that chimney sweeps are supposed to remove soot, not apply it. An observer who knew nothing of literature might expect this fact to work against the reading: it is appropriate for sweeps metaphorically to cleanse the church since their job is to remove literal soot, but it is absurd to have 'appall' mean 'make dirty.' There is much to be said for such a line of reasoning, and it indicates just how peculiar the properties of literary language are. It is a fact about the conventions of literary interpretation that such reversals or paradoxes work as a kind of proof of the poem, a demonstration of logical and semantic density. As we see here, conventions of interpretation let us perform quite radical acts of semantic transference, moving blackness and soot around from chimneys to sweeps to the church to its moral authority.

The critics I have cited may disagree about what the lines mean, but they are all following the same convention of unity, performing interpretive operations to fill, in their different ways, a structure they have all posited. And, as I have emphasized, the interpretive operations or semantic transformations that they employ are not in any sense personal and idiosyncratic acts of free association; they are common and acceptable formal strategies.

What I want to stress here are the interpretive operations at work in producing perfectly ordinary interpretations. It is often difficult to see what kinds of moves lead from text to interpretation, but that does not mean that these moves are in any way unique or even idiosyncratic. For example, the poem tells us that 'the hapless Soldier's sigh / Runs in blood down Palace walls.' It may be difficult to explain what figures, what interpretive moves and semantic shifts, are employed when a reader transforms this statement to something like 'The despair and pain of the soldier brands the people and institutions he has been defending with the guilt of causing his suffering.' But no matter how difficult it is to make explicit the interpretive operations responsible for his reading, we admit that they are not idiosyncratic moves when we recognize that the poem's statement could very well mean this. In granting the plausibility of this interpretation we are in effect identifying as public, reproducible operations the interpretive strategies we find hard to describe. A primary task of the study of reading is to describe the operations responsible for interpretations we find plausible. Questions such as to what extent individual readers perform the same operations or how far these operations are confined to a tiny community of professional critics cannot really be answered until we are better able to describe the operations in question.

The full complexity of these operations is revealed in readings of the last stanza of 'London.' Of course, it requires some imagination to see how a harlot's curse blasts an infant's tear and blights the marriage hearse, but this difficulty does not in itself explain the amount of interpretive labor which readers and critics have expended on the stanza. It would, after all, be at least plausible to say that the narrator hears a youthful harlot first curse her child for crying and then, shouting at a marriage procession, curse the institution of marriage. But those who attempt to interpret this poem are not content with such readings. Michael Riffaterre, whose semiotics of poetry we shall consider in the next chapter, would say that the attempt at an initial, mimetic reading, which this paraphrase crudely represents, breaks down (what is a 'marriage hearse' and how does the harlot blight it with plagues?), and the reader must undertake a second reading in which the constituents are interpreted as transformations of literary and conventional forms. It is at least true that primary determinants of the various interpretations of this final stanza are, first, a structural convention, and then the interplay between a convention of formal patterning and a topos or descriptive system.

Structural conventions require that the final stanza bring the poem to a close, produce an appropriate conclusion. There are, of course, various ways in which this may be done, but in a poem organized as a series of perceptions the critic's inclination is to read the final stanza as the climax of the vision, its most intense and typical moment.[39] This leads to large claims. The harlot, says Edwards, 'blasts the prospects of innocent children . . . and blights the healthful possibilities of marriage,' because her existence is 'a gross parody of sanctified mutuality in love.'[40] For others the institution of marriage is a manacle and the harlot one of its victims: 'If there were no marriage there would be no ungratified desires, and therefore no harlots. Thus it is ultimately the marriage hearse itself and not the youthful harlot which breeds the pestilence that blights the marriage hearse.'[41]

These different readings seem the result of a choice between interpretive strategies. One may, in one's attempt to produce unity, follow the parallelism that links sweep, soldier, and harlot: the narrator hears the sweep cry, the soldier sigh, and the harlot curse. The insistent syntactic parallelism brings them together as victims. The harlot's curse becomes her characteristic cry, another instance, as the poem has told us, of mind-forged manacles.

This parallelism makes the harlot a victim, even though she blasts the infant's tear and blights the marriage hearse; and a critic following the convention that parallelism of expression begets parallelism of thought is encouraged to consider whether infant and hearse should not take their place in the series of institutions affected or tainted by the victims' cries. No critic I have encountered reads 'infant' as a figure for a repressive institution (left out of the series, the infant becomes an extra victim), but 'marriage hearse' is subjected to various interpretive transformations. Generally, it seems to be read as a complex double figure combining two sorts of metonymy: first, the wedding carriage is taken as a metonymy for the institution of matrimony itself, as a crown may figure the institution of monarchy; and second, the carriage becomes the *marriage hearse* by a metonymy that places an effect before its cause. The carriage is treated as a hearse even before it has been cursed. It is marked by a curse, just as the palace, in a less compressed figure, is marked by the blood of the soldier's sighs and the church is blackened by the sweep's cry. Of course, interpreters do not spell out their interpretive moves in such detail, but operations of this sort must be posited to account for the conclusions they reach: that marriage, like church and palace, is an oppressive institution and that in this last stanza the harlot's cry, in blighting the marriage hearse, accuses the chartered institution that excludes and exploits her. Without marriage, Hirsch claims, there would be no harlots. It is the marriage hearse (i.e. marriage as an institution which is then marked by the accusations of the oppressed) that breeds the pestilence.

Other critics resist this view and reach the conclusion that the harlot herself is the figure of a social system that blights the prospects of innocent children and destroys marriage. What conventions and operations bring them to this rather different conclusion? It would seem that instead of following the syntactic parallelism that places the harlot among the victims, they grant precedence to the cultural convention that associates 'innocence' with new-born infants, especially a new-born infant whose 'tear' is invoked. In a context where oppressors are set against victims, there are powerful cultural conventions urging us to place a new-born infant on the side of innocent victims. But if, granting precedence to the descriptive system that associates infants with innocence, one makes them the primary victims, then the parallelism that links 'infant's tear' with 'marriage hearse' as what the harlot's curse blasts and blights leads one to perform different interpretive operations on 'marriage hearse.' The transformation of carriage to hearse is no longer treated as an accusatory marking, like the blackening of the church or the bloodying of palace walls. The reference to death becomes the heart of the figure: in the most common interpretation, the harlot collapses the distance between wedding carriage and hearse by spreading venereal disease and making death follow hard upon marriage. Her curse is not, therefore, as it was for the other group of readings, her characteristic cry, like the sweep's 'weep' and the soldier's sigh, but a figure for a specific disease.

However, numerous critics, while making the babe and the newly-weds the principal victims, find this explanation too narrow and specific to serve as climax ('But *most* thro' midnight streets I hear . . .') to a poem that insists on its generality. They broaden the vision by synecdochic expansion: 'The harlot's curse is therefore something more than simply a figure for the venereal disease that "blasts . . . and blights."'[42] The harlot is a synecdoche for the exploitative social system of which she is a provocative and garish part; the babe and the newly-weds stand for the general possibilities of innocence and love, which are blighted not just by disease or by the existence of prostitution but by the social injustice and exploitive relations of a society based on charters and privilege.

Whether one insists on the parallelism that makes the harlot the primary victim or on the conventions that make the infant the victim, the subsequent interpretive procedure seems to be a move from part to whole that makes the poem a political statement. Readers disagree about what the poem indicts: 'faults which Englishmen have brought upon themselves'; 'kings, priests, and the marriage hearse . . . All the woes of "London" are owing to these artificial institutions'; 'Reason, whose "mind-forged manacles" have restricted every natural joy into a terrible agony.'[43] But a limited number of formal interpretive operations give them the structures that they flesh out with their own referential and ethical discourse.

This attempt to make explicit the interpretive operations that underlie critics' remarks about 'London' is not, one should insist, a semiotic interpretation of the poem. It is an attempt to explain on what basis a range of interpretations such as those provided by our critical sample could be produced: what conventions and interpretive procedures enable critics to draw the inferences and make the statements they do. Of course, readers, when confronted with this sort of exposition, will be inclined to prefer some operations to others. The exposition itself may cast some in a more favorable light, but this should not be taken to suggest that one might hope to determine, by some kind of semiotic analysis, what 'appalls' really means here or how the harlot should be interpreted. In the corpus of readings various procedures can be observed, some more common than others, some granting more importance to semantic features of the lexical items, others to structures of the context in which they occur, still others to possibilities of paranomasia and semantic decomposition. At a particular moment or within a particular interpretive community some of these procedures will be more readily accepted than others. Every interpretation employs the pathways of rhetorical transformations and draws upon conventions of literary structure or of topoi and descriptive systems, and for even the most unexpected reading one may hope to determine a basis, but one cannot judge it to be aberrant except in relation to some standard. In pedagogic situations these standards are readily available, though still open to question. 'You should look up that word,' we say to a student whose interpretation seems to involve a particular misunderstanding, but the dictionary is not a standard to judge by in cases where the relevance of the dictionary meaning is questioned and critics claim that other considerations take priority. One can only determine a correct reading in relation to a standard, and such standards are ultimately imposed by varying sorts of cultural authority.

But the fact that this analysis has not tried to promote or eliminate particular readings should not be presumed to mean that for a semiotics the meaning of the poem is a grand synthesis of all these readings, an appreciation of its infinite ambiguity. One is always tempted by the synoptic view. The desire to reach an understanding which includes all other understandings and explains their misunderstandings is a powerful force in interpretation; but there is no justification for thinking that what would emerge from an attempt to put together all these readings would be anything like a 'meaning' of the poem. We can say that poems, by the conventions of our culture, welcome a variety of interpretations and that this variety is part of their significance, but it seems likely, as the work of each of these critics implies, that to give the poem any force one must make choices. A reading that refused all choice and sought to live happily with all possibilities would be a strange experience, certainly not something one would recommend as an encounter with the poem.

This discussion has not pointed towards a semiotic reading but has sought to demonstrate that interpretation is a highly conventional activity, drawing on a series of operations that can be described—though our rhetorical vocabulary needs further development if our descriptions are to attain the sort of precision we should wish. Above all, this example illustrates the status of interpretive disagreements for the study of reading. Against anyone who maintained that a semiotics of reading is impossible because no two people read and interpret in the same way, one can reply that even when they reach different conclusions about the significance of a line, a stanza, or a poem, they are employing interpretive conventions that can be defined and which will make the relation between their interpretive statements more comprehensible.

More generally, it is important to stress that if we want to understand the nature of literature and of our adventures in language we will have to recognize that the 'openness' and 'ambiguity' of literary works result not from vagueness nor from each reader's desire to project himself into the work, but from the potential reversibility of every figure. Any figure can be read referentially or rhetorically. 'My love is a red, red rose' tells us, referentially, of desirable qualities that the beloved possesses. Read rhetorically, in its figurality, it indicates a desire to see her as she is not: as a rose. 'Charter'd street' in the first stanza of 'London' tells us, referentially, of an ordered city, its streets full of chartered institutions. Rhetorically, it is hyperbole: to speak as if even the streets had royal charters is excessive, ironic. One can, of course, go on to read this irony referentially, as a suggestion that too many charters enslave: London is so restrictive that even streets need charters to exist. But one could also in turn reverse this figure and, reading the irony in its figurality, say that the act of seeing streets as if they were chartered is an example of another kind of enslavement: enslavement to one's own fiction. These four readings are generated by two elementary operations which, as a pair, constitute the possibility of figural reading.

On a larger scale, for example, the repetitive movement of 'London''s opening stanzas can, referentially, tell us of visionary power to perceive the common misery beneath the variety of outward appearances: 'Only the poet hears what is *in* each cry or sees *how* it looks and acts—in short, what it means,' writes Martin Price.[44] But, rhetorically, to hear manacles in every cry of every person, to connect through a figure of repetition all surfaces and sounds, is itself an obsession, a mind-forged manacle, the danger always courted by the visionary poet.

This kind of reversal is inherent in the possibilities of reading, in the possibilities of literary language as we know it. The opposing, even contradictory, readings engendered in this way depend not on prior 'opinions' of the subject but on formal operations that constitute the activity of interpretation. Opposed readings which stand in the same relation to one another can be produced for most texts: the interpretive move that treats a linguistic sequence as figurative opens the possibility of a series of reversals, which will produce other readings. The content of these readings will differ according to the nature of the text, but their formal properties will be a result of definable operations of reading. To understand interpretive disagreements, to understand the ambiguity or openness of literary meaning, one must study the reading process. No other area of literary criticism offers such an interesting and valuable program. For further investigation of its possibilities, we can now turn to an ambitious and impressive recent contribution, Michael Riffaterre's *Semiotics of Poetry*.

4

Riffaterre and the Semiotics of Poetry

Michael Riffaterre's *Semiotics of Poetry* is an ambitious work of literary theory that proposes 'a coherent and relatively simple description of the structure of meaning in a poem' (p. 1).[1] His earlier work in structural stylistics treated meaning as a function of the perceptions and expectations of the reader—expectations correlated with the probabilities of occurrence established by the 'macro-context' of work and genre and by the 'micro-context' of the surrounding phrases.[2] The statistical orientation occasionally present in his earlier work has now been abandoned, but the study of meaning is still seen as a study of reading, and a semiotics of poetry is in essence an account of the way readers process or make sense of a text. He writes (pp. 1–2):

> The literary phenomenon is a dialectic between text and reader. If we are to formulate rules governing this dialectic, we shall have to know that what we are describing is actually perceived by the reader; we shall have to know whether he is always obliged to see what he sees or if he retains a certain freedom; and we shall have to know how perception takes place.

These are stiff but pertinent requirements. A theory attempting to live up to such standards will have important things to say about reading.

Riffaterre begins with two axioms, that poetic signification is indirect—'a poem says one thing and means another' (p. 1)—and that the unit of meaning in poetry 'is the finite, closed entity of the text' (p. ix). He does not argue for this second assumption, which is a cornerstone of this theory, but follows a long and authoritative tradition in claiming that unity is a condition of poetry: 'the characteristic feature of the poem is its unity' (p. 2). Reading a poem is a quest for unity, and unity is achieved or perceived only when the reader abandons the apparent referential or representational meaning of the discourse and grasps the unifying feature or factor that the various signs of the poem express by indirection.

There are thus two stages of reading. In the initial or 'heuristic' reading, readers comprehend linguistic signs in a primarily referential fashion; they assume that the poem is the representation of an action or a statement about objects and situations. But they encounter difficulties or, as Riffaterre calls them, 'ungrammaticalities': some signs give bizarre or contradictory results when interpreted referentially. Moreover, the results of this heuristic reading are unsatisfying for two further reasons. The text characteristically displays prominent patterns of a metrical, phonological, or rhetorical sort which cannot be interpreted referentially; these patterns impose themselves on the reader's attention as signs that should be interpreted, but they can only be dealt with at another level. Furthermore, at the mimetic level the poem is a string of representations: it says first one thing, then another. But since, according to Riffaterre, readers know that the characteristic feature of a poem is its unity, they must, if they are to interpret the text properly, seek another level at which that unity can be identified and the text become a single whole.

These difficulties give rise to a second, 'retroactive' or 'hermeneutic' reading in which the obstacles that arose when one tried to read mimetically become the keys to a new reading, 'the guideline to semiosis, the key to significance in the higher system' (p. 6). Here is Riffaterre's description of this process (p. 4):

> The ungrammaticalities spotted at the mimetic level are eventually integrated into another system. As the reader perceives what they have in common, as he becomes aware that this

common trait forms them into a paradigm, and that this paradigm alters the meaning of the poems, the new function of the ungrammaticalities changes their nature, and now they signify as components of a different network of relationships. This transfer of signs from one level of discourse to another, this metamorphosis of what was a signifying complex at a lower level of the text into a signifying unit, now a member of a more developed system, at a higher level of the text, this functional shift is the proper domain of semiotics. Everything related to this integration of signs from the mimesis level into the higher level of significance is a manifestation of *semiosis*.

All those items which resist a straightforward mimetic reading, including the expressions that readers have identified as requiring metaphorical interpretation, are said to have some common trait which makes them emerge in the second or retroactive reading as 'variants of the same structural matrix.' One of the most striking features of Riffaterre's theory is his conception of semiotic unity. At this higher level of significance, everything in the poem is a variant of an original word or sentence: 'The poem . . . results from the transformation of a *word* or *sentence* into a text' (p. 164). Sentences which appear to be making statements about the world must, if the poem is to be construed as a unity, be grasped as variants of this kernel or matrix, which is another verbal structure. As Riffaterre states (p. 19):

> The poem results from the transformation of the *matrix*, a minimal and literal sentence, into a longer, complex and non-literal periphrasis. The matrix is hypothetical, being only the grammatical and lexical actualization of a structure. The matrix may be epitomized in one word, in which case the word will not appear in the text. It is always actualized in successive variants; the form of these is governed by the first or primary actualization, the model. Matrix, model, and text are variants of the same structure.

The expansion or conversion of a matrix into a text produces a series of apparently representational signs, some of which are 'poetic signs.' A word or phrase is poeticized and comes to function as a poetic sign 'when it refers to (and if a phrase patterns itself upon) a preexistent word group' (p. 23). This preexistent word group Riffaterre calls a *hypogram*. A hypogram may be a cliché, a quotation, or a group of conventional associations which Riffaterre calls a 'descriptive system' or a thematic complex. In any event, the hypogram is not located in the text itself but is the product of past semiotic and literary practice, and it is in perceiving a sign's reference to this preexisting phrase or complex that the reader identifies the sign as 'poetic.' The apparently mimetic sign is seen as a transformation of past poetic discourse. But 'for the poeticity to be activated in the text, the sign referring to a hypogram must also be a variant of that text's matrix' (p. 23). In other words, poetic signs in a text are powerfully overdetermined: they both refer to a preexisting hypogram and are variants or transformations of a matrix.

A poet creates a poem in taking a word or sentence and expanding it into a text by using a series of hypograms, modifying each in some way so as to make it a variant of his original structure. The reader interprets a poem by recognizing references to hypograms once the language has failed to work mimetically, and reconstructing the original matrix detectable in the common feature of the transformations to which the hypograms have been subjected. The need to discover the hypograms and the matrix makes poetry 'more of a game than anything else' (p. 14) and Riffaterre's theory of poetic structure makes it possible for the reader to solve the mystery of a poem, to come up with the right answer (p. 12):

> Then suddenly the puzzle is solved, everything falls into place, indeed, the whole poem ceases to be descriptive, ceases to be a sequence of mimetic signs, and becomes a single sign, perceived from the end back to its given as a harmonious whole, wherein nothing is loose, wherein every word refers to one symbolic focus.

To witness Riffaterre solving the puzzle in a way that illustrates his strong and surprising claims about poetic unity and poetic

structure, let us consider an example where his argument is clear
and his interpretive results quite striking, Rimbaud's 'Fêtes de la
faim':[3]

FÊTES DE LA FAIM

Ma faim, Anne, Anne
Fuis sur ton âne.

Si j'ai du *goût*, ce n'est guères
Que pour la terre et les pierres.
5   Dinn! dinn! dinn! dinn! Je pais l'air,
Le roc, les Terres, le fer.

Tournez, les faims, paissez, faims,
Le pré des sons!
Puis l'aimable et vibrant venin
10   Des liserons;

Les cailloux qu'un pauvre brise,
Les vieilles pierres d'église,
Les galets, fils des déluges,
Pains couchés aux vallées grises!

15   Mes faims, c'est les bouts d'air noir;
L'azur sonneur;
—C'est l'estomac qui me tire.
C'est le malheur.

Sur terre ont paru les feuilles!
20   Je vais aux chairs de fruit blettes
Au sein du sillon je cueille
La doucette et la violette.

Ma faim, Anne, Anne!
Fuis sur ton âne.

[Feasts of Hunger. My hunger, Anne, Anne, run away on your

donkey. If I have any taste, it is for hardly anything but earth's soil and stones. Dinn! dinn! dinn! dinn! I feed on air, rock, soil, iron. Turn round and round, hungers, graze the meadows of sound! Then the nice vibrant venom of the morning glories; the stones a poor man breaks, the old slabs of churches, the beach pebbles, children of deluge, bread loaves lying in the gray valleys! My hungers, they are crumbs of black air; the azure bellringer; it's my stomach that aches. It's unhappiness. Leaves have come out on earth! I am going to the flesh of overripe fruit, from the heart of the furrow I pick lamb's lettuce and the violet. My hunger, Anne, Anne! run away on your donkey.]

This is certainly a poem that poses difficulties for the reader. First, there are mimetic difficulties: how can the speaker, as he says, feed on air, rock, soil, iron, the venom of morning glories and old slabs of churches? These ungrammaticalities call out for a figurative or metaphorical reading, but the poem provides no clear indications of what semantic transformations would be appropriate (is it evoking, for example, a taste or liking for all objects of the earth?). Blocked in his mimetic reading, the reader must, says Riffaterre, consider each of these images as a transformation of a cliché or hypogram and a variant of the matrix. The inedibility of these various objects, the obstacle to a mimetic reading, becomes the clue to the hermeneutic reading. Noting that the last stanza shifts to edibles from inedibles, Riffaterre (p. 78) argues that

the entire poem is an expansion on two polar opposites, the narrative potentialities derivable from the sememe 'hunger': a tale of unsatisfied hunger, and a tale of its satisfaction. *Avoir faim* has two lexical facets, a negative and a positive: you starve or you have a good appetite. In either case the craving for food can be expressed in terms of eating, hence a matrix: *eating the inedible, eating the edible*, which covers the whole story of the poem's given, that is, of the title.

If this is the matrix, then each image is a variant of this theme modeled on or referring to a hypogram, as Riffaterre proceeds to argue in a passage that must be cited at length since one of the issues at stake is the comprehensiveness of his mode of explanation (pp. 78–9):

> Each variant of this non-food is in fact guaranteed by, and ritualistically refers to, clichés. The air (line 5): *vivre de l'air du temps*, a proverbial phrase applied to impecunious individuals or dieting ladies. The puzzling *bouts d'air noir* uses air as a hyperbolic substitute for the famine cliché *des bouts de pain noir*. Whereas *air noir* is sheer nonsense referentially, it carries on the conversion by replacing stale and scanty crusts with the illusion of food, and, as a variant on the model of the stereotype, it makes sense. Again, the deadly convolvulus brings us to familiar warnings to children about poisonous plants. And the revolving hungers refer to the revolving wooden horses of the carousel ('Tournez, tournez, bons chevaux de bois,' Verlaine is writing at about the same time) by way of the colloquial *manger avec les chevaux de bois* [eat when the wooden horses eat]—that is, starve. Hence too *paissez*, the verb for cattle or horses browsing on grass. Hence *sons*, a pun on the two meanings, 'bran,' horse fodder, and in the plural, 'sounds.' Sounds, of course, because of the bell in line 5, the refectory bell that summons to the table. We need not be wildly imaginative to find this a nice instance of tautology, since 'dinn! dinn! dinn! dinn! mangeons' sounds like 'dine! dine! mangeons!' (as we would say, 'Dinner! Dinner! Let's eat!'). A hollow invitation, this being a mineral dinner–wherefore the bitterness concerning *l'azur sonneur*, which unites *l'air du temps* of our aforementioned proverb with the delusive call to dinner. Whence also the bitterness of the allusion to the Mallarmé intertext—the only possible explanation for this strange phrase—a poem in which the blue sky serves as image for a 'sterile desert,' a haunting emptiness, where 'l'Azur triomphe . . . qui chante dans les cloches . . . il se fait voix pour plus nous faire peur avec sa victoire méchante' [Azure triumphant sings in the bells; it turns itself into a voice the better to frighten us with its victorious wickedness].

In sum, then, the matrix here is *hunger* (eating) and its expansion into a text employs first a negative then a positive converter, to yield a vision of eating, first, the inedible, and then, with an inversion of the key features of the inedible, the edible. Presumably, although Riffaterre does not explicitly say so, the sentence of lines 2–3, 'Si j'ai du *goût*, ce n'est guères/Que pour la terre et les pierres,' would be the *model*, since the subsequent images of eating are interpreted according to the formula made explicit here. Finally, each representation of eating is determined by a cliché, quotation or colloquial phrase to which it alludes or which it takes literally.

Riffaterre sums up his demonstration as follows (p. 80):

Thus, while every single representation in the poem is well nigh incomprehensible to start with, it becomes capable of metaphorization or symbolization as soon as it is perceived as functionally identical with the others, as soon as we perceive the sequence that develops one word of the title, or rather one seme of that word, into a text. And once again, maximal catachresis at the lexematic level of individual words and phrases coincides with significance at the textual level.

The poem is not an account of acts of eating or of the failure to eat but is rather organized around those possibilities and impossibilities of eating that are enshrined in discourse.

If 'Fêtes de la faim' illustrates the way in which idioms and clichés of a language can be transformed into variants of a matrix, and thus the way in which the reader's identification of matrix and hypograms can demonstrate the poetic unity which he began by assuming, it must nevertheless seem a very special case: a poem which resists mimetic interpretation and encourages the reader to go to great lengths to unify it and make it intelligible. One might well wonder how Riffaterre's account of the reading process would work for a different sort of poem. A useful example is Baudelaire's first 'Spleen' from *Les Fleurs du Mal*, which critics have had less trouble interpreting and which is usually taken as a powerful statement of despair rather than as a puzzle to be solved:[4]

Pluviôse, irrité contre la ville entière,
De son urne à grands flots verse un froid ténébreux
Aux pâles habitants du voisin cimetière
Et la mortalité sur les faubourgs brumeux.

Mon chat sur le carreau cherchant une litière
Agite sans repos son corps maigre et galeux;
L'âme d'un vieux poëte erre dans la gouttière
Avec la triste voix d'un fantôme frileux.

Le bourdon se lamente, et la bûche enfumée
Accompagne en fausset la pendule enrhumée,
Cependant qu'en un jeu plein de sales parfums,

Héritage fatal d'une vieille hydropique,
Le beau valet de cœur et la dame de pique
Causent sinistrement de leurs amours défunts.

[Pluvius, annoyed at the whole city, pours torrents of dark cold out of his urn down onto the pale tenants of the cemetery next door, torrents of mortality over the foggy suburbs. On the tiling, my cat is looking for a litter to bed down on; he shifts his thin mangy body about restlessly. The soul of an old poet wanders through the rainspout with the sad voice of a chilly ghost. The great bell is lamenting, and the smoke-blackened log, in falsetto, accompanies the wheezy clock, the while, in a deck of cards filled with foul perfumes—fatal bequest of a dropsical old hag—the handsome knave of hearts and the queen of spades talk of their dead loves sinisterly.]

Here the matrix 'would be something like *no refuge from misery*, but the cliché *all-pervading gloom* would do as well' (p. 68). It seems very likely that in most readings what unifies the poem is a feeling of dismal disagreeableness expressed or implied in each stanza. Most readings of the poem probably do, in effect, treat it as an expansion of this sort of kernel. More striking is Riffaterre's claim that the expansion of this matrix into a text is mediated by the descriptive system associated with *maison*. A descriptive system is a set of associated commonplaces: the descriptive system of 'home sweet home' in English involves, for example, the fireside, a peaceful pet, security, intimacy, perhaps a sunny green lawn, etc. Riffaterre argues that in 'Spleen' the expansion of the gloomy matrix involves conversion of the various elements of the equivalent French descriptive system into negative images. By convention the system of *maison* has a positive orientation, but 'Spleen' takes various elements of the system and transforms each into a variant of *all-pervading gloom*, so that the home which should protect us against discomfort becomes an instance of it.

Earlier Riffaterre has described what is involved in this conversion of the hypogram (pp. 63–4):

> If he is to perceive the converted verbal sequence [i.e. perceive it as indirection and hence as poetic], the reader must make a mental comparison between the sequence and a hypogram that is the text imagined by him in a pretransformation state. This hypogram (a single sentence or a string of sentences) may be made out of clichés, or it may be a quotation from another text, or a descriptive system. Since the hypogram always has a positive or negative 'orientation' (the cliché is meliorative or pejorative, the quotation has its position on an ethical and/or esthetic scale, the descriptive system reflects the connotations of its kernel word), the constituents of the conversion always transmute the hypogram's markers—in some cases the conversion consists of nothing more than a permutation of markers.

Ordinarily the *maison* system opposes a warm, protective inside to a hostile outside, but here, Riffaterre argues, 'the conversion dictated by *pervasive gloom* transforms this opposition *inside* vs *outside* into an equivalence.' The disagreeable discomfort that reigns outside is also to be found inside, as in the second stanza, where the description of the cat inverts the features the descriptive system would lead us to expect. Given a sleek, contented, fireside cat, 'the markers' permutation derives *maigre*, ''skinny,'' from the ideal cat body, *galeux*, ''mangy,'' from the ideal coat. The soft rug becomes *carreau*, and *carreau* never generates any adjective but *dur* or *froid*, which negate cosiness' (p. 69), and so on. Similarly, in the first tercet familiar sounds become harsh or dissonant; but most interesting is the transformation that takes place in the puzzling final stanza. Riffaterre argues that knicknacks, packs of cards, etc., are part of the system of *maison*, in which they are 'common motifs in scenes of intimacy' and when no one is about 'symbolize the essential continuity of living.' A familiar hyperbolic variant of this motif gives these things a secret life: at night they come alive. The animation of inanimate household objects is an everpresent possibility in the case of playing cards, and love among kings, queens, and knaves is 'a logical result.' Riffaterre concludes (p. 70):

> The whole motif, a complicated story, is verily a subsystem of the *maison* system. It has now been integrated into the overall conversion of 'Spleen' and functions as a word—no matter how broad all its connotations—would function, as one constituent in a sentence, on a par with the other words. The conversion within the subsystem (adjectives and adverbs: *sales parfums*, *héritage fatal*, *causent sinistrement*, *amours défunts*) has no independent meaning; no symbolism of their own attaches to the details of this pathetic story. Their complex negativizations are just a marker like the others, an embedding within the syntagmatic continuum of the sonnet's conversion. The realistic mimesis of the whole tercet has been semioticized into being one word of *maison*'s transformation into *non-maison*, that is of the transformation of *maison*'s systematic significance into a code of that significance's contrary.

One striking feature of this passage, particularly remarkable in a book that is supposed to describe the process of reading and interpreting poems, is its deviation from the conventions of ordinary critical writing. Readers and critics are generally inclined to insist on the richness of meaning in a poem, the depth of significance of each detail. Riffaterre provocatively denies that the details of the final stanza have any independent or symbolic significance: this mysterious little story is nothing more than a negation of one aspect of *maison*. Many readers will find this confident reductionism somewhat objectionable, but one can argue that in fact Riffaterre is describing in a rather emphatic way what, in effect, occurs in readings of this poem. The final tercet is difficult and puzzling; readers are likely to be fascinated precisely because the scene of playing cards seems gratuitous and sinister in its gratuitousness; and though they would seldom claim that the details of the scene are unimportant (since one powerful convention has it that no detail of a good poem can be unimportant), what they respond to and what they succeed integrating into an interpretation of the sonnet is nothing other than this general sense of something sinister and disagreeable in this enclosed space of a home.

One could say much the same about other formulations of Riffaterre's. He violates critical decorum in claiming that reading a poem is a matter of discovering the word or sentence from which it is generated and of which its every element is a variant. This seems much too crude and reductive to be an accurate account of how readers and critics proceed; most interpretations require considerable time or space to explain all the things a poem is about and how it integrates these concerns in a complex balance of attitudes that can be experienced but not described. It is a far cry from critics' rich interpretations of Blake's 'The Sick Rose' to the matrix which, according to Riffaterre, the poem simply repeats over and over again in different guises: 'the rose is sick.'[5] Moreover, by describing the identification of a unifying matrix as the goal of poetic interpretation, he encourages reductionism. If the reader of 'Spleen' is supposed to see every line as the transformation of a hypogram into a variant of gloom, he will have every reason to treat the strange first stanza as simply, in Riffaterre's words, 'the conventional language of traditional allegory' asserting 'Nature's hostility to man' (p. 67). Since the emblematic figure pours cold on the inhabitants of the cemetery and mortality on the suburbs, one might be inclined to seek a more complex explanation—something more than Nature's hostility to man seems to be at work. But Riffaterre's theory suggests not only that readers fail to make anything of these details but that there is no more meaning to be had. Like the details of the final stanza, they have no significance except as variants of the misery from which there is no escape.

There are two answers to this charge of reductionism, which doubtless will be frequently levelled at *Semiotics of Poetry*. First, Riffaterre makes it clear that the matrix is not the meaning of the poem. To discover the matrix is to unify the poem, but meaning, or significance (for Riffaterre restricts 'meaning' to representational meaning), is something else. (p. 12):

> Significance, and let me insist on this, now appears to be more than or something other than the total meaning deducible from a comparison between variants of the given. That would only bring us back to the given, and it would be a reductionist procedure. Significance is, rather, the reader's praxis of the transformation, a realization that it is akin to playing, to acting out the liturgy of a ritual—the experience of a circuitous sequence, a way of speaking that keeps revolving around a key word or matrix reduced to a marker. It is a hierarchy of representations imposed upon the reader despite his personal preferences, by the greater or lesser expansion of the matrix's components, an orientation imposed upon the reader despite his linguistic habits, a bouncing from reference to reference that keeps on pushing the meaning over to a text not present in the linearity.

The meaning of the poem is not the matrix but the entire experience of moving from mimetic reading to the pursuit of hypograms to the discovery of semiotic unity.

Second, in reply to the charge of reductionism one can argue that Riffaterre's positing of a matrix is an attempt to identify the structure which enables readers to discover unity when they are interpreting the poem. As the discussion of 'Spleen' makes clear, Riffaterre's description of hermeneutic reading as the hypothesizing of a matrix is a claim that we go beyond the mimetic reading of individual lines and phrases by finding some basic topic of which we can see everything as a variant. This is probably true even for the most complex critical interpretations, though one may wish to question Riffaterre's insistence that the matrix is 'a word or sentence,' since in many cases readings unify a poem with the aid of some elementary binary opposition, as in 'Fêtes de la faim.' There seems no compelling reason why the basic unifying structure should be expressed as a word or sentence.

In numerous cases one can argue that Riffaterre's formulations, despite their air of reductionism, do in fact describe what readers and interpreters actually do, but if one tries consistently to maintain this position one repeatedly confronts a major obstacle. Though claiming to describe how readers do and must respond, Riffaterre likes nothing better than outdoing previous readers, citing the feebler efforts of prior interpreters and triumphantly proposing his own solution to the puzzle that has baffled them. We thus repeatedly encounter the questions Riffaterre himself posed at the beginning: is what he describes actually perceived by readers and are they obliged to perceive it, or do they retain a certain freedom (p. 2)? For instance, Riffaterre's first major example of the passage from a mimetic to a hermeneutic reading is Gautier's 'In Deserto,' which appears to be an objective description of a deserted Spanish sierra. At the end of the poem, Riffaterre argues, this objectivity is 'cancelled or made subservient to another representation, because the reader now knows that the whole sequence is not an independent description allegiant only to the truth of the outside world, but is the constituent of a trope.' He interprets the poem, convincingly, as a derivation from the cliché *a heart of stone* and from the phrase alluded to by the title, *vox clamens in deserto*. However, in this account of what the reader knows, does, or realizes, the only reading cited is that of 'the learned editor of the one and only critical edition we have,' who sticks faithfully to mimesis and 'comes to the conclusion that Gautier is fairly accurate, although he does seem to have made the sierra more of a desert than it really is' (p. 7). The poem explicitly relates the barrenness of the landscape to the speaker's inner barrenness, but 'in spite of this, our scholar, a seasoned student of literature, pursues his habit of checking language against reality.' Similarly, in presenting his account of 'Fêtes de la faim' Riffaterre notes that previous interpreters have simply given up and called the poem 'free childish association' or else have offered miscellaneous mimetic rationalizations of various images. 'These lame explanations are quite unnecessary,' he announces, unveiling his own new interpretation.

What are we to make of this combination? There is clearly a tension in Riffaterre's writing between the desire to outdo previous critics by offering a new and superior interpretation, and the desire to develop a semiotics of poetry that would describe the processes by which readers interpret poems. Both the rhetoric and the goals of these two enterprises are very different; it is difficult to treat the efforts of previous readers simultaneously as the phenomena one wishes to explain and as the errors one is attempting to surpass. Instead of attempting a mild-mannered compromise, which would probably fail and deprive the book of its excitement and energy, Riffaterre has boldly opted for contradiction, rejecting the conclusions of previous readers whenever he cites them, claiming to describe their procedures whenever he does not cite them.

In brief, the tone rejects previous readings, the theory encompasses them. One might be tempted to argue that Riffaterre is in fact describing how a particularly sophisticated group of readers interpret, but he explicitly rejects such a notion. Readers do not have the freedom to read as they will. Poetic signs form patterns that cannot be ignored. The reader is 'under strict guidance and control as he fills in the gaps and solves the puzzle' (p. 165). 'Because of the complexity of its structures and the multiple motivations of its words, the text's hold on the reader's attention is so strong that even his absentmindedness or, in later eras, his estrangement from the esthetic reflected in the poem or its genre, cannot quite obliterate the poem's features or their power to control his decoding' (p. 21). Finally, 'the reader's freedom of activity is further limited because of the poem's saturation by the semantic and formal features of its matrix; in other words, continuity and unity, that is, the fact that the semiotic unit is the text itself, forbid the attention to wander, deny the opportunities for hermeneutic deviance' (p. 165).

There is no way of reconciling these affirmations with the evidence presented in *Semiotics of Poetry* that earlier readers of Rimbaud and Gautier, who were neither absentminded nor ignorant (Gautier's editor is a 'scholar' and a 'seasoned student of literature'), found opportunities for hermeneutic deviance, failed to notice the repetition of the matrix, and were not compelled to shift from mimesis to semiosis. If the theory is to include readers other than Riffaterre himself, one needs to reformulate some of his principles.

First, Riffaterre speaks of the shift from mimesis to semiosis as something enforced by the text, but the example of Gautier's editor and Rimbaud's earlier interpreters shows that readers may not make this shift. We are dealing not with an inexorable textual force but with a convention of reading—more specifically, with a hierarchy of conventions. At the lowest level there is the common convention by which 'ungrammaticalities' are converted not so much into semiosis in Riffaterre's sense as to second-order referential meanings. When readers encounter the ungrammaticality of 'my love is a red, red rose,' they suspend the reference to actual roses but do so in favor of a reference to the woman's precious and fragile beauty. Riffaterre has devoted considerable energy and acumen to arguing that such conversions in the interpretation of figurative language do not depend upon knowledge of the world but only upon hypograms of various sorts: connections previously established in clichés, descriptive systems, and past poetic texts. The interpretation of 'my love is a red, red rose' is based on the recognition of a code, just as the interpretation of 'Spleen' depends upon the values and associations of the descriptive system of *maison*, and therefore these conversions are examples of an overcoming of mimesis. However, one must make a distinction here. Riffaterre has indeed done much to show the crucial role of intertextuality and descriptive systems; most interpretation does perhaps rely more on the identification of codes and discursive associations than on a scanning of the actual features of objects referred to (it is cultural codes alone that tell us that if a woman is compared with a swan she is not being given a deformed neck or feathers). But though all interpretations rely on these intertextual, cultural codes, there is a difference between interpretive moves that use these codes to reestablish a reference at a second level (not to the rose but to the woman's beauty) and interpretive moves that treat the figure as primarily a reference or allusion to the code itself (the primary significance of 'my love is a red, red rose' is compliance with the most traditional stereotyped figures of love poetry). It is only the second interpretive move that truly exemplifies Riffaterrean semiosis, and what is involved here is a further convention, generally applied at a later stage and by a more restricted group of readers, that an important meaning of figures is what they tell us about figurative language.

The prior convention by which ungrammaticalities are converted to second-order referential meanings operates unless there are good reasons to suspend it (Riffaterre argues, for example, that in 'Fêtes de la faim' we need not attempt to interpret the request to Anne to run away on her donkey, because by convention refrains need not have meaning). When it does operate, there are conventions governing the ranking of subjects or topics toward which interpretation moves. Weather, for example, ranks extremely low, and statements about the weather or climate are interpreted as referential at another level. A common convention of the lyric makes the speaker's mood or state of mind a topic to which they may be referred. Riffaterre may well be surprised, given the importance of this convention, that Gautier's editor did not interpret statements about the sierra and its climate as images of the speaker's imaginative aridity, especially since figures in the poem explicitly established this connection; but the editor doubtless thought that the convention of unifying a poem by relating its statements to the self of a speaker was a romantic convention relevant to certain kinds of lyric but not to the genre of descriptive poetry, to which 'In Deserto' was presumed to belong. The distinguishing feature of descriptive poetry would be that the conversion of first-order mimesis to second-order mimesis need not take place, and therefore that comparisons between the scene described and the speaker's inner state can be interpreted as thoughts provoked by the scene in question rather than as the true subject of the poem, for which all other elements are figures.

Riffaterre treats the transcending of mimesis as a necessary effect of all poetic language, whereas in fact it is a convention for the interpretation of most poetic genres, and even in these cases there are intermediary levels of mimesis. In the interpretations of Blake's 'London' discussed in Chapter 3 the vast majority of interpretive conversions were explicitly designed to make the poem a mimetic, referential statement. Asking 'How the Chimneysweeper's cry/ Every black'ning Church appalls', critics naturally relied on the semiotic codes relating to sweeps and churches, but they sought to produce statements about the Church's guilt for the exploitation of child sweeps. Most readings of the poem, treating it as a powerful indictment of human misery (though disagreeing about the nature and causes of that misery), sought to unify the poem at an explicitly referential level. The kind of semiosis that most interests Riffaterre, the consideration of the sources of figures and the inferring of poetic unity from the obstacles to mimesis, seemed to become important only at a late stage, in the possibility—always open to readers and critics and now more encouraged than it used to be—of reading figures rhetorically, in their figurality. In so far as each image in the text is an instance of the poetic ability to hear marks of weakness and woe in every particular, the poem can be seen as the expansion of a matrix via the topoi of city life into a series of scenes or images.

Whenever Riffaterre considers the readings of other critics, he is inclined to reject them in favor of his own. He thus has at best an ambiguous relation to the activities of reading he claims to describe, and this is doubtless one reason why, instead of speaking of conventions of reading, he prefers to speak of properties of texts which compel readers to perform certain operations. If this preference has unfortunate consequences, leading to inconsistencies and inadequacies in the theory, it nevertheless does have some excellent results. It enables Riffaterre to describe astutely and convincingly various poetic devices, particularly the properties of words and phrases that are conventionally regarded as 'poetic'. Someone interested primarily in conventions might be content to note that certain phrases function as conventional indicators of the poetic,[2] but Riffaterre attempts to specify their properties—*agile*, he suggests, like certain other adjectives, is not poetic in French when it is a predicate; 'the agent of poeticity is a specific relationship between epithet and noun, which designates a quality of the noun's referent, or a seme of that signifier, as characteristic or basic' (p. 28). *Le soleil agile* or *la toupie agile* is poetic because the epithet characterizes the sun or the top as permanently or basically nimble. In other cases, what is responsible for the poetic nature of a term, especially nouns, is an underlying descriptive system whose 'grammar and lexical distribution [is] characterized by polar oppositions . . . polarization is responsible for the noun's exemplariness and consequently for its poetic nature' (p. 43). *Soupirail* means an opening or vent that lets light and air into a cellar, but it has great poetic vitality because '*soupirail* does not designate a referent but serves as a kind of lexical shorthand for an abstract dialectic between a *here* and a *beyond*, between oppression here and a fantasy of imagined release elsewhere' (p. 46).

This detailed work on the reasons for the effects of poetic images and especially on the role of descriptive systems and commonplaces in poetic discourse is a valuable contribution to the semiotics of poetry, but Riffaterre's enterprise is continually deflected by the temptations of interpretation. At one moment he is explaining why a form or construction necessarily works in a certain way and produces a particular response; at the next moment he claims to be solving a puzzle that has always baffled readers and to have discovered the true but hitherto unknown meaning of a poem. The temptations are understandable, for Riffaterre is very good at providing new and striking interpretations, particularly for baffling Surrealist texts or laconic prose poems.

The more interested one becomes in these interpretations, the more it seems that Riffaterre is not undertaking the semiotics he originally proposed, not describing how readers do and must read, but offering, rather, a genetic theory, a method of interpretation based on a theory of origins. To discover the true meaning of a poem, one must interpret it in accordance with the principles by which it was constructed. Poems are generated by the expansion of a matrix through various hypograms into a text, so the correct interpretation, the solution to the puzzle, will be one that recovers the matrix and the hypograms. As he puts it when grappling with one apparently incoherent construction, 'the incompatibility vanishes once the text is read the way texts are built to be read' (p. 85). Previous readers and critics usually have not understood how poems are built to be read and thus have failed to reach correct conclusions.

Since Riffaterre is explicit about the conventions and strategies he applies to texts, his book has much to contribute to an analysis of reading. An extended discussion of prose poems, for example, illustrates very nicely the procedures open to readers struggling to make sense of the laconic, enigmatical fragment or narrative, and demonstrates the importance of generic conventions in interpretation of this sort. One may occasionally wish that Riffaterre had stuck to his program of describing 'the dialectic between text and reader' and not yielded to interpretation, but in general his interpretations are so engaging that one cannot wish them eliminated. When interpreting, he can write with energy and arrogance, avoiding the banality that always threatens a descriptive semiotics. The semiotician courts banality because he is committed to studying meanings already known or attested within a culture in the hope of formulating the conventions that members of that culture are following. The fact that one's labors, if successful, will lead to an explicit account of what is implicitly known, explains why the semiotician may be tempted by inter-pretation. Why not offer a new reading instead of trying to explain the conditions of old readings? Why not, after all, do both? Riffaterre has indeed tried to do both, and the result is a theory torn between its general and its specific claims. To ap-preciate what is valuable in his book one must separate the two enterprises that he has tried to join.

5

Presupposition and Intertextuality

Nous ne faisons que nous entregloser.
                                    Montaigne

Suppose that you had to explain to an outsider, a stranger from a culture that knew nothing about such matters, why you are reading this page. It would not be an easy task, for you would have to explain, in general terms, why people read works of literary theory, what sort of expectations bring them to engage in this activity and what expectations they bring to it. If we were to tell this stranger that a discussion of literary criticism is expected to instruct us in some aspect of the study of literature, we should not have done much to advance his understanding, for we should still have to tell him something about the discursive space or order of words which we call 'literary criticism' and explain that a book or essay should, within this framework, offer significant propositions.

If he pressed us on this point and asked us what we meant by 'significant,' we should no doubt have to reply that a book must say things which one has not explicitly thought or read but are related in some positive way to what one has in the past thought or read. Within the context of what is known, it must propose elaborations or modifications. For a discussion to be significant it must stand in a relationship, which doubtless would be difficult to describe, to a body of discourse, an enterprise, which is already in place and which creates the possibility of new work.

One would hope that any real stranger would by this time have become bored, but if he did continue to question we should find it extremely difficult to explain precisely what are the expectations with which we approach a book on an aspect of literary criticism and how such a discussion is rendered intelligible and significant by a whole body of already existing discourse. Indeed, we would be tempted, I think, to take evasive action, to say that the expectations of each individual reader, like his knowledge, are different, and that consequently there can be no talk of the general presuppositions of a discussion or of the general expectations of readers which will give it meaning. But even if it is thus personalized, the question remains difficult. How will you, as an individual, know whether what I say is significant or not? What are the individual expectations and norms which will enable you to make such a judgment? It is worth pointing out that, however difficult you may find it to formulate these norms and expectations, you will make a judgment about the significance of this discussion. You will, very shortly, evaluate it in relation to the critical enterprise.

So even this retreat from the general to the individual—an evasion one respects in that it bears the marks of truth—even this does not offer easy answers. Moreover, it is not an option which can always be exercised: the lecturer or writer of an article, for example, cannot accept it as truth, he cannot live or act by it. When he speaks or writes, his discourse makes a decision about a general and implicit contract, about what is known and what will be significant, about the state of literary studies as manifested in the intersubjectivity of his audience. Postulating general expectations, implicit and explicit knowledge which will make his discourse intelligible, cannot be an impossible thing to do, for the author or lecturer does it; indeed, he cannot avoid doing it. In the act of writing or speaking he inevitably postulates an intersubjective body of knowledge.

In saying that my discussion is intelligible only in terms of a prior body of discourse—other projects and thoughts which it implicitly or explicitly takes up, prolongs, cites, refutes, transforms—I have posed the problem of intertextuality and asserted the intertextual nature of any verbal construct. We can pose the problem another way by asking what a piece of writing presupposes. What does it assume, what must it assume to take on significance? This is not essentially or even primarily a question of what the writer knows, certainly not a question of what he has in mind, for the relevant presuppositions may be deeply sedimented in his past or in the past of his discipline; and indeed it is a characteristic experience that one's presuppositions are best revealed by another. They are, perhaps, that which must be revealed by another, or by an effort of *dédoublement*: of thinking from the point of view of the other.

I do not, then, propose to describe the presuppositions of my own discourse. Rather, I offer it and its situation as an example of the necessarily intertextual nature of formal utterance and of the difficulty of formulating presuppositions or of describing intertextuality. Even for simple facts which we know quite explicitly to be presuppositions, we cannot cite a source. How do we know that an article is supposed to tell us something new and significant? This is not exactly the fruit of experience, the necessary inference from the overwhelming evidence of past cases, nor is it part of an original covenant of the discipline. Even in such simple cases we seem faced with an infinite intertextuality where conventions and presuppositions cannot be traced to their sources and thus indubitably identified as grounds of signification. Roland Barthes speaks of intertextual codes as a 'mirage of citations,' likely to prove evasive and insubstantial as soon as one attempts to grasp them. The codes are nothing other than the 'déjà lu,' and readers, in whom these codes dwell, may be thought of as the representatives of a general intertextuality. '*I*,' writes Barthes, 'is not an innocent subject that is anterior to texts. . . . The *I* that approaches the text is itself already a plurality of other texts, of infinite or, more precisely, lost codes (whose origins are lost).'[1]

That conventions such as the convention of significance have lost origins should not be thought of as an accident that has befallen them. It is not that each convention or moment of a code had a determinate origin which the accidents of history have obscured. Rather, it is part of the structure of discursive conventions to be cut off from origins. Doubtless, the signs and grammatical rules of English have origins in some sense, but a pursuit of their origins would never yield an event that could truly count as an origin. The first recorded use of a form or grammatical construction is not an origin, because what originates in this event is not yet a constituent of the code; it becomes an element of the system or code in a process that excludes origination. It makes no sense to ask of a child 'what was the first word he spoke?' and it is similarly problematic to ask at precisely what moment 'cattle' became a sign of English.

This is, of course, a paradoxical situation, and one function of the notion of intertextuality is to allude to the paradoxical nature of discursive systems. Discursive conventions can only originate in discourse; everything in *la langue*, as Saussure says, must have first been in *parole*. But *parole* is made possible by *la langue*, and if one attempts to identify any utterance or text as a moment of origin one finds that they depend upon prior codes. A codification, one might say, can only originate or be originated if it is already encoded in a prior code; more simply, it is the nature of codes to be always already in existence, to have lost origins.

'Intertextuality' thus has a double focus. On the one hand, it calls our attention to the importance of prior texts, insisting that the autonomy of texts is a misleading notion and that a work has the meaning it does only because certain things have previously been written. Yet in so far as it focuses on intelligibility, on meaning, 'intertextuality' leads us to consider prior texts as contributions to a code which makes possible the various effects of signification. Intertextuality thus becomes less a name for a work's relation to particular prior texts than a designation of its participation in the discursive space of a culture: the relationship between a text and the various languages or signifying practices of a culture and its relation to those texts which articulate for it the possibilities of that culture. The study of intertextuality is thus not the investigation of sources and influences as traditionally conceived; it casts its net wider to include anonymous discursive practices, codes whose origins are lost, that make possible the signifying practices of later texts. Barthes warns that from the perspective of intertextuality 'the quotations of which a text is made are anonymous, untraceable, and nevertheless *already read*'; they function—this is the crucial thing—as 'already read.'[2]

Julia Kristeva also defines intertextuality as the sum of knowledge that makes it possible for texts to have meaning: once we
think of the meaning of a text as dependent upon other texts that
it absorbs and transforms, she writes, 'in place of the notion of
intersubjectivity is installed that of intertextuality.'[3]

The concept of intertextuality is thus central to any structuralist
or semiotic description of literary signification, but it proves
somewhat difficult to work with. For example, Laurent Jenny, in
an excellent recent article entitled 'La Stratégie de la forme,'
begins with the broad strokes and synoptic vision that mark so
many definitions of intertextuality: 'Outside of intertextuality,'
he writes, 'the literary work would be quite simply imperceptible,
in the same way as an utterance in an as yet unknown language.'[4]
The comparison leaves no room for doubt: what makes a series of
noises perceptible as a sequence of meaningful elements is the
entire phonological, grammatical and semantic system of a
language, and intertextuality, through this analogy, designates
everything that enables one to recognize pattern and meaning in
texts. But when Jenny comes to work with the concept, his
perspective changes quite surprisingly: 'The notion of intertextuality,' he continues, 'poses immediately a delicate problem
of identification. At what point can one start to speak of the
presence of one text in another as an instance of intertextuality?'[5]
He proposes to distinguish intertextuality proper from 'simple
allusion or reminiscence': in the latter case a text repeats an
element from a prior text without using its meaning; in the former
it alludes to or redeploys an entire structure, a pattern of form and
meaning from a prior text. He thus excludes from intertextuality
proper an allusion in Lautréamont's *Maldoror* to Musset: the
unusual image of the pelican offering its breast for its little ones to
devour. The allusion is immediately recognizable but, argues
Jenny, the symbolism of Musset's pelican is simply set aside:
'Even if the romantic reminiscence is mocked by the general
emphaticness of the discourse, there are not relations between
two texts as structured units.'[6]

There are good reasons for wishing to exclude such allusions
from the domain one is investigating, and this restriction of
intertextuality allows Jenny to produce an interesting study of

various ways of using structures from prior texts and different ways of transforming intertextual citations (according to the models of various rhetorical figures), but the intertextuality he describes does not stand in the decisive relation to a text that he originally claimed. It is evident, for example, that even though Lautréamont's text ignores the meaning of Musset's pelican, Lautréamont's mockery of Romanticism is made possible by empty allusions to or, if one prefers, misuses of romantic images and topoi. If intertextuality is what makes the later text 'perceptible,' then it clearly must include these relations to romantic discourse, even the superficial repetition of the pelican.

A restriction of the concept of intertextuality may seem a reasonable price to pay for a good essay on the uses of citation, but it does pose questions about the implications of the larger concept. Riffaterre and others have employed the broad concept of intertextuality to discuss the special referentiality of literary works: what appears to be a reference to an object, a state of affairs, etc., can and should be read as a reference to other texts and to the clichés and descriptive systems of a culture that result from the repetition of connections and associations in texts. Since Jenny wants to exclude some repetitions and allusions from intertextuality proper, what happens to them? Are cases like the pelican to be ignored by accounts of literary signification? Are they to be read referentially instead of intertextually, as involving actual pelicans, or are they to be treated on some as yet unspecified model? To restrict the concept of intertextuality for practical reasons—to mark out a manageable area of investigation—is not an innocent strategy. It poses questions about the claims made for the larger concept.

A particularly interesting case is that of Julia Kristeva, who is generally credited with having formulated and developed the notion of intertextuality. What happens when she undertakes the description of a work's intertextual space? 'Whatever the semantic content of a text,' she writes, 'its condition as a signifying practice presupposes the existence of other discourses. . . . This is to say that every text is from the outset under the jurisdiction of other discourses which impose a universe on it.'[7] But it seems difficult to make that universe itself the object of attention:

'The poetic signified refers to (relates to) other discursive signifieds, so that in a poetic utterance can be read numerous other
discourses.'[8] The attempt to demonstrate the importance of intertextuality leads one to focus on the other discourses identifiable
in and behind a discourse and to try to specify them. Thus the
intertextuality of Lautréamont's *Chants de Maldoror* and *Poésies* is
described as a dialogue with texts that are in principle (and
generally in practice as well) identifiable:

> The other text, the object of 'mockery,' is absorbed by the
> poetic paragram either as a *reminiscence* (the *ocean*—Baudelaire?
> the *moon*, the *child*, the *gravedigger*—Musset? Lamartine? the
> *pelican*—Musset? and the whole code of Romanticism that is
> dislocated in the *Chants*), or as a *citation* (the other text is taken
> up literally and dismembered in the *Poésies*).[9]

Particularly striking is Kristeva's choice of what she calls a 'striking example of this intertextual space which is the birthplace of
poetry.' Lautréamont's *Poésies*, which contain a very large
number of explicit negations or deformations of identifiable
maxims and sententiae, are the principal example of intertextuality in *Semiotiké* and the only example in the discussion of 'the
presupposed context' in *La Révolution du langage poétique*.[10] *Poésies
II*, in particular, practically imposes on the analyst a detailed
study of the relationship between undeniable sources (usually in
Pascal, Vauvenargues, or La Rochefoucauld) and disrespectful
deformations. Anyone thinking that the point of intertextuality is
to take us beyond the study of identifiable sources is brought up
short by Kristeva's observation that 'in order to compare the
presupposed text with the text of *Poésies II*, one needs to
determine what editions of Pascal, Vauvenargues, and La
Rochefoucauld Ducasse could have used, for the versions vary
considerably from one edition to another.'[11]

The point is not that such questions are uninteresting or insignificant but only that a situation in which one can track down
sources with such precision cannot serve as the paradigm for a
description of intertextuality, if intertextuality is the general discursive space that makes a text intelligible. Kristeva's procedure

is instructive because it illustrates the way in which the concept of intertextuality leads the critic who wishes to work with it to concentrate on cases that put in question the general theory. A criticism based on the contention that meaning is made possible by a general, anonymous intertextuality tries to justify the claim by showing how in particular cases 'a text works by absorbing and destroying at the same time the other texts of the intertextual space' and is happiest or most triumphant when it can identify particular pretexts with which the work is indubitably wrestling. Critical practice guides the theorist toward the claim that 'the poetic text is produced in the complex movement of a simultaneous affirmation and negation of another text.'[12]

One critic who has unhesitatingly taken this road, who has embraced the concept of intertextuality and compressed it to a relationship between a text and a particular precursor text, between a poet and his major predecessor, is Harold Bloom. The French proponents of intertextuality would have no quarrel with Bloom's formulation when he asserts the intertextual nature of text and meaning:

> Few notions are more difficult to dispel than the 'common-sensical' one that a poetic text is self-contained, that it has an ascertainable meaning or meanings without reference to other poetic texts. . . . Unfortunately, poems are not things but only words that refer to other words, and *those* words refer to still other words, and so on into the densely overpopulated world of literary language. Any poem is an inter-poem, and any reading of a poem is an inter-reading.[13]

This is the case because prior linguistic acts are the ground, the conditions of possibility of one's own discursive actions. What happens, Bloom asks,

> if one tries to write or to teach or to think, or even to read without the sense of a tradition? Why, nothing at all happens, just nothing. You cannot write or teach or think or even read without imitation, and what you imitate is what another

person has done, that person's writing or teaching or thinking
or reading. Your relation to what informs that person is tradition.[14]

Here we can already detect that shift from texts to persons
which will assume greater importance until it becomes the central
feature of Bloom's theory, setting it in radical opposition to the
theory of his French predecessors. For Barthes, one might say,
the model for textual production is Bouvard and Pécuchet, whose
lives are generated by an infinite network of anonymous citations. For Bloom, on the contrary, the intertextual is not a space of
anonymity and banality but of heroic struggles between a sublime poet and his dominant predecessor ('A poetic "text," as I
interpret it, is not a gathering of signs on a page, but is a psychic
battlefield upon which authentic forces struggle for the only
victory worth winning, the divinating triumph over oblivion').[15]
Turning from texts to persons, Bloom can proclaim intertextuality with a fervor less circumspect than Barthes's, for Barthes's
tautologous naming of the intertextual as the 'déjà lu' is so
anticlimactic as to preclude excited anticipations, while Bloom,
who will go on to name precursors and describe the titanic struggles which take place on the battlefield of poetic tradition, has
grounds for enthusiasm. Indeed, his use of intertextuality is a
daring move which cannot but tempt the critic who is frustrated
by the prospect of working in a Barthesian space of infinite and
anonymous citations. It is a daring move, for, while proclaiming
the dependence of every text on other texts, it produces a
cosiness which even a Kabbalistic rhetoric cannot disguise. The
function of Bloom's theory of influence, certainly the function of
the Freudian analogies which structure it, is to keep everything in
the family. Intertextuality is the family archive; when one explores it one stays wholly within the traditional canon of major
poets. The text is an intertextual construct, comprehensible only
in terms of other texts which it prolongs, completes, transforms,
and sublimates; but when we ask what these other texts are, they
turn out to be the central poems of a single great precursor. And if
we ask why this should be so, why the intertextual should be
compressed to a relationship between two individuals, the

answer seems to be that a man can have only one father: th\
scenario of the family romance gives the poet but one progenitor.
It is from this family romance, this cosy and murderous intertextuality of sublime poets, that Bloom's intertextuality derives.
There are origins after all; the precursor is the great original, the
intertextual authority. Locate the key precursor text, by a process
which *A Map of Misreading* scarcely elucidates, and you have your
intertextual space: a space whose articulations can be named by a
series of gaudy and exotic tropes.

Bloom's theory looks like an account of intertextuality and
presupposition, but when intertextuality is narrowed to this
point, where it is a relationship between a given poem and a
single great precursor poem which the poet was striving to overcome, one begins to have doubts. Is not Bloom's account of
influence and misreading actually a theory of origins, aimed, like
most theories of origin, at persuading us to take a different view
of the nature and meaning of the object in question? Though he
asserts that poems do not have meanings but only relations to
other poems, Bloom's writing consists of new and powerful
interpretations of poems, grounded on a claim about how poems
come into being. Like Riffaterre, he claims to reveal the secret of
the text by describing an act of origination: the troping on or
misreading of a previous poem instead of a troping on hypograms or clichés. If we are persuaded that this is indeed how
poems come into being, then we will interpret them as Bloom
urges, using one text as the intertextual space of the other.

If Bloom's 'antithetical criticism' is ultimately a genetic theory
rather than a theory of the conditions of signification, it nevertheless illustrates the dangers that beset the notion of intertextuality:
it is a difficult concept to use because of the vast and undefined
discursive space it designates, but when one narrows it so as to
make it more usable one either falls into source study of a traditional and positivistic kind (which is what the concept was designed to transcend) or else ends by naming particular texts as the
pre-texts on grounds of interpretive convenience.

Bloom's work is not to be dismissed: on the contrary, he has
done much to reinvigorate interpretive criticism, which had lost
its sense of purpose as the moderate humanism of the New

Criticism came to seem dated. Asserting that 'humane letters' is an oxymoron, that 'the imagination's gift comes necessarily from the perversity of the spirit' and that the main tradition of Western poetry since the Renaissance 'is a history of anxiety and self-saving caricature, of distortion, of perverse, wilful revisionism without which modern poetry as such could not exist,'[16]—with assertions like these Bloom will inspire a whole generation of critics to read poems as acts of self-saving caricature.

He is also to be admired for raising so forcefully and frequently the problem of intertextuality; but those of us who lack his strength must contend with the fact that poems do seem to presuppose more than a single precursor poem: what makes possible reading and writing is not a single anterior action which serves as origin and moment of plenitude but an open series of acts, both identifiable and lost, which work together to constitute something like a language: discursive possibilities, systems of convention, clichés and descriptive systems.

Intertextuality is more complicated and also more banal than the model of sublime poetry may suggest. Indeed, Neil Hertz has subtly demonstrated that one function of the sublime is precisely to transform a disordered multiplicity into a focussed drama. What Kant calls the 'mathematical sublime' arises out of cognitive exhaustion, when confronting sheer proliferation, with no hope of bringing a long series or a vast scattering under some sort of conceptual unity, the mind experiences a 'momentary checking of its vital powers,' followed by a compensatory positive movement, an exultation in its own confrontation of the unmasterable. Finding this drama repeated in the scholar's contemplation of the proliferation of data, publications, and interpretations, Hertz writes:

> the goal . . . is the oedipal moment, that is, the goal is the sublime of conflict and structure. The scholar's *wish* is for the moment of blockage, when an indefinite and disarrayed sequence is resolved (at whatever sacrifice) into a one-to-one confrontation, when numerical excess can be converted into that supererogatory identification with the blocking agent that is the guarantor of the self's own integrity as an agent.[17]

Bloom transforms intertextuality from an endless series of anonymous codes and citations to an oedipal confrontation, one of whose effects is to preserve the integrity of his poets as agents of the poetic process. But even if we eschew Bloom's dramatic maneuvers, the general scenario is difficult to avoid. Theories of intertextuality set before us perspectives of unmasterable series, lost origins, endless horizons; and, as I have been suggesting, in order to work with the concept we focus it—but that focusing may always, to some degree, undermine the general concept of intertextuality in whose name we are working.

But this is no reason to abandon the project. It suggests, rather, the need for multiple strategies, for different focuses and restrictions, even though one cannot have any confidence that these could eventually contribute to a grand synthesis. One valuable project is Riffaterre's attempt, described in the previous chapter, to reconstruct the clichés and descriptive systems that underlie particular uses of poetic language. Another possibility would be to follow the linguistic model as far as one can by exploring the notion of presupposition in linguistics and the literary analogues it suggests.

In discussing the presuppositions at work in a natural language linguists find it convenient to distinguish between *logical* and *pragmatic* presuppositions. The former are best thought of as the presuppositions of a sentence, as when we recognize that *Have you stopped beating your wife?* is a loaded question because any answer gives assents to what the sentence presupposes: that one previously made a habit of beating one's wife. An explicit definition of logical presupposition is as follows: 'A sentence *S* logically presupposes a sentence *S'* just in case *S* logically implies *S'* and the negation of *S*, ~*S*, also logically implies *S'*.'[18] Presuppositions are what must be true in order that a proposition be either true or false. Thus, *It surprised me that John bought a car* presupposes that *John bought a car*, as does *It didn't surprise me that John bought a car*. A whole series of grammatical constructions and lexical items carry presuppositions of this sort: factive predicates (as in the example above), cleft sentences (*It was John who caught the thief*), temporal subordinate clauses (*John left before Mary called*), non-restrictive relative clauses (*The hotel, which was built in the nineteenth century, is decrepit*), certain aspectuals (*John stopped [or continued, resumed] writing at two o'clock*), iteratives (*John called again*), presuppositional quantifiers (*Everyone but John died*), and definite names, including all those syntactic constructions which function as names (*John married Fred's sister* presupposes that Fred has a sister and *John lost the paper that Fred gave him to read* presupposes the existence of a paper that Fred gave John to read). We can also extend this notion of logical presupposition to questions (*Where did he go?* presupposes that he went somewhere) by saying that the presuppositions of a question are those sentences which are the logical presuppositions of every one of its answers.[19]

This notion of presupposition, which is not defined in terms of speaker's or author's beliefs, introduces a modest intertextuality in relating sentences of a text to another set of sentences which they presuppose. This kind of presupposition is of considerable importance in literature. If the presuppositions of a sentence are all those propositions which it and its negation logically entail, then we can say, more informally, that they consist of all the assertions made by a sentence *except* the assertion made by its surface structure predicate. It is of considerable importance which propositions a work chooses to assert directly and which it chooses to place in this intertextual space by presupposing them.

Thus, when Baudelaire begins a poem

> Quand le ciel bas et lourd pèse comme un couvercle
> Sur l'esprit gémissant en proie aux longs ennuis

[When the low and heavy sky weighs like a lid on the spirit groaning from the long anxieties that prey on it][20]

and when he carries on in temporal subordinate clauses for three stanzas, he is choosing to presuppose the most important assertions of his discourse, to relegate them to the intertext or pre-text, to identify them as part of the *déjà lu*, as a set of sentences already in place. There is implicit reference to prior poetic discourse, to a poetic tradition, even though no poet may ever have described the sky as the lid of a pot. If Baudelaire had begun 'Parfois le ciel bas et lourd pèse comme un couvercle,' he would be claiming to have discovered something about the world, and we might expect explanation, justification, a narrative which located this fact in an experiential context. The decision to presuppose undermines referentiality at this level by treating the fact in question as already given. In cases like this, logical presupposition is an intertextual operator which implies a discursive context and which, by identifying an intertext, modifies the way in which the poem must be read.

Again, when Baudelaire begins 'Bénédiction' with

> Lorsque par un décret des puissances suprêmes
> Le Poète apparaît en ce monde ennuyé
>
> [When by a decree of the supreme powers
> The poet appears in this bored world][21]

by presupposing this fact about the poet he takes up a different relationship to it: treating it as prior discourse, part of the intertext, a myth of the poet which he can cite, he opens the question of the mode in which his poem will treat this prior discourse. Presupposition opens an intertextual space which can easily become ironic.

In poetry it makes a difference whether a proposition is asserted directly or presupposed. Ted Hughes begins a poem 'October is marigold.'[22] This direct assertion of a metaphor, especially of an unusual one, is a way of acquiring a reputation for energy and forthrightness. To have begun 'In marigold October' would have been to treat the conjunction of *October* and *marigold* as presupposed, to have relegated to a prior text the creation or discovery of that relationship, and to have suggested (even though we know of no other poem which treats October as marigold) that he was using a metaphor already implicit in poetic vision, in poetic discourse. 'October is marigold' eschews the citational mode, perhaps because it seeks to avoid irony.

Finally, poems containing questions explicitly assert their intertextual nature, not just because they seem to request an answer and hence designate themselves as incomplete, but because the presuppositions carried by their questions imply a prior discourse. In Blake's 'The Tyger' we have a series of questions:

> What immortal hand or eye
> Could frame thy fearful symmetry?
>
> In what distant deeps or skies
> Burnt the fire of thine eyes?
> On what wings dare he aspire?
> What the hand dare seize the fire?[23]

By presupposing that the fearful symmetry was framed by some immortal hand, that the fire of the eyes burned in some distant deep or sky, etc., the poem identifies these latter sentences as part of a discourse or mode of discourse already in place, as a text or set of attitudes prior to the poem itself. Thus the problem of interpreting the poem becomes essentially that of deciding what attitude the poem takes to the prior discourse which it designates as presupposed.

This kind of presupposition is useful for the study of intertextuality for, though it is clearly very limited (in no way an infinite repertory of possibilities), it indicates with perfect clarity the truth of Barthes's claim about the intertext: that a text refers to or cites bits of discourse which are 'anonymous, undiscoverable, and nevertheless already read.' When works presuppose sentences they treat them as prior discourse, as an intertext to which the poem relates. We may or may not find in earlier poems sentences similar to those presupposed; that is in no way crucial. They function as already read; they present themselves as already read by virtue of the simple fact that they are presupposed.

Logical presupposition does not, however, exhaust the notion of presupposition. Indeed, it is not difficult to produce examples which set in striking contrast the logical presuppositions of linguistics and the rhetorical and literary presuppositions which are central to the process of reading literary works.

Consider the matter of opening sentences in novels: logical

presuppositions have an important role here, as the basic figures which determine a hermeneutic strategy. *The boy stood by the strange object pretending that nothing had happened* implies a very rich set of prior sentences, and as opening sentence in a novel or story would, by the very weight of its presuppositions, put us *in medias res* and program our reading as an attempt to discover the elements of this 'prior' text: What boy? What object? What had happened? But logically the opening sentence with the fewest presuppositions would be something like *Once upon a time there lived a king who had a daughter*. Poor in logical presuppositions, this sentence is extremely rich in literary and pragmatic presuppositions. It relates the story to a series of other stories, identifies it with the conventions of a genre, asks us to take certain attitudes towards it (guaranteeing, or at least strongly implying, that the story will have a point to it, a moral which will govern the organization of detail and incident). The presuppositionless sentence is a powerful intertextual operator.

If we think about this kind of case, we shall see that there are many ways in which literary or pragmatic presuppositions are signaled and produced by elements or constructions which carry no logical presupposition. For example, in most cases the logical presuppositions of positive and negative propositions are the same, but rhetorically, pragmatically, literally, negations are much richer in presuppositions. Thus, in Baudelaire's 'Un Voyage à Cythère,' after the line 'J'entrevoyais pourtant un objet singulier!' [I glimpsed, however, an unusual object], the poem continues as follows:

> Ce n'était pas un temple aux ombres bocagères,
> Où la jeune prêtresse, amoureuse des fleurs,
> Allait, le corps brûlé de secrètes chaleurs,
> Entrebaîllant sa robe aux brises passagères.

> [It was not a temple with bosky shades
> Where the young priestess, in love with flowers,
> Passed, her body consumed by secret flames,
> Her robe blowing open in the fleeting breezes.][24]

Logically, *it was not a temple* presupposes only that there was something, but rhetorically it presupposes that someone would have expected it to be a temple or had claimed that it was. The length of the following description intensifies this presupposition and makes the whole stanza the negation of an intertextual citation, the negation of something already in place as a discursive supposition, the negation of the language which poetic tradition might have applied to Cythère. The rhetorical presupposition which opens an intertextual or dialogical space in the poem is of a different order from the logical presuppositions we have previously been considering.

To describe rhetorical or literary presupposition would be to analyze the various interpretive operations which are brought into play by special kinds of discourse. This enterprise is related to the program which linguistics must develop to deal with its second type of presupposition: pragmatic presupposition. These presuppositions are defined not on the relations between sentences but on the relations between utterance and situation of utterance: 'An utterance of a sentence pragmatically presupposes that its context is appropriate.'[25] That is, the context must be such as to allow one to interpret the utterance as the kind of speech act which it is. *Open the door* presupposes, pragmatically, the presence, in a room with a door that is not open, of another person who understands English and is in a relation to the speaker which enables him to interpret this as a request or command.

The analogies with the case of literature are not very rich, except in this respect: we take literary utterance as a special kind of speech act, detached from a particular temporal context and placed in a discursive series formed by other members of a literary genre, so that a sentence in a tragedy, for example, is appropriately read according to conventions which are different from those which would apply in comedy. In trying to formulate the pragmatic presuppositions of sentences which *warn*, *promise*, *command*, etc., one is working on the conventions of a genre of speech act.

Attempts to formulate pragmatic presuppositions for speech acts have only recently got under way and have generally focussed on the criteria for successful accomplishment of speech acts such as promising, ordering, warning. It is not clear that literary studies would learn much from the details of such investigations. The point is, simply, that formally the investigation of pragmatic presuppositions is similar to the task which confronts poetics. To work on the presuppositions of a sentence which *promises* is to relate it to a whole series of other sentences, to place it in a discursive or intertextual space which gives rise to the conventions that make this sentence intelligible and significant as a speech act. In relating this sentence to other acts of promising which form, as it were, its conditions of possibility, one need not enquire whether the speaker of the sentence has previously encountered these other sentences which promise, nor even whether anyone has actually produced these sentences. None of these sentences is a point of origin or moment of authority. They are simply the constituents of a discursive space from which one tries to derive conventions.[26]

This is precisely the kind of enterprise which poetics must undertake. Focusing on the conditions of meaning in literature, it relates a literary work to a whole series of other works, treating them not as sources but as constituents of a genre, for example, whose conventions one attempts to infer. One is interested in conventions which govern the production and interpretation of character, of plot structure, of thematic synthesis, of symbolic condensation, and displacement. In all these cases there are no moments of authority and points of origin except those which are retrospectively designated as origins and which, therefore, can be shown to derive from the series for which they are constituted as origin. As in explaining the conventions of a lecture, it is a matter of working out what conventions are necessary to account for what happens, not of surveying the members of a class and inductively discovering common properties.

Paul Valéry, who thought that a true history of literature would be 'a history of the mind as a producer and consumer of literature,' saw that such a project would be 'a study aimed at gaining as exact an idea as possible of the conditions of existence and development of literature, an analysis of this art's modes of action, its means, and the diversity of its forms.'[27] A poetics of this kind would be justified above all by the intertextual nature of literary works and would attempt to describe the plethora of languages, themes, conventions, and commonplaces in relation to which language occurs.

The linguistic analogy suggests two limited approaches to intertextuality. The first is to look at the specific presuppositions of a given text, the way in which it produces a pre-text, an intertextual space whose occupants may or may not correspond to other actual texts. The goal of this project would be an account of how texts create presuppositions and hence pre-texts for themselves and how the ways of producing these presuppositions relate to ways of treating them. The second enterprise, the study of rhetorical or pragmatic presupposition, leads to a poetics which is less interested in the occupants of that intertextual space which makes a work intelligible than in the conventions which underlie that discursive activity or space.

These are both, of course, partial approaches. By its very nature, perhaps, the description of intertextuality can only be accomplished by projects that distort and restrict the original theoretical program. But the impossibility of ever mastering and presenting, making present, the intertextuality of a particular text, much less a culture, does not mean that the project can be abandoned in favor of interpretation which applies one text to another in order to produce new readings. Bloom and others have shown us that one can often produce heat and light by rubbing two texts together, but even when the proponents of interpretation call their activity 'misreading' and announce that 'strength' is the criterion of success, a question arises about the source of strength. And to answer that question one must engage with all the pragmatic presuppositions, the conventions of discourse, and the sedimentation of prior texts designated by 'intertextuality.' Strength comes from a strategic positioning in the discourses of a culture, and to produce a strong discourse one must be an acute analyst of intertextuality.

6

Stanley Fish and the Righting of the Reader

Stanley Fish's criticism in *Self-Consuming Artifacts* and *Surprised by Sin* has many virtues, and it is a harsh man indeed who would not be impressed by a simple list of the various things it is supposed to do: it presents a theory without creating an elaborate theoretical apparatus or a special metalanguage; it stresses the rights of the reader against the claims of the professional critic; it presents reading as an active and creative process rather than a state of passive receptivity; it claims, therefore, to proceed from and contribute to a true humanism, ignored in its essentials by critics who treat the work as an a-temporal object or artifact; it welcomes the temporality of the work rather than seeking refuge from it in spatial fictions; it openly espouses and promotes the modern axiom that critical understanding proceeds through the ways of self-consciousness; and finally, it offers a hermeneutic method, a strategy for producing new interpretations, which nevertheless remains faithful to, or explicitly predicated upon, the actual experience of reading. As such a list suggests, Fish's work is fundamentally attractive, a repository of good causes, and if one admits, as I am quite happy to do, that it combines its theoretical ambitions with intelligent readings of seventeenth-century texts, which are thoroughly acceptable as independent critical studies, then one is forced to concede that it deserves all its success, as a program which manages to be pleasantly progressive while retaining most of the tasks and values traditionally assigned to criticism.

Doubts arise when one questions this success, when one

wonders whether a theory which challenges a host of traditional assumptions about literature should not encounter rather more resistance to its critical practice, when one enquires whether a theory worth proclaiming ought not to have more radical consequences than this. If it is easier to welcome Fish than to judge him, it is no doubt because both theory and practice seem eminently valid in their own terms, even if the values to which they minister be different. The problem, one might say, lies precisely in the fact that it is equally possible to praise him for performing the traditional tasks of criticism with taste and elegance and to cite his theory as a splendid and forceful attack on traditional modes of descriptive and interpretive criticism.

It would seem, then, that the best way to evaluate Fish's work is to drive a wedge between the theory of literature and the practice of criticism, to break those links which he has so conscientiously forged, and to see what happens if one tries to reconstruct them oneself on the evidence of the now separate enterprises. And since, if one may say so, the publication of additional interpretations of some seventeenth-century literature is a relatively common affair, whereas the formulation of a major reorientation in the theory of literature is rarer and of greater moment, it seems appropriate to concentrate initially on the latter, to ask what is Fish's theory of literature and what are its logical consequences, before comparing these consequences with the criticism Fish actually practices.

The essential points of the theory are easily stated and grasped: to enquire about the meaning of a word, phrase, or other element of a literary work is to enquire what it *does* in the work, and one cannot give an account of what it does without specifying how it is received, organized, and generally experienced by the reader as he proceeds through the text. The meanings of elements of a work are not intrinsic properties of some kind but the functions they have for readers in context and, by virtue of the temporal nature of the reading process, that context is a temporal one. It follows that the literary work itself is a false object, or at least that the kind of statements which can be made about the hypostatized object (roughly, statements about the words which it contains and the order in which they are deployed) have only an indirect bearing on the meaning and value of the work. If one wishes to discuss meaning and value, one must describe not an object but an event, and this involves, as Fish says, 'an analysis of the developing responses of the reader in relation to the words as they succeed one another in time.'[1]

One does not, then, attempt to describe 'the work itself'—a concept to which Fish attributes many of the difficulties of Anglo-American criticism. Other critics assume, Fish argues, that the text is already 'filled with significances and what the reader is required to do is get them out. In short, the reader's job is to extract meanings that formal patterns possess prior to, and independently of, his activities. In my view, these same activities are constitutive of a structure of concerns which is necessarily prior to any examination of meaningful patterns because it is itself the occasion of their coming into being.'[2] The activity of the reader, his attempt to make sense of the text by positing various structures and anticipating what may come, is a necessary condition of the emergence of patterns. Significance is not a property of the text but what is experienced during a series of interpretive acts, on which criticism must focus.

This theoretical reorientation has several advantages. First of all, it frees us from the notion that the poem is some kind of autonomous object which 'contains' its meaning as an inherent property. That notion has unfortunate consequences; it suggests that the reader, like a good empiricist, should approach the poem without any preconceptions so as to read only what is there in the text. The implication that the ideal reader is a *tabula rasa* on which the text inscribes itself not only makes nonsense of the whole process of literary education and conceals the conventions and norms which make possible the production of meaning but also insures the bankruptcy of literary theory, whose speculations on the properties of literary texts become ancillary and *ex post facto* generalizations which are explicitly denied any role in the activity of reading.

Secondly, as Fish himself points out, a theory which proclaims the importance of analyzing interpretive acts is 'from the very beginning organizing itself in terms of what is significant,' whereas any theory which invokes the text as object and sees description as bearing on the text itself will have great difficulties in finding ways of distinguishing the significant from the insignificant.

> If one sets out to describe in the absence of that which marks out the field of description [the experience of the reader], there is no way of deciding either where to begin or where to stop, because there is no way of deciding what counts. In such a situation, one either goes on at random and forever (here we might cite the monumental aridity of Jakobson's analyses of Baudelaire and Shakespeare) or one stops when the accumulated data can be made to fit a preconceived interpretive thesis.[3]

That is to say, if one tries to analyze the poem as object and does not ask which of its properties are significant for the reader, then one will either operate with no principle of relevance at all (any discernible properties will have an equal claim upon one's attention) or else import some principle of relevance which may be only contingently connected with the experience of the poem. This is an important point. It enables us to see, for example, that the error of the New Criticism did not lie in its critical practice, which clearly did make the experience of a particular type of reading the principle of relevance (other poems, says Cleanth Brooks, 'were to be read as one has learned to read Donne and the moderns'). Where it erred was in its claim that it was merely describing objective structures and that therefore it had no need for a theory of reading except in a negative and polemical form, as an attack on the preconceptions of other critics.

The third advantage of this orientation is that it paves the way for a proper theory of literature and avoids the difficulties encountered by theories predicated upon the work as object. If one assumes that works are autonomous entities which contain their own meaning, then literary theory is simply a set of generalizations about these objects. Any theory about 'the language of poetry,' for example, must identify objective qualities common to poems but not found in the language of prose—a requirement which disqualifies most significant claims, such as Brooks's 'the language of poetry is the language of paradox,' and leads to the spurious notion that poetic language is characterized by grammatical or semantic deviance. Or again, a literary theory which generalizes about the 'inherent qualities' of texts is embarrassed by works which can be read either as literature or as history, philosophy, theology, biography, for since the objective properties of such works do not change, they constitute a challenge to the distinctiveness of literature. Finally, for such a theory genres are simply taxonomic classes. Any series of works which share a number of properties can be grouped together as a genre, and there is no principled reason why 'tragedy' should be a more valid category than, say, 'novels about the lives of aristocrats.'

If, however, one claims that the qualities of literary works can be identified only in the structure of the reader's response, then literary theory has a crucial and explanatory task: it must outline the conditions and parameters of response; it must account for responses by investigating the conventions and norms which enable responses and interpretations to be as they are. The embarrassments cited above disappear. No longer need one maintain, in the face of the evidence, that the language of poetry is objectively different from the language of prose. The same sentence can have different meanings in poetry and prose because there are conventions that lead one to respond to it differently. Nor is one upset by the fact that some works can be read either as literature or as something else. On the contrary, such cases offer valuable evidence about the norms and responses which characterize literature, as opposed to other modes of discourse. The notion of 'reading something as literature' becomes central, as do notions of reading something as a lyric, as comedy, as tragedy. A description of a genre, as Fish says, 'can and should be seen as a prediction of the shape of response.'[4] Genres are no longer taxonomic classes but groups of norms and expectations which help the reader to assign functions to various elements in the work, and thus the 'real' genres are those sets of categories or norms required to account for the process of reading.

In general, then, though at this point Fish would no longer agree, an approach predicated upon the process of reading makes clear the importance of literary theory: it is a theory of how literary communication is possible and hence an attempt to make explicit the knowledge and interpretive operations which readers deploy as they move from a series of sentences to an understanding of a literary work. Interpretations of individual texts, in this view, are simply a display of that literary competence which a poetics must attempt to analyze. Indeed, the interpretation of individual works is only indirectly related to the study of literature. If the critic wishes to produce new and subtle readings, he is at perfect liberty to entertain himself in this way, but he should not do so in the belief that he is thereby making important contributions to the study of literature. An understanding of literature, both as an institution and an activity, involves an understanding of the conventions and operations which enable works to be written and read.

The first and most obvious objection to such a theory bears on the notion of 'the reader.' Since readers differ in their responses and interpretations, the complaint might run, are you not forced either simply to describe and analyze your own responses, thus forfeiting all claims to objectivity, or else to discount the variations and idiosyncrasies of actual readers by appealing, implicitly, to something very much like 'what the text actually says'? In other words, if you make some pretense of objectivity, as you seem bound to do, is not the only source of objectivity the text itself, as hypostatized object?

There are at least four points to be made in reply to such objections. First, even if one were only to describe, as explicitly as possible, the norms and operations on which one's own reading is based, the results would be extremely useful, and others could judge where these norms deviated from their own. But even in this case there would be a large common ground, for the simple reason that learning to read is an interpersonal activity: one sees how others respond, grasps intuitively or through explicit demonstration what kinds of questions and operations they deploy. Second, variations in interpretation are not an obstacle; they are rather the fact with which one starts. What one is attempting to explain—and it is something which deserves detailed explanation—is the fact that for any work there is a range of interpretations which can be defended within the conventions of reading. We have little difficulty setting aside the idiosyncratic response whose causes are personal and anecdotal (simple discussion with other readers can eliminate these). The problem is to make explicit the operations and conventions which will account for a range of readings and exclude any we would agree to place outside the normal procedures of reading. Third, one should stress that the whole institution of literary education depends upon the assumption that is being defended here: the assumption that one can learn to become a more competent reader and that therefore there is something (a series of techniques and procedures) to be learned. We do not judge students simply on what they know about a given work; we presume to evaluate their skill and progress as readers, and that presumption ought to indicate our confidence in the existence of public and generalizable operations of reading. Finally, it is clear that any literary criticism must assume general operations of reading: all critics must make decisions about what can be taken for granted, what must be explicitly argued for, what will count as evidence for a particular interpretation and what would count as evidence against it. Indeed, the whole notion of bringing someone to see that a particular interpretation is a good one assumes shared points of departure and common notions of how to read. In short, far from appealing to 'the text itself' as source of objectivity, one must assert that the notion of 'what the text says' itself depends upon common procedures of reading.

The task of literary theory or poetics, then, is to make explicit the procedures and conventions of reading, to offer a comprehensive theory of the ways in which we go about making sense of various kinds of texts. But here Fish's theoretical enterprise quite abruptly vanishes; to the question, how does the reader create meaning, he has no general reply to make. Whether he has glimpsed the radical consequences of his theory and taken fright at the prospect of Herculean labors, or whether his attachment to the traditional tasks of criticism is so strong as to prevent him from even considering the possibility of a new program, he raises the question of a general theory of reading only once, and then in order to beg it: the informed reader, he tells us, is assumed to be 'sufficiently experienced as a reader to have internalized the properties of literary discourse, including everything from the most local of devices (figures of speech, etc.) to whole genres.'[5] It is not a little ironic that a man who has so imperiously thrust the reader before us, announced a new age of criticism focussed on the reader, and insisted that meaning and value lie not in the text itself but in the activity of reading, should then turn and tell us that we need not enquire what this activity involves. Indeed, it is not ironic but bathetic.

There are several reasons for it, of course. The first is probably sheer difficulty. To set out the conventions and operations for reading sentences as, say, lyric poems would require considerable analysis and great theoretical acumen. One would have to specify, for example, which elements of discourse are immediately treated differently from the way they would be in other modes (obvious candidates are deictics—I, you, here, now, yesterday—which no longer take their meaning from a moment and situation of utterance but are devices which enable one to construct a fictive situation). How do we go about identifying poetic *personae* and what is the possible significance for the poem of these identifications? What are the varieties of structure which serve us as images of completion or coherence and toward which we work in our organization of elements? What are the complex paths of inference which govern the interpretation of what we call 'symbols' and give us a sense of plausible and implausible moves? What are the varieties of incongruity and insignificance which trigger the processes of symbolic reading? In short, the task is one of setting out a whole series of codes and models which underlie the experience of literature and which, inter-subjective in essence, enable the reader to act as a local manifestation of Reading. The task is a daunting one, and it is small wonder that Fish should retreat to the easier activity of interpreting poems—which, as he repeatedly tells us, is simply a matter of describing his experience of them.

But Fish is also compelled to flee the consequences of his theory by a moral position which he appears to prize. He sees his own focus on the reader as an admirable humanism, enhancing the dignity of men by insisting that they create meaning, and he thinks that any attempt to formulate the operations by which meaning is created would in some way desecrate this 'infinitely flexible ability.' We are supposed not to investigate the conventions which permit the production of meaning but simply to revel in 'the recognition that meaning is human.' But, of course, any ability can in principle be described as a system of operations, and to make the ability less mysterious is not to slight it. Obeisance to the 'creativity' of individual readers is an obstacle to achievement because reading is worth analyzing only in so far as it is an interpersonal process. Meaning is not an individual creation but the result of applying to the text operations and conventions which constitute the institution of literature. A misplaced desire to praise man as the originator of meanings can only hamper the attempt to explain how these meanings arise.

Fish is also attracted to interpretive criticism because he wishes to argue for the moral value of literature: 'it is didactic in a special sense; it does not preach the truth but asks its readers to discover the truth for themselves.'[6] And since he knows what these truths are, he sees his own function as that of describing the discovery of the truth, of offering interpretations of individual works rather than analyzing the conventions of reading.

His commitment to interpretive criticism, in the face of his theory, does, of course, create problems for him. To claim simultaneously that one is recounting the experience of readers and that one is producing new and striking interpretations is indeed a difficult act, and Fish brings it off with great skill. He must tread very carefully indeed to maintain both claims, which is no doubt why his attention cannot stray to other, more important matters.

Surprised by Sin: The Reader in Paradise Lost is his greatest success, primarily because he does maintain an elegant balance between his two claims. He cites other critics' interpretations as evidence that they, too, have responded as he assumes readers do, and then shows how their preconceptions lead them to base false interpretations on a true response. *Surprised by Sin* is successful also because he is treating a single work and can spend much time discussing the knowledge seventeenth-century readers would have brought to the text. His sketch of current theories of language, theological background, and expectations about religious discourse, helps to account for the operations of reading which lead to the experience Fish postulates. Finally, the work succeeds because *Paradise Lost* is a poem in which the concept of the reader has a distinctive hermeneutic role. The reader, as fallen man, is the subject of the poem, and 'Milton's method is to recreate in the mind of the reader the drama of the Fall, to make him fall again exactly as Adam did.'[7]

The function of this notion is to give Fish a dialectical method—and it is a sad reflection on Anglo-American criticism that the dialectic must be smuggled in this way. Whereas other critics note contradictions (we are attracted by the heroism of Satan's speeches and then are told by the narrator that he is not heroic at all) and feel compelled either to explain one term away or to condemn the poem, Fish is able, by an elementary dialectical move, to argue that the contradiction is crucial: we are supposed to be jolted by it, to see that as fallen men we are indeed prey to Satan's wiles, so that the contradiction becomes, at a higher level, the point of the poem. The virtue of *Surprised by Sin* is to have made available a dialectical method and to have shown in detail how it resolves and transcends the difficulties encountered by less dialectically-minded critics.

Self-Consuming Artifacts: The Experience of Seventeenth-century Literature is less successful, partly because the focus on a series of authors squeezes out the discussion of codes that make reading possible, partly because the reader no longer enjoys the special hermeneutic role assigned him in *Paradise Lost*, but primarily because Fish's concept of the 'self-consuming artifact' is suspect. He presents it as a historical category: in the seventeenth century there are works which undermine the distinctions, categories, and conclusions they offer. Of course, most interesting works could be read in this way—as self-reflective, self-critical—and it is an important modern convention that we should try to read them thus. Conceived as a convention of reading, the notion is valuable, but Fish tries to make it a historical category bearing on the properties of works. Indeed, the arbitrariness of his grouping is nicely illustrated by his decision to exclude Sir Thomas Browne, who meets all the formal criteria but who continually calls attention to what he is doing and lacks the brand of moral strenuousness which Fish particularly values. Instead of creating the self-consuming artifact as the result of a particular type of reading, Fish retreats to traditional interpretive criticism and makes it a rather arbitrary thematic classification.

But this is a local complaint. The central flaw of the argument is more severe. Fish has not thought clearly about his major methodological claim: that since the activity of reading is temporal interpretation is a linear process which takes in one word at a time. The sentence *That Judas hanged himself is uncertain* is a self-consuming artifact, Fish argues, because the proposition *that Judas hanged himself* is posed as if it were a certainty and then destroyed by the last two words—whereas *It is uncertain that Judas hanged himself* is not self-destructive. By this criterion the sentence *Between fancy and imagination there is no real difference* is self-consuming (it poses a distinction and then obliterates it), whereas *There is no real difference between fancy and imagination* is not self-destructive. Now it could be argued quite plausibly that in most modes of discourse the two members of each pair are synonymous and that it is by convention only, within a specific mode of reading, that we recognize and value a difference. Fish appears to deny this, to claim that there is a 'natural' difference between the two sentences because of the temporal nature of the reading process. To confirm such a claim he would have to investigate the actual psychological processes involved (How long a stretch is taken in simultaneously? How far has one actually gone in registering *that Judas hanged himself* as a positive proposition before one's eyes light upon the next two words?). Fish shows no interest in such questions—quite rightly so, because we are dealing not with natural processes but with conventions about interpretation. But there is considerable duplicity in his refusal to discuss the conventions and in his assumption that he may blithely proceed as if we registered and interpreted one word at a time.

Indeed, there is overwhelming evidence that Fish is dealing with conventions and nòt, as he claims, with a transcription of his natural and creative experience of the text. One may put it crudely by saying that the experience of reading to which *Self-Consuming Artifacts* constantly refers is quite obviously faked. If we were to take seriously the suggestion that he is describing and analyzing his experience of reading these texts, we would be brought up short by the fact that he never learns anything from his reading. In poem after poem he starts off with the expectation that the categories or distinctions proposed at the beginning of sentences or of texts are going to be preserved, developed, made essential; and time after time he is surprised, discomfited, demoralized to discover that they are destroyed. Time after time he is chastened and purified by the experience which forces him to abandon intellect. In any empirical case such experience would create new expectations; he would anticipate that self-destructive movement of the next poem and would read it as fulfilling his expectations.

Of course, he is quite right not to proceed in this way. We would object if he gave an account of the experience of reading a poem which depended on the fact that immediately before this he had read a particular series of poems. He is observing an important convention: namely, that one may discuss poems as independent entities, as if the reader came to them only with general expectations about poetry and not specific expectations about this kind of poem. He is analyzing each poem in terms of conventions of reading and not in terms of a particular sequential experience. This, as I say, is thoroughly proper, but he should recognize what he is doing.

Moreover, despite all his claims about the chastening lessons of this literature, he obviously has not been taught that he must abandon all distinctions and rationality itself. Fortunately he knows, at least implicitly, that such claims about the teachings of literature are generally interpretive strategies and that, when we describe with admiration the movement by which a Herbert poem suggests we should abandon ourselves to God, we are not claiming that we have been actually convinced by the lesson but that we have enjoyed and profited from seeing it worked out. It is too bad that a man who enjoins us to think about reading should have so vague an idea of the nature of the conventions by which he himself is reading.

Of course, this is not the first time that a potentially valuable formalism has taken fright and nullified its own insights with a retreat to thematic interpretation. One might wish that the retreat were a little less disorderly and more self-conscious, but fortunately Fish's readers can rescue much from the general collapse and self-destruction of his theory and can find in it an implied project of considerable importance: an investigation of reading as a rule-governed, productive process.

PART THREE

7

Apostrophe

Apostrophes are forbidden on the funicular
                          Wallace Stevens

Quintilian, speaking of oratory, defines apostrophe as 'a diversion of our words to address some person other than the judge'; and though he cautions against it, 'since it would certainly seem to be more natural that we should specifically address ourselves to those whose favor we desire to win,' he allows that occasionally 'some striking expression of thought is necessary . . . which can be given point and vehemence when addressed to some person other than the judge.'[1] The effects here cited to justify apostrophe do not, of course, distinguish it from other tropes, which also are said to seek 'greater point and vehemence.' But apostrophe is different in that it makes its point by troping not on the meaning of a word but on the circuit or situation of communication itself. If we posit for this essay, 'Apostrophe,' a communicative process linking an 'authorial voice' and the readers of *The Pursuit of Signs*, an apostrophe seems to mark a deflection of the message: O mysterious apostrophe, teach us to understand your workings! Show us your varied talents here!

Such apostrophes may complicate or disrupt the circuit of communication, raising questions about who is the addressee, but above all they are embarrassing: embarrassing to me and to you. Even an apostrophe delivered during a lecture on apostrophe, whose title might have prepared listeners for occasional apostrophes, will provoke titters. This minor embarrassment that apostrophes produce may be taken as a sign of a larger and more

135

interesting embarrassment which leads literary critics to turn aside from the apostrophes they encounter in poetry: to repress them or rather to transform apostrophe into description. Whether this is because writing, in some innate hostility to voice, always seeks to deny or evade the vocative, it is a fact that one can read vast amounts of criticism without learning that poetry uses apostrophe repeatedly and intensely. Classic essays such as M. H. Abrams's 'Structure and Style in the Greater Romantic Lyric' do not discuss apostrophe, though it is a feature of most of the poems mentioned. Earl Wasserman found it possible in *The Subtler Language* to write fifty pages on the highly apostrophic *Adonais* without addressing the problem.[2] One could multiply examples of this sort, but a single central case may illustrate more effectively the systematic and non-accidental character of this evasion.

Consider George N. Shuster's *The English Ode from Milton to Keats*. The problem of apostrophe ought to lie right at the heart of this book, since it is the central feature shared by the poems he discusses, but from the outset Shuster engages in instructive maneuvers to exclude apostrophe from his domain: 'The element of address,' he notes in the introduction, 'is of no especial significance, being merely a reflection of the classical influence. All the verse of antiquity was addressed to somebody, primarily because it was either sung or read and the traditions of song and recitation required that there be a recipient.'[3] Thus apostrophe is insignificant because conventional: an inherited element now devoid of significance. And if one asks what significance it had in the classical period, one is told that then it was already a convention: the traditions of song and recitation required a recipient.

Nor is apostrophe an important formal feature of the ode. This meaningless convention is also, Shuster argues, a purely 'accidental characteristic' of the genre; and he suggests that one pernicious effect of Wordsworth's ode 'Intimations of Immortality' was to have given currency to the misconception that the ode was a lyric

characterized by a note of address couched in relatively august terms. We have seen that virtually all the melic verse of antiquity was addressed to someone, primarily because the forms of ancient rhetoric and music required it. . . . The Romantic poets were so close to the classical tradition that they accepted the element of address as a matter of course; and we of the present are so remote from it that it seems a thing established in its own right.[4]

Proximity and distance are, it seems, equally good excuses for denying significance: to the Romantics apostrophe was natural and insignificant; to us it is wholly artificial and insignificant. It can always be ignored, though for changing reasons.

Shuster's evasions identify apostrophe as a genuine embarrassment. The fact that it is systematically repressed or excluded by critics suggests that it represents that which critical discourse cannot comfortably assimilate. Indeed, one might be justified in taking apostrophe as the figure of all that is most radical, embarrassing, pretentious, and mystificatory in the lyric, even seeking to identify apostrophe with lyric itself.

This might seem wilfully perverse, but there is good reason for it. Northrop Frye, for example, argues in the *Anatomy of Criticism* that genre theory is essentially based on 'the radical of presentation' and that in this schema the lyric is defined by John Stuart Mill's aphorism: the lyric is not heard but overheard. 'The lyric poet normally pretends to be talking to himself or to someone else: a spirit of nature, a Muse, a personal friend, a lover, a god, a personified abstraction, or a natural object. . . . The poet, so to speak, turns his back on his listeners.'[5]

This suggests that if we would know something of the poetics of the lyric we should study apostrophe, its forms and meanings. Such a project would confront at the outset complex problems of definition and delimitation, which I here leave aside in order to focus on cases which will be apostrophic by any definition:

> O Rose, thou art sick!
> O wild West Wind, thou breath of Autumn's being!
> Thou still unravished bride of quietness . . .
> Sois sage, ô ma douleur!

Such invocations, which turn away from empirical listeners by addressing natural objects, artifacts, or abstractions, will doubtless prove central to any systematic account of apostrophe and they are themselves an interesting and problematic case.

What role do apostrophes play in poems? Most obviously they serve as intensifiers, as images of invested passion. This is a matter on which rhetoricians seem to agree, and in so agreeing they invoke a rudimentary psychology to naturalize the figure: to explain its meaning by treating it as the natural effect of an unexceptionable cause. Thus Fontanier in his *Figures du discours*: 'But what can give rise to apostrophe? It can only be feeling, and only the feeling stirred up within the heart until it breaks out and spreads itself about on the outside, as if acting on its own. . . [as if it were] the spontaneous impulse of a powerfully moved soul!'[6] Apostrophe, by this tale, is a figure spontaneously adopted by passion, and it signifies, metonymically, the passion that caused it. If one were to accept Fontanier's claim, repressing one's suspicion that few things are more artificial than apostrophic addresses to inanimate objects, one might conclude that apostrophes indicate intense involvement in the situation described. 'O Rose, thou art sick' differs from 'The rose is sick' in that the former marks a powerful outburst of concern.

There may be some truth in this, but for many apostrophes, including 'O Rose, thou art sick,' the moderate, controlled, or admonitory tone does not justify tales of an outburst of passion. And even in exuberant poems it may be difficult to argue that apostrophe reinforces description, attaching intensified emotion to what is described. Consider Blake's invocation of spring in the *Poetical Sketches*:

> O thou with dewy locks, who lookest down
> Through the clear windows of the morning, turn
> Thine angel eyes upon our western isle,
> Which in full choir hails thy approach, O Spring!
>
> The hills tell each other, and the listening
> Valleys hear; all our longing eyes are turned

Up to thy bright pavilions: issue forth,
And let thy holy feet visit our clime.

Come o'er the eastern hills and let our winds
Kiss thy perfumed garments; let us taste
Thy morn and evening breath; scatter thy pearls
Upon our love-sick land that mourns for thee.

O deck her forth with thy fair fingers; pour
Thy soft kisses on her bosom; and put
Thy golden crown upon her languished head,
Whose modest tresses were bound up for thee![7]

To say that the act of addressing spring signifies the speaker's intense feelings about that season would be too simple, for the poem evokes not a love for an empirical season of the year so much as an intense feeling for the act of addressing this season. As Geoffrey Hartman writes about Blake's four poems to the seasons,

> We feel at once their intensely vocative nature—that the prophetic or speaking out and the invocational or calling upon are more important than their conventional subject. Their mood is never purely descriptive but always optative or imperative: what description enters is ritual in character. It evokes an epiphany so strongly as to carry the poet towards it.[8]

We can see why this might be the case if we ask why rhetoricians should claim that passion spontaneously seeks apostrophe. The answer would seem to be that to apostrophize is to will a state of affairs, to attempt to call it into being by asking inanimate objects to bend themselves to your desire. In these terms the function of apostrophe would be to make the objects of the universe potentially responsive forces: forces which can be asked to act or refrain from acting, or even to continue behaving as they usually behave. The apostrophizing poet identifies his universe as a world of sentient forces.

Harold Bloom, in the days when he thought that poetry was

about poets' relationship to the world as well as their relationship to Milton, interpreted Shelley's major poems as manifestations of an *I–Thou* relationship to the universe, but he insisted that in addressing Mont Blanc or the West Wind Shelley is invoking an unseen power behind them, an ultimate Thou: 'To invoke the Spirit that is in the west wind is not to invoke the wind or the autumn only.'[9] Doctrinally, this is a thoroughly plausible interpretation, for the poems themselves display considerable interest in a pervasive unseen power. But in defining this ultimate Thou as the true auditor the critic reduces the strangeness of apostrophe: while the poems directly address natural objects, the critic identifies the true addressee as a divine spirit. The student of apostrophe must resist this reduction. Whatever sort of pantheism the poems embody, when they address natural objects they formally will that these particular objects function as subjects; they perform the radical act of Keat's charioteer:

> The charioteer with wondrous gesture talks
> To the trees and mountains; and there soon appear
> Shapes of delight, of mystery, and fear[10]

This Keatsian claim makes apparent the connection between apostrophe and embarrassment. Readers temper this embarrassment by treating apostrophe as a poetic convention and the calling of spirits as a relic of archaic beliefs. What is really in question, however, is the power of poetry to make something happen. 'Poetry makes nothing happen,' says Auden, speaking for an ironic age. It can express an attitude—so we speak of the pantheism of apostrophic poems, reducing vocative to description and eliminating precisely that which attempts to be an event: the moment of apostrophe. Poetry makes nothing happen but, Auden admits,

> it survives,
> A way of happening, a mouth.[11]

Apostrophe reflects this conjunction of mouth and happening. The vocative of apostrophe is an approach to the event because its animate presuppositions are deeply embedded, asserted the more forcefully because they are not what the sentence asserts. Just as the question 'Have you stopped beating your wife?' thrusts its presuppositions on the listener with something of the force of an event, constitutes an event against which he must struggle, so the presuppositions of apostrophe are a force to be reckoned with. A nicely self-reflexive example is Lamartine's apostrophic question, 'Objets inanimés, avez-vous donc une âme?' [O inanimate objects, do you have a soul?], which presupposes a form of that which it asks about. [12]

The vocative posits a relationship between two subjects even if the sentence denies the animicity of what is addressed, as in Baudelaire's apostrophe to a portion of the self:

> Désormais tu n'es plus, O matière vivante,
> Qu'un granit entouré d'une vague épouvante
>
> [Henceforth, O living matter, you are no more
> than a piece of granite shrouded in vague horror] [13]

The assertion of the sentence contradicts its presupposition. Or consider Rousseau's complaint to inanimate objects: 'Etres insensibles et morts, ce charme n'est point en vous; il n'y saurait être; c'est dans mon propre coeur qui veut tout rapporter à lui.' [Insensitive and dead beings, this charm is not at all in you; it could not be there; it is in my own heart which wishes to draw everything back to itself.] [14] The animicity enforced by the apostrophe is independent of any claims made about the actual properties of the object addressed.

At this second level of reading the function of apostrophe is to constitute encounters with the world as relations between subjects, but the simple oppositional structure of the *I–Thou* model leaves out of account the fact that a poem is a verbal composition which will be read by an audience. What is the effect of introducing this third term? A prosaic example may assist reflection here.

Imagine a man standing on a corner in the rain cursing buses: 'Come on, damn you! It's been ten minutes!' If he continues apostrophically when other travellers join him on the corner, he makes a spectacle of himself; his apostrophes work less to establish an *I–Thou* relation between him and the absent bus than to dramatize or constitute an image of self. We might posit, then, a third level of reading where the vocative of apostrophe is a device which the poetic voice uses to establish with an object a relationship which helps to constitute him. The object is treated as a subject, an *I* which implies a certain type of *you* in its turn. One who successfully invokes nature is one to whom nature might, in its turn, speak. He makes himself poet, visionary. Thus, invocation is a figure of vocation. This is obvious when one thinks how often invocations seek pity or assistance for projects and situations specifically related to the poetic vocation, but it can also be inferred from the functionally gratuitous invocations which mark so many poems. If asking winds to blow or seasons to stay their coming or mountains to hear one's cries is a ritualistic, practically gratuitous action, that emphasizes that voice calls in order to be calling, to dramatize its calling, to summon images of its power so as to establish its identity as poetical and prophetic voice.

Shelley's 'Ode to the West Wind' is perhaps the clearest example of the way in which the apostrophic mode, making the wind a *thou*, poses the problem of the poetic subject as a problem of the wind's relation to him. If the wind is spirit, it can make the speaker either an *it* or a *thou* to its *I*. So Bloom writes, 'He can either surrender himself to the wind as an object for it to experience ("O lift me as a wave, a leaf, a cloud"), as the leaf, cloud, and wave are objects for it, or else he can attempt to call upon the wind to take up a stand in relation to him, to enter into him and he into the wind.'[15] ('Be thou, Spirit fierce/ My spirit! Be thou me, impetuous one!') Of course, it is in his ability effectively to sustain this apostrophic discourse that the speaker produces the poetic event and is constituted as poetical spirit.

Whitman says that 'I and mine'—which is to say, strong poets—'do not convince by arguments, similes, rhymes. We convince by our presence.'[16] The poet makes himself a poetic presence through an image of voice, and nothing figures voice better than the pure *O* of undifferentiated voicing: 'the spontaneous impulse of a powerfully moved soul.' A phrase like 'O wild West Wind' evokes poetic presence because the wind becomes a *thou* only in relation to a poetic act, only in the moment when poetic voice constitutes itself.

If we think of what the vocative represents in this process, we can see why apostrophe should be embarrassing. It is the pure embodiment of poetic pretension: of the subject's claim that in his verse he is not merely an empirical poet, a writer of verse, but the embodiment of poetic tradition and of the spirit of poesy. Apostrophe is perhaps always an indirect invocation of the muse. Devoid of semantic reference, the *O* of apostrophe refers to other apostrophes and thus to the lineage and conventions of sublime poetry.

When we as critics reduce apostrophe to description we can state the alternatives which confront the subject in a poem like the 'Ode to the West Wind,' but we eliminate the vocative, which is precisely the attempt to bring about the condition to which it alludes: the condition of visionary poet who can engage in dialogue with the universe. If, as we tend to assume, post-enlightenment poetry seeks to overcome the alienation of subject from object, then apostrophe takes the crucial step of constituting the object as another subject with whom the poetic subject might hope to strike up a harmonious relationship. Apostrophe would figure this reconciliation of subject and object. But one must note that it figures this reconciliation as an act of will, as something to be accomplished poetically in the act of apostrophizing; and apostrophic poems display in various ways awareness of the difficulties of what they purport to seek. Poems which contain apostrophes often end in withdrawals and questions. The 'Ode to a Nightingale' affirms the deceptive power of fancy:

> Adieu! the fancy cannot cheat so well
> As she is famed to do, deceiving elf.[17]

Fancy deceives by not deceiving as effectively as it is said to. This problematic structure leaves open the questions with which the poem concludes:

> Was it a vision or a waking dream?
> Fled is that music:—Do I wake or sleep?

The question about the status of the event is a way of suspend-
ing the referential aspect of the poem and focusing on a poetic
event.

   Other poems, instead of posing questions about the efficacy of
the apostrophic act, parody their own apostrophic procedures.
Baudelaire's 'Le Cygné,' which begins with the apostrophe
'Andromâque, je pense à vous,' tells of a swan who, nostalgically
seeking his 'beau lac natal' in a 'ruisseau sans eau', supplies an
'O' apostrophizing nature: 'Eau, quand donc pleuvras-tu? quand
tonneras-tu, foudre?' [Water, when will you fall? when will you
sound, thunderbolts?] The coincidence of *'O'* and *Eau* can be
variously interpreted: the nostalgic quest for a moment or place of
origin, the 'eau' of a 'beau lac natal,' yields only an 'O' of a trope;
or the pun identifies the potential addressee of every apostrophe
as the apostrophic 'O' itself and makes every apostrophe an
invocation of invocation. However one develops the implications
of the pun, the result is a foregrounding of apostrophe as trope: a
verbal equivalent of the Cygne's ineffective writhing ('Sur son
cou convulsif tendant sa tête avide'). In so far as the swan is
identified with an apostrophizing poet,

> Je pense à mon grand cygne, avec ses gestes fous,
> Comme les exilés, ridicule et sublime,
> Et rongé d'un désir sans trêve.
>
> [I think of my great swan with his frenzied gestures,
> Ridiculous and sublime like all exiles,
> Gnawed by an unremitting desire.][18]

the poem offers a critique of the apostrophic gesture, which is
ridicule as well as *sublime*: when it seeks something other than
itself (*eau*), it finds only itself (*O*), which may also be nothing (O).
In these terms, the opening apostrophe, 'Andromâque, je pense
à vous,' which seeks nothing but merely accomplishes what it
states, is a demystified apostrophe. But anyone who wished to
affirm this conclusion would have to contend with the fact that
insistence on the futility of the swan's apostrophic gesture has,
by adding to the pathos, made the swan a powerful symbol of

nostalgia for many readers (of whom the poem's narrator, who already sees the swan as a 'mythe étrange et fatal,' was only the first). The feeble apostrophic *cygne* becomes a powerful apostrophic *signe*, as readers adopt the emotion which the futility of the swan's apostrophe seems to be exposing.

A last instance of subtle and self-conscious commentary on apostrophe comes at the end of Rilke's ninth *Duino Elegy*. When you speak to the angel, 'Sag ihm die Dinge.' Tell him things.

> Und diese, von Hingang
> lebenden Dinge verstehn, dass du sie rühmst; vergänglich,
> traun sie ein Rettendes uns, den Vergänglichsten, zu.
> Wollen, wir sollen sie ganz im unsichtbarn Herzen verwandeln
> in—o unendlich—in uns! wer wir am Ende auch seien.
>
> Erde, ist es nicht dies, was du willst: unsichtbar
> in uns erstehn?—Ist es dein Traum nicht,
> einmal unsichtbar zu sein? Erde! unsichtbar!
> Was, wenn Verwandlung nicht, ist dein drängender Auftrag?
> Erde, du liebe, ich will.
>
> [These things that live on departure
> Understand when you praise them: fleeting, they look for
> rescue through something in us, the most fleeting of all.
> Want us to change them entirely, within our invisible hearts,
> into—oh, endlessly—into ourselves! Whosoever we are.
>
> Earth, isn't this what you want? an invisible
> rearising in us? Is it not your dream
> to be one day invisible? Earth! Invisible!
> What is your urgent command if not transformation?
> Earth, you darling, I will!][19]

Addressing Earth, the poem embraces the apostrophic fiction: that the things of earth function as *thous* when addressed. If they are subjects they seek, like all subjects, to transcend a purely material condition, they aspire to transcendence. If Earth can be addressed and has desires, it wants to be invisible, to be spirit; it seeks rearising in us. That we, the agents of this 'rescue,' are 'the most fleeting of all' is an irony which gives the transformation of earth a fictional quality. But the poem goes further: what the narrator boldly agrees to do is to produce an invisible earth— which is not the easiest claim to verify. One could argue that in treating the earth as a subject the poem has in fact made it invisible, but one can never maintain with confidence that this has actually happened.

To read apostrophe as sign of a fiction which knows its own fictive nature is to stress its optative character, its impossible imperatives: commands which in their explicit impossibility figure events in and of fiction. This line of thought has already led beyond the third level of reading, at which apostrophe was a way of constituting a poetical persona by taking up a special relation to objects. It has led to a fourth level at which one must question the status so far granted to the *thou* of the apostrophic structure and reflect on the crucial though paradoxical fact that this figure which seems to establish relations between the self and the other can in fact be read as an act of radical interiorization and solipsism. Either it parcels out the self to fill the world, peopling the universe with fragments of the self, as in Baudelaire's apostrophes to his pain, his mind, his soul, his living matter ('Sois sage, ô ma douleur,' 'Mon esprit, tu te meus avec agilité,' 'Recueille-toi, mon âme, en ce grave moment,' 'Désormais tu n'es plus, ô matière vivante,'), or else it internalizes what might have been thought external (things, says Rilke, 'want us to change them entirely . . . into ourselves'). The techniques of the first procedure, though not its consequences, are obvious. The second may be explained as follows: if *I* implies a *you* (in that 'I' means 'your *vis-à-vis* intends himself'), to name as a *you* something which in its empirical state cannot be a you (such as the earth) is a way of preempting the place of the *you*, placing there what can only fill that role through 'an invisible rearising in us.' It is only as a product of poetic intervention that the object can occupy the places of the addressee.

This emerges from another Rilke poem, an early apostrophic lyric from *The Book of Hours*:

Ich liebe dich, du sanftestes Gesetz,
an dem wir reiften, da wir mit ihm rangen
du grosses Heimweh, das wir nicht bezwangen,
du Wald, aus dem wir nie hinausgegangen,
du Lied, das wir mit jedem Schweigen sangen,
du dunkles Netz,
darin sich flüchtend die Gefühle fangen.

Du hast dich so unendlich gross begonnen
an jenem Tage, da du uns begannst,—
und wir sind so gereift in deinen Sonnen,
so breit geworden and so tief gepflanzt,
dass du in Menschen, Engeln und Madonnen
dich ruhend jetzt vollenden kannst.

Lass deine Hand am Hang der Himmel ruhn
und dulde stumm, was wir dir dunkel tun.

[I love you, gentlest law, through which we yet
were ripening while with it we contended,
you great homesickness we have not transcended,
you forest out of which we never wended,
you song that from our silence has ascended,
you somber net
where feelings taking flight are apprehended.

You made yourself a so immense beginning
the day when you began us too,—and we
beneath your suns such ripeness have been winning
have grown so broadly and deep-rootedly,
that you, in angels, men, madonnas inning,
can now complete yourself quite tranquilly.

Let your right hand on heaven's slope repose
and mutely bear what darkly we impose.][20]

Following conventions of the ode, this poem is a series of apostrophes that name an addressee in various metaphorical ways,

but the variety of designations makes the addressee mysterious and impalpable. Moreover, as Paul de Man argues in his reading of the poem,

> The object of the apostrophe is only addressed in terms of an activity that it provokes in the addressing subject: if it is said to be a forest, it is only with reference to our behavior toward this forest; the net exists only as an obstacle to *our* flight; law is, per definition, that which governs our behavior, and the song is at once identified as *our* song (or silence). The metaphors therefore do not connote objects, sensations, or qualities of objects, but refer to an activity of the speaking subject. The dominating center, the 'du' of the poem, is present in the poem only to delegate, so to speak, its potential activity to the speaking voice; this becomes the explicit theme of the poem in the two concluding lines.[21]

The strange series of predicates in this poem may alert the reader to the fact that the apostrophic postulation of addressees refers one to the transforming and animating activity of the poetic voice. The 'you' is a projection of that voice. As Shelley says, 'the words *I*, *you*, *they* are not signs of any actual difference subsisting between the assemblage of thoughts thus indicated but are merely marks employed to denote the different modifications of the one mind.'[22]

The fact that apostrophe involves a drama of 'the one mind's' modifications more than a relationship between an *I* and a *you* emerges with special clarity in poems with multiple apostrophes. Wordsworth's 'Immortality Ode,' for example, brings together in a single unreal space 'Thou child of joy,' 'ye blessed creatures,' 'Thou whose exterior semblance dost belie thy soul's immensity,' 'ye birds,' and 'ye fountains, meadows, hills, and groves.' Brought together by apostrophes, they function as nodes or concretizations of stages in a drama of mind.

This internalization is important because it works against narrative and its accompaniments: sequentiality, causality, time, teleological meaning. As Shelley put the matter with high poetic disdain,

there is this difference between a story and a poem, that a story
is a catalogue of detached facts which have no other connection
than time, place, circumstance, cause and effect; the other is
the creation of actions according to the unchangeable forms of
human nature as existing in the mind of the creator, which is
itself the image of all other minds.[23]

This puts the case for apostrophic poetry against narrative. If
one brings together in a poem a boy, some birds, a few blessed
creatures, and some mountains, meadows, hills and groves, one
tends to place them in a narrative where one thing leads to
another; the events which form ask to be temporally located; soon
one has a poem which would provoke Shelley's strictures. But if
one puts into a poem *thou shepherd boy, ye blessed creatures, ye birds*,
they are immediately associated with what might be called a
timeless present but is better seen as a temporality of writing.
Even if the birds were only glimpsed once in the past, to apostrophize them as 'ye birds' is to locate them in the time of the
apostrophe—a special temporality which is the set of all
moments at which writing can say 'now.' This is a time of discourse rather than story. So located by apostrophes, birds,
creatures, boys, etc., resist being organized into events that can
be narrated, for they are inserted in the poem as elements of the
event which the poem is attempting to be.
   Such considerations suggest that one distinguish two forces in
poetry, the narrative and the apostrophic, and that the lyric is
characteristically the triumph of the apostrophic. A poem can
recount a sequence of events, which acquires the significance
lyric requires when read synecdochically or allegorically. Avoiding apostrophe, Wordsworth wrote lyrical ballads: anecdotes
which signify. Alternatively, a poem may invoke objects, people,
a detemporalized space with forms and forces which have pasts
and futures but which are addressed as potential presences.
Nothing need happen in an apostrophic poem, as the great
Romantic odes amply demonstrate. Nothing need happen because the poem itself is to be the happening.
   The tension between the narrative and the apostrophic can be
seen as the generative force behind a whole series of lyrics. One

might identify, for example, as instances of the triumph of the apostrophic, poems which, in a very common move, substitute a fictional, non-temporal opposition for a temporal one, substitute a temporality of discourse for a referential temporality. In lyrics of this kind a temporal problem is posed: something once present has been lost or attenuated; this loss can be narrated but the temporal sequence is irreversible, like time itself. Apostrophes displace this irreversible structure by removing the opposition between presence and absence from empirical time and locating it in a discursive time. The temporal movement from A to B, internalized by apostrophe, becomes a reversible alternation between A' and B': a play of presence and absence governed not by time but by poetic power.

The clearest example of this structure is of course the elegy, which replaces an irreversible temporal disjunction, the move from life to death, with a dialectical alternation between attitudes of mourning and consolation, evocations of absence and presence. In Shelley's *Adonais*, for example, the apostrophes give us an alternation which is reversible in the temporality of discourse:

> O, weep for Adonais—he is dead!
> Wake, melancholy Mother, wake and weep!
> Yet wherefore? Quench within their burning bed
> Thy fiery tears . . .
>
> Most musical of mourners, weep again!
> Lament anew, Urania!
>
> Mourn not for Adonais . . .
> Ye caverns and ye forests, cease to moan![24]

Moving back and forth between these two postures, the poem displaces the temporal pattern of actual loss and, focusing on these two apostrophic commands, makes the power of its own evocativeness a central issue.

A poem of a very different sort, Yeats's 'Among School Children,' can be shown to follow a similar pattern. Reiterated contrasts between age and youth form a structure from which the poem suddenly turns in the penultimate stanza with an apostrophe:

> O Presences
> That passion, piety or affection knows,
> And that all heavenly glory symbolize—
> O self-born mockers of man's enterprise.[25]

The transcendental presences evoked here, the images which are objects of strong feelings that generate them, make the transient projects of human life seem paltry indeed. However, a second apostrophe calls forth against these images another set of presences which seem to be both empirical and transcendental and which are presented as possible examples of organic unity:

> O chestnut tree, great-rooted blossomer,
> Are you the leaf, the blossom, or the bole?
> O body swayed to music, O brightening glance,
> How can we know the dancer from the dance?

The opposition is no longer an irreversible temporal move from youth to age but an a-temporal juxtaposition of two sorts of images, evoked as presences by apostrophes. The question of whether we can indeed choose between these alternatives and precisely what such a choice would entail is extremely difficult, but the poem has, through its apostrophic turn, made this the central issue.

Even poems which explicitly narrate a loss which they know to be irreversible may find this knowledge undermined by the apostrophes they use. Wordsworth's 'Elegiac Stanzas' recount a loss:

> A power is gone, which nothing can restore . . .
> A deep distress hath humanized my Soul.[26]

But by addressing Peele Castle,

> I was thy neighbour once, thou rugged Pile!
> Four summer weeks I dwelt in sight of thee:
> I saw thee every day,

the narrator places it beyond the movement of temporality; the poem denies temporality in the very phrases—recollections—that acknowledge its claims. Indeed, it is because the apostrophes produce a fictional and a-temporal castle that the narrator can identify with the 'huge castle standing here sublime' and find, in his poetic ability to invoke it as a transcendent presence, a sense of his own transcendent continuity. The fact that the stanzas are, as the subtitle says, 'Suggested by a Picture of Peele Castle, in a Storm, Painted by Sir George Beaumont,' reinforces rather than attenuates the apostrophic movement: the painting makes the castle a transcendent presence, and the narrator accomplishes the same movement in his turn through his apostrophes.

Apostrophe resists narrative because its *now* is not a moment in a temporal sequence but a *now* of discourse, of writing. This temporality of writing is scarcely understood, difficult to think, but it seems to be that toward which the lyric strives. Proverbial definition calls the lyric a monument to immediacy, which presumably means a detemporalized immediacy, an immediacy of fiction, or in Keats's phrase from 'To J. R.,' 'one eternal pant.' This is, of course, the condition which Keats describes in 'Ode on a Grecian Urn': a fictional time in which nothing happens but which is the essence of happening.

But if apostrophe works to produce this effect, there seems to be no reason why criticism should seek to avoid or repress it. Far from experiencing embarrassment at moves which appear to neutralize or transcend time, critics are generally delighted to proclaim that poetry transmutes the temporal into the eternal, life into art. Why then avoid discussions of apostrophe? Apostrophe must be repressed precisely because this high calling of poetry must not be seen to depend on a trope, an *O*. This trope proclaims its artificial character rather too obviously, and the craft of poetry would be demeaned if it were allowed that any versifier who wrote 'O table' were approaching the condition of sublime poet.

However, the very brazenness with which apostrophe declares its strangeness is crucial, as indication that what is at issue is not a predictable relation between a signifier and a signified, a form and its meaning, but the uncalculable force of an event. Apostrophe is not the representation of an event; if it works, it produces a fictive, discursive event.

To follow the complex play of mystification and demystification at work in the neutralization of time through reference to a temporality of writing, one might consider what is perhaps Keats's most fascinating poem, 'This Living Hand.' The fact that it eschews apostrophe for direct address makes it possible to speak with more confidence about its effects and the way in which they are produced. It may be, in fact, as de Man has suggested in a discussion of Wordsworth's *Essays upon Epitaphs*, that there is an intimate relation between apostrophes addressed to the dead or the inanimate and prosopopoeia that give the dead or inanimate a voice and make them speak. De Man notes 'the latent threat that inhabits prosopopoeia, namely that by making the dead speak, the symmetrical structure of the trope implies, by the same token, that the living are struck dumb, frozen in their own death.' The fiction of address, as in the 'Stay, traveller' of an epitaph, 'thus acquires a sinister connotation that is not only the prefiguration of one's own mortality but of our actual entry into the frozen world of the dead.'[27] The problem of apostrophe may be elucidated by the study of poems that exploit this sinister reciprocity, poems which capture the time of the apostrophic *now* and thrust it provocatively at the reader:

> This living hand, now warm and capable
> Of earnest grasping, would, if it were cold
> And in the icy silence of the tomb,
> So haunt thy days and chill thy dreaming nights
> That thou wouldst wish thine own heart dry of blood
> So in my veins red life might stream again,
> And thou be conscience-calm'd—see, here it is—
> I hold it towards you.[28]

We know too little about apostrophes to assert what actually happens when an apostrophe succeeds, but this poem, whose deictics—'This living hand, now warm . . .,' 'see, here it is'— give it the special temporality of apostrophic lyrics, is a daring and successful example of the attempt to produce in fiction an event by replacing a temporal presence and absence with an apostrophic presence and absence. There is here a complex play of mystification and demystification, which one might describe as follows.

The poem baldly asserts what is false: that a living hand, warm and capable, is being held towards us, that we can see it. One might expect our reaction to be an ironic smile; we see no hand, and if we imagine the hand of a speaker it will be one which we know is in the tomb, so that the poem would be a pathetic document testifying to misplaced poetic pride. We might expect to smile ironically at the speaker's naïveté. We do not however. Whether read aloud to audiences or read silently to oneself, the poem does not provoke this response. On the contrary, readers seem to do precisely what the poem predicts. The narrator contrasts his life with his death, proleptically predicting that when he is dead the reader will seek to overcome his death, will blind himself to his death by an imaginative act. We fulfill this icy prediction, not by seeking actually to sacrifice our lives that Keats might live, but by losing our empirical lives: forgetting the temporality which supports them and trying to embrace a purely fictional time in which we can believe that the hand is really present and perpetually held toward us through the poem. The poem predicts this mystification, dares us to resist it, and shows that its power is irresistible. It knows its apostrophic time and the indirectly invoked presence to be a fiction and says so but enforces it as event. 'See, here it is, I hold it towards you.' This is the kind of effect which the lyric seeks, one whose successes should be celebrated and explained.

8

The Mirror Stage

Natura voluit orationem esse speculum animi
Erasmus

The Mirror and the Lamp is now such a classic that it is easy to forget the peculiar power it had for many readers in its first decade. Those of us who had been nurtured on the New Criticism and thought Donne and the Moderns the supreme examples of poetic achievement were inclined to find romantic poetry the aberration of an age and sensibility out of tune with our own. The Romantics, we had heard, thought poetry a spontaneous overflow of feeling rather than a verbal construct, an expression of personality rather than an impersonal and comprehensively ironic form. We needed precisely such a guide as *The Mirror and the Lamp*, which would judiciously explain romantic theory, enabling us to grasp its relation to other theories of poetry and to see romantic literature as a comprehensible historical phenomenon. We thus came to read romantic poetry as a reflection of the projects Abrams had described: expression rather than imitation, and 'an attempt to overcome the cleavage between subject and object, between the vital, purposeful, value-full world of private experience and the dead postulated world of extension, quantity, and motion' (p. 65).[1]

The Mirror and the Lamp became the glass in which we saw Romanticism, but it also, unexpectedly, claimed to show us ourselves. Seeking to understand the assumptions of a literary tradition very different from the one we prized, we turned to it for

155

enlightenment about a historical past. Imagine our bewilderment at its opening sentence: 'The development of literary theory in the lifetime of Coleridge was to a surprising extent the making of the modern critical mind.' Much of the power of *The Mirror and the Lamp* came from its demonstration that a whole series of contemporary critical concepts, including those which one had thought of as anti-romantic, had in fact been formulated by Coleridge and other romantic critics: the notion of the poem as heterocosm, or self-contained universe, which must display organic unity and achieve the resolution of contraries; the conception of organic form and the inseparability of form and content; and finally the conception of good poetry as the product of a unified sensibility, or imagination, which fused together thought and feeling—in general, the notion that a poem must not mean but be.

In identifying the romantic sources of current critical notions *The Mirror and the Lamp* did indeed serve as a mirror: we looked into it and saw ourselves. It thus inaugurated what psycho-analysis calls the mirror stage, in which the child discovers his 'self' by identifying with the image he perceives in a mirror.[2] The other which he sees in a mirror and which he can grasp as a totality turns out to be himself; thus the constitution of the self is dependent on the perception of the self as other. *The Mirror and the Lamp*, in describing romantic theory, became a mirror in which the contemporary critic could discover who and what he was. Various notions one had picked up here and there, various interpretive operations one was accustomed to perform, assumptions of which one may have been unaware, were here explicitly integrated, shown to cohere in a totality. Through this image of the other, this specular representation, the budding critic discovered that he had a theory of literature.

Such specularity carried with it certain dangers. When the mother of Narcissus, the nymph Liriope, asks Tiresias whether her son will live to an old age, the blind seer replies, 'If he never recognizes himself.' Narcissus's initial failure to recognize his reflection in the pool fueled an illusory hope, but when he did recognize himself there, this brought a graver dilemma. To look in the mirror and discover that one is a romantic, when one had thought one was anti-romantic or, at the very least, post-romantic, is not the most pleasing of fates, but it seems to be an unavoidable mirror stage. Not to recognize ourselves in the image that appears in *The Mirror and the Lamp* would be a wishful error, like Narcissus's failure to recognize himself. But to recognize ourselves in *The Mirror and the Lamp* brings cold comfort.

Cold comfort, because to look into the mirror with a good lamp, to see the self as other, is to inaugurate the complex specular play of identification and alienation. The account of romantic critical principles in *The Mirror and the Lamp* initiates a critique of modern critical principles by showing us the self as other. In particular, these historical analyses reveal critical theory as an economy of metaphors. Consider the notion of *organic form*—linchpin, as it were, of the New Criticism—which more than any other concept regulates our analysis of poems. Here is *The Mirror and the Lamp* on Coleridge:

> It is astonishing how much of Coleridge's critical writing is couched in terms that are metaphorical for art and literal for a plant; if Plato's dialectic is a wilderness of mirrors, Coleridge's is a very jungle of vegetation. Only let the vehicles of his metaphors come alive, and you see all the objects of criticism writhe surrealistically into plants or parts of plants, growing in tropical profusion. Authors, characters, poetic genres, poetic passages, words, meter, logic, become seeds, trees, flowers, blossoms, fruit, bark, and sap (p. 169).

This passage, of course, is having some fun at the expense of Coleridge and the succeeding critics who have adopted his plants, but it is also extremely astute: 'only let the vehicles of his metaphors come alive,' Abrams says. This is what is at issue here, the 'life' of language and figure. Coleridge's organic language insists that poems, 'the objects of criticism,' are not the lifeless products of fancy, dead figures, mechanical contrivances, but the living products of imagination, language with a life of its own. But a language come alive, as Abrams suggests, is a language unable to control its own tropology, writhing surrealistically 'in tropical profusion.' Though Abrams may be poking fun at

Coleridge for his metaphors, his own language shows that Coleridge has a point, that language can lead a life of its own, even run wild. Planted in Abrams's lively language is a plant effect, a tropism, a tropical profusion; the pun on tropes and tropics might even count as mild 'surrealistic writhing.'

This passage can be treated as the beginning of what we now call a deconstructive reading of organicist theory: the revelation of a self-deconstructive movement within romantic theoretical discourse, whose major insights are aporias revealed by the very attempt to conceal them. *The Mirror and the Lamp* helps us to follow this movement in romantic theory by illuminating what Jacques Derrida calls the structured genealogy of certain key figures and distinctions, showing how an opposition on which the theory relies subverts itself in the course of theoretical argument.[3]

A central distinction contrasts mechanism with organicism, and proposes, as Abrams says, 'the replacement of a mechanical process by a living plant as the implicit paradigm governing the description of the process and product of literary invention' (p. 158). This replacement distinguishes the freedom and creativity of the poetic Imagination from the mechanical processes of Fancy. Fancy operates according to mechanistic principles of associationist psychology; it is determined; it cannot originate but only combine. Imagination, on the other hand, is essentially vital, undetermined, and originary; it exercises a creative freedom like the freedom of God: 'a repetition in the finite mind of the eternal act of creation in the infinite I AM.'[4] While the works of Fancy are lifeless, mechanistic artifacts produced by the imposition of a pre-determined form or by the operation of laws of association, the products of Imagination display organic form, which, Coleridge says, 'is innate. It shapes as it develops itself from within.'[5] However, as Abrams remarks, 'to substitute the concept of growth for the operation of a mechanism in the psychology of invention seems merely to exchange one kind of determinism for another, while to replace the mental artisan-planner by the concept of organic self-generation makes it difficult, analogically, to justify the participation of consciousness in the creative process' (p. 173).

Organicist language was introduced in order to distinguish the servile and combinatory operations of Fancy from the creativity and freedom of the Imagination, but this representation of freedom ends by denying the freedom it was supposed to represent. Free will, conscious origination, becomes a crux in Coleridge, Abrams says, 'because it runs counter to an inherent tendency in his elected analogue' (p. 174). The problem of the 'elected analogue' illustrates the very issue that is at stake here: the freedom and power of the mind in relation to language. Coleridge's imagination imagined a new concept of Imagination; he chose a new analogue in an act of freedom and origination. But his elected analogue turned out, Abrams says, to have an inherent tendency. It developed according to laws of its own, determined less by an act of origination than by an autonomous logic.

This organicist logic thus deconstructs itself, revealing the irresoluble paradox that is one of its greatest insights into the nature of language. The very figures which state the freedom and creativity of imagination and its products illustrate the limitations of that freedom which they were supposed to represent. More generally, one can say that no account of language can escape the aporia of structure and event. On the one hand, language seems the realm or medium in which consciousness can truly produce events, display its freedom in creative acts of origination. Language thus seems the realm of fresh starts and discontinuity. But, on the other hand, language is the realm of structures always already in place, as a plant is always already present in its prior state. Creative acts of imagination, like the sudden flowering of a plant, turn out to depend on and be limited by structures already in place; and linguistic creations, such as Coleridge's organic metaphors, function outside the control of an originating consciousness. Note that one cannot resolve this problem by seeking a compromise, in which linguistic structures are said to make possible a limited creativity and freedom—as if it were possible to divide language into what is free and what is determined. This is impossible, because the most common, banal, or resilient structures must have been produced, must once have been singular and creative events, while, on the other hand, the most radical creative acts turn out to be determined in various ways and to develop according to laws which are not the intentions of their 'creators.' In *The Mirror and the Lamp* this aporia is revealed in the attempt to make 'organic' the name of both free origination and structural continuity.

This paradox or figure reproduces itself in surprising ways. Abrams argues, for example, that Coleridge's theory of mind— his description of mind in terms of the organic processes of a living plant—'was, as he insisted, revolutionary; it was in fact part of a change in the habitual way of thinking, in all areas of intellectual enterprise, which was as sharp and dramatic as any the history of ideas can show' (p. 158). The description of mind as a plant, the representation of thought as a process of organic growth and continuity, is said to constitute a decisive rupture in the development of thought; and Coleridge's theory thus, by its very success, calls into question the appropriateness of character-izing thought as organic continuity and exfoliation.

Of course organicism is not merely a natural analogue. It is also a theological idea, one of the many modern critical concepts whose theological functions and origins *The Mirror and the Lamp* identifies. What is important here is not that individual concepts should have theological sources—that might be a matter of merely antiquarian interest—but that we are dealing with an economy, a system of terms based on the analogy, whether hidden or expressed, between the poet and God. 'This analogy,' Abrams writes, 'opened the way for the introduction into criti-cism of a rich stock of linked ideas, accumulated over centuries of theological speculation' (p. 239). This 'theocritical' system is what has made possible the wealth of critical speculation in our own day, and indeed, Abrams argues, holding up a mirror that shows us the self as other, if we fail to recognize to what extent the concepts and structures of literature and criticism are a displaced theology,

> that is because we still live in what is essentially, though in derivative rather than direct manifestations, a Biblical culture and readily mistake our hereditary ways of organizing ex-perience for the conditions of reality and the universal forms of thought.[6]

Abrams discusses one particularly striking case in which critics who thought they were challenging a romantic and theological position were in fact simply occupying another position generated by the system of secularized theology, as if the system itself had determined in advance the possibilities of critical disagreement. This is the case of the poem as heterocosm:

> This parallel between God and the poet, and between God's relation to his world and the poet to his poem, fostered the earliest appearance of the doctrine, so widespread today, that a poem is a disguised self-revelation, in which its creator, 'visibly-invisible,' at the same time expresses and conceals himself. It turns out that the same parallel helped generate a conception of the work of art which seems equally modern, is hardly less widely current, and (having largely lost the marks of its origin) is often presented in explicit opposition to the cognate thesis that a poem is the expression of personality. This is the concept, at the heart of much of the 'new criticism,' that poetic statement and poetic truth are utterly diverse from scientific statement and scientific truth, in that a poem is an object-in-itself, a self-contained universe of discourse of which we cannot demand that it be true to nature, but only, that it be true to itself (p. 272).

One could argue, following Abrams's lead, that it was no accident that the New Criticism found itself implicated in a theological system; that indeed any criticism predicated upon the autonomy and teleological unity of the work will have a theological character.[7] What Abrams has done is to demonstrate the pervasiveness of what one might call the 'theocritical system,' which determines even opposing polemical positions; and he provides no expectation of escape from the logocentrism of this system.

But he does suggest that we can escape and indeed have escaped from the mimetic conception of mind and art: rejecting notions of the mind or work as mirror, we have, since the romantic period, thought of the mind as lamp and the work as plant. And this shift from mirror to lamp is, he claims, part of 'a change in the habitual way of thinking . . . as sharp and dramatic as any the history of ideas can show' (p. 158). If we are persuaded, as Abrams's readers usually are, that we have indeed made this decisive move from mirror to lamp, it is because we are convinced that *The Mirror and the Lamp* is an accurate mirror. It can convince us that this shift away from representation has taken place only by convincing us that it is accurately representing or reflecting what has taken place—accurately mirroring what is to be found in the texts. This persistence of mimesis, as the very ground of arguments which reject it, ought to arouse our suspicions that perhaps we have not left the order of mirrors and mirroring and that perhaps, on the contrary, lamps are only another version of mirrors and belong to the same system of specularity and representation.

Once these suspicions are aroused, there are a number of things that confirm them. First, the notion of poem as heterocosm, which is supposed to have displaced the notion of the poem as imitation, is always justified by an appeal to mimeticism: the poet imitates the creative act of God or, at the very least, the generative activity of nature. The work can only be a world in itself rather than an imitation of nature if it is produced in a process that imitates the production of the world. Second, it could be argued that this notion of generative activity, supposed to be distinctive of lamps, is already implicit in conceptions of the mind as mirror. Here is Ernst Cassirer explicating the philosophy of the Enlightenment: 'When the mind becomes a mirror of reality it is and remains a living mirror of the universe, and it is not simply the sum total of mere images but a whole composed of formative forces.'[8] Here the mirror already has formative power; it is implicitly a lamp.

The difficulty of using the distinction between mirror and lamp for historical periodization is compounded when one looks to Yeats, whose remarks in the introduction to the *Oxford Book of Modern Verse* provide the epigraph for *The Mirror and the Lamp*: 'it must go further still; that soul must become its own betrayer, its own deliverer, the one activity, the mirror turn lamp.'[9] What is this movement from mirror to lamp which Yeats, in 1936, says must go further still? It is the shift from Stendhal (who 'described a masterpiece as a "mirror dawdling down a lane"'), novelists 'from Huysmans to Hemingway,' Victorian poets, and modern poets who, Yeats says, 'feel they can write a poem by recording the fortuitous scene or thought . . ."I am sitting in a chair, there are three dead flies on a corner of the ceiling"'—a shift from these writers of the mirror to three Georgian poets: Walter James Turner, Herbert Read, and Dorothy Wellesley.[10] Yeats goes on to claim, in remarks which he subsequently proposes to dismiss as 'ancient history,' that the Elizabethan and seventeenth-century poets and the Romantics can be classified with the Georgians, and the poets of the eighteenth century grouped with the Victorians and the Moderns. This suggests that his distinction, whose historical content is variable and idiosyncratic, is primarily evaluative. (When poetry turns from lamp to mirror it loses, Yeats says, 'bravado.') Since Abrams takes his epigraph from Yeats's discussion, one must at least consider the possibility that his separation of two historically distinct esthetic theories may be a way of establishing an evaluative distinction, persuading us to prefer romantic to eighteenth-century poetry by drawing upon the theological notions implicit in the romantic description of the poet.

The mind or the poet as lamp: what is the force of that image? A lamp illuminates when it is dark, when there is not enough light to see. The light of a lamp stands in a determined relation to natural light, which it replaces or imitates. The meaning of *lamp* depends on this system, which makes it a substitute sun or source of light; its significance is established by a relation of mimesis. Doubtless there is a difference between the poet as lamp, projecting, by God's grace, a light like God's own, and the poet as mirror, reflecting the light provided by God; but both give us a system based on visibility, presence, and representation, where the mind or author casts light upon that which he perceives and represents. To put it bluntly, a mirror is no use without light, and there is no point in illuminating a scene unless something will register or reflect what is there. The economy of mimesis presupposes light; the lamp fits into that economy.

Abrams cites as an example of the romantic view the famous lines in which Coleridge, after hearing portions of *The Prelude*, speaks of its 'theme hard as high!'

of moments awful,
Now in thy inner life, and now abroad,
When power streamed from thee, and thy soul received
A light reflected, as a light bestowed . . . (p. 60).

The passage seems to claim that Wordsworth thought he was a mirror when he was in fact a lamp, and it explains why it might be hard to tell the difference: in both cases light comes to one from nature, and the question is whether the light is bestowed by nature or whether nature is reflecting light which one originally cast in its direction. But wherever the light comes from, we have a system in which subject and object are present to one another in a light which makes possible a specular relationship, a relationship of correspondence: subject reflected in object and object in subject. The most compelling evidence for this view—that romantic poetry of the lamp does not break with the economy of specularity but is part of it—comes from Abrams himself. When he identifies the exemplary romantic project in *Natural Supernaturalism* he selects as 'the manifesto of a central romantic enterprise' not a passage about lamps but the high argument of Wordsworth's preface to *The Excursion*:

How exquisitely the individual mind
. . . to the external world
Is fitted, and how exquisitely too,
Theme this but little heard of among men,
The external world is fitted to the mind.[11]

There is light here also (a good fitting requires light): light provided by the dread power

Whose gracious favour is the primal source
Of all illumination.

This light makes possible the mirroring relationship, 'fitting and fitted,' between subject and object. In showing the centrality of this passage to the projects enunciated by romantic theory, Abrams has identified for us a mirror stage, in which the subject grasps itself as object and attains self-awareness through this specular fitting. Yeats, Abrams's expert on mirrors and lamps, writes:

Mirror on mirror mirrored is all the show.[12]

'Mirror on mirror mirrored is all the show,' I am suggesting, when we are dealing with mirrors and lamps. It is the only show on the mirror stage. But there are other shows on other stages, and Abrams has given us a preview of some of them. Some of his analyses are the beginnings of what one might call a deconstructive reading of romantic theory: a reading attentive to its self-deconstructive logic, to what exceeds the economy of mimesis and specularity—such as plants that get out of hand and put in question the power of origination that they were supposed to represent. These analyses alert us to a tropology, a play of language, which cannot be arrested by centering systems. Indeed, Abrams's whole approach is predicated, as he tells us, upon the insight that since critical terminology is borrowed and hence figurative, the logic of the figures themselves will, to a considerable extent, determine critical thinking. A working out of that logic invariably reveals a certain excess, something which is neither fitting nor fitted to the mirroring, specular relationship between subject and object.

The seductiveness of the mirror stage is its offer of totality and a vision of the self as a unified whole. What lies 'beyond' the mirror stage is a loss of totality, the fragmentation of the body and the self—what Lacan calls the symbolic order. The child is born into the symbolic order in that he has a name which stands for him in the order of language and because he already figures in an oedipal triangle that lies beyond the binary order of reflection. Though the child never leaves the mirror stage altogether—for he continues to identify with images of wholeness—he enters the symbolic order by accepting the fragmentation of the body (more specifically, in technical terms, castration) and by accepting the possibility which language brings of the discontinuity of the self.[13]

A reading of Romanticism attentive to what lies beyond the

specularity of the mirror stage and the focus on correspondence between subject and object would follow two lines of enquiry. First, it would stress that even if poems are presented as specular encounters of mind and nature they are intertextual constructs, revisionary responses to other texts, moments or fragments of a poetic process which, like the oedipal triangle, always precedes and exceeds the subject. Analysts working in this mode will be tempted to personalize the intertextual and reduce it to a specular struggle between a poet and a single great precursor (in whom he sees himself). This reduction can generate powerful readings but must appeal to a totalizing notion of the self which is irreparably subverted by aspects of language such readings must neglect: the uncertain status of citation and allusion, whose interpretation can never be limited by an authorial project and the uncanny displacements of figural logic from one text to another.

A second focus for a reading which sought to go beyond the mirror stage would be language itself, and in particular the written character which, for example, plays such strange roles in *The Prelude*. Language disrupts or displaces the self-sufficient visual presence of object to subject in the mirror stage. Poets may, of course, hope for a perfect correspondence between language and thought, knowing, as Wordsworth wrote, that

> If words be not an incarnation of the thought but only a cloth-
> ing for it, then surely they will prove an ill gift; such a one as
> those poisoned vestments, read of in the stories of super-
> stitious times, which had power to consume and to alienate
> from his right mind the victim who put them on. [14]

The child, told that in the language of adults he is 'William' or 'George' or 'Mary,' might well, if he could rise to philosophic complaint, find language an ill gift, garments he is loth to put on; but it is a gift he must accept—in the hope, as Wordsworth says, that it will become a sustaining yet invisible medium, like the air we breathe, or else a stable operative principle that can be taken for granted, like the force of gravity. 'Language,' Wordsworth continues after raising the spectre of poisoned vestments, 'Language, if it do not uphold and feed, and leave in quiet, like the power of gravitation or the air we breathe, is a counter-spirit, unremittingly and noiselessly at work to derange, to subvert, to lay waste, to vitiate, and to dissolve.'

Today we are less sanguine than readers of Wordsworth have often been about the possibility that language might simply 'leave in quiet.' We are more inclined to subscribe to the doubts and uneasiness that Wordsworth here expresses with such power. (Indeed, with the current interest in how the language of texts deranges, subverts, lays waste, vitiates, dissolves, and deconstructs, if one were to write *The Mirror and the Lamp* today one would have to give it a different title, such as, perhaps, *The Mire and the Swamp*.) But Abrams has already pointed the way to the mire, directing us in *The Mirror and the Lamp* to Wordsworth's 'Essay on Epitaphs,' which, he says, 'has not received adequate attention from students of Wordsworth's literary theory' (p. 111). When it does receive adequate attention, and this has begun with an excellent book by Frances Ferguson, *Wordsworth: Language as Counter-Spirit* (Yale University Press, 1977), we may be able to answer questions such as why many of Wordsworth's most important statements on poetry come in comments on funerary inscriptions, the type of verse furthest removed from the specular relation between subject and object, and what we can learn about the function of 'sincerity' in Wordsworth's theory from its prominence in this particular context, where ordinary notions of sincerity become problematic. This kind of enquiry would lead to an identification of what in romantic theory and practice lies beyond the mirror stage.

This enquiry is already begun in *The Mirror and the Lamp*, in its exploration of the play of figure within the theological economy of critical discourse, but it must go further still. Recent work suggests that distinctions such as mirror and lamp, fancy and imagination, organic and mechanical, free origination and imitation, *natura naturans* and *natura naturata* have a special function. They hypostatize a transcendent principle of some kind (an absolute origin or plenitude) that commands the field covered by the two terms, but by providing it with an opposite they protect it from anything that might taint it. By distinguishing imitation from true creativity one sets aside the imitative aspect of creation so as to produce, as the norm for poetic activity, an ideal, God-like act of free origination. But in such operations the repressed term always inhabits its opposite. Accounts of true creativity, for example, cannot escape from a notion of imitation; they always rely on it in one way or another, so that what is called 'free origination' can in fact be seen as a particular version of imitation. [15]

If we are now better placed to see how the privileged terms in such hierarchical oppositions are inhabited by their opposites—if we are now able to explain how this relationship deconstructs the opposition itself—this does not mean that we can relegate the distinctions of romantic esthetics to the past and view them as errors. On the contrary, we continue to work and think within this system even as we deconstruct its oppositions. We continue, for example, to 'reflect'; we attempt to 'illuminate' or 'make clear' even as we try to undo the system and describe what breaches it. We do not escape mirrors and lamps.

9

Story and Discourse in the Analysis of Narrative

> More and more there is embarrassment all around
> when the wish to hear a story is expressed.
> Walter Benjamin

So much work has been done in the field of narratology that to attempt any sort of synthesis, identifying areas of fundamental agreement and the principal issues in dispute, would be a massive task. Limiting oneself to the obvious cases, there is the work of the Russian Formalists, particularly Propp and Schlovsky; an American tradition, running from Henry James's prefaces, through Lubbock and Booth, to modern attempts at synthesis such as Seymour Chatman's *Story and Discourse*, has been especially concerned with problems of point of view. French Structuralism has undertaken the development of narrative grammars (Barthes, Todorov, Bremond, Greimas, Thomas Pavel, Gerald Prince) and description of the relations between story and narration (Genette). In German the writings of Wolfgang Kayser, Eberhard Lämmert, Franz Stanzl, and Wolf Schmid come to mind; important work has been done in the Netherlands, notably by Teun Van Dijk and Mieke Bal; and there is an active group in Tel Aviv (Benjamin Hrushovski, Meir Sternberg, Menakhem Perry).[1] There is considerable variety among these traditions, and of course each theorist has concepts or categories of his own, but if these theorists agree on anything it is this: that the theory of narrative requires a distinction between what I shall call 'story'— a sequence of actions or events, conceived as independent of their manifestation in discourse—and what I shall call 'discourse,' the discursive presentation or narration of events.

In Russian Formalism this is the distinction between *fabula* and *sjuzhet*: the story as a series of events and the story as reported in the narrative. Other theorists propose different formulations, whose terms are often confusing: *récit*, for example, is sometimes *fabula*, as in Bremond, and sometimes *sjuzhet*, as in Barthes. But there is always a basic distinction between a sequence of events and a discourse that orders and presents events. Genette, for instance, distinguishes the sequence of events, *histoire*, from the presentation of events in discourse, *récit*, and also from a third level, *narration*, which is the enunciation of narrative; but from the way in which Genette uses his categories Mieke Bal argues, rightly I believe, that 'in the end Genette distinguishes only two levels, those of Russian Formalism.'[2]

The American tradition has been less inclined than the others to formulate this distinction explicitly. It has been primarily concerned with the problems of point of view: the identification and discrimination of narrators, overt and covert, and the description of what in the novel or short story belongs to the perspective of the narrator. In order to do this, however, one must posit a distinction between actions or events themselves and the narrative presentation of those actions. For the study of point of view to make sense, there must be various contrasting ways of viewing and telling a given story, and this makes 'story' an invariant core, a constant against which the variables of narrative presentation can be measured. But to describe the situation in this way is to identify the distinction as a heuristic fiction, for except in rare cases the analyst is not presented with contrasting narratives of the same sequence of actions; the analyst is confronted with a single narrative and must postulate what 'actually happens' in order to be able to describe and interpret the way in which this sequence of events is organized, evaluated, and presented by the narrator.

Thus the American tradition, though it has never been much concerned to formalize its categories or attempt a grammar of plot, has relied on the same basic distinction that European narratology explicitly formulates, a distinction which, I claim, is an indispensable premise of narratology. To make narrative an object of study, one must distinguish narratives from nonnarratives, and this invariably involves reference to the fact that narratives report sequences of events. If narrative is defined as the representation of a series of events, then the analyst must be able to identify these events, and they come to function as a nondiscursive, nontextual given, something which exists prior to and independently of narrative presentation and which the narrative then reports. I am not, of course, suggesting that narratologists believe that the events of a Balzac story actually took place or that Balzac conceived the events first and then embodied them in narrative discourse. I am claiming that narratological analysis of a text requires one to treat the discourse as a representation of events which are conceived of as independent of any particular narrative perspective or presentation and which are thought of as having the properties of real events. Thus a novel may not identify the temporal relationship between two events it presents, but the analyst must assume that there is a real or proper temporal order, that the events in fact occurred either simultaneously or successively. Mieke Bal defines this assumption with an explicitness that is rare among theorists of narrative: 'the story [*l'histoire*] consists of the set of events in their chronological order, their spatial location, and their relations with the actors who cause or undergo them.' And more specifically, 'The events have temporal relations with one another. Each one is either anterior to, simultaneous with, or posterior to every other event.'[3]

The analyst must assume that the events reported have a true order, for only then can he or she describe the narrative presentation as a modification or effacement of the order of events. If a novel does not identify the temporal relation between two events, one can treat this as a distinctive feature of its narrative point of view only if one assumes that the events themselves do have an order of succession.

Of course, it is only reasonable to assume that events do occur in some order and that a description of events presupposes the prior existence, albeit fictive, of those events. In applying these assumptions about the world to the texts of narrative we posit a level of structure which, by functioning as a nontextual given, enables us to treat everything in the discourse as a way of interpreting, valuing, and presenting this nontextual substratum.

This has been a fruitful way of proceeding. Indeed, it is indispensable, even for the analysis of contemporary fictions that seem to reject the very notion of 'event.' The assumption that narrative presents a series of events is necessary to account for the effect of narratives, such as Robbe-Grillet's *Le Voyeur*, that make it impossible for the reader to work out what the real events are and in what order they occurred. Without the assumption of a real order of events, the repetitions of the narrative discourse would not be at all confusing and would be interpreted, flatly, as a repetition of motifs. However, indispensable as this perspective may be, its premise about the nature of narrative and the organization of narrative discourse is frequently questioned in narratives themselves, at moments when the hierarchy of narrative is inverted—moments that must be carefully investigated if one is not to oversimplify the way in which narratives function and fail to account for their force. Positing the priority of events to the discourse which reports or presents them, narratology establishes a hierarchy which the functioning of narratives often subverts by presenting events not as givens but as the products of discursive forces or requirements.

To illustrate the issues involved, let us start with a familiar example, the story of Oedipus. The analysis of narrative would identify the sequence of events that constitutes the action of the story: Oedipus is abandoned on Mt Cithaeron; he is rescued by a shepherd; he grows up in Corinth; he kills Laius at the crossroads; he answers the Sphinx's riddle; he marries Jocasta; he seeks the murderer of Laius; he discovers his own guilt; he blinds himself and leaves his country. After identifying the *fabula*, one could describe the order and perspective in which these events are presented in the discourse of the play. Treating these events as the reality of the story, one then seeks to interpret the significance of the way in which they are portrayed. In the case of *Oedipus*, as in many other narratives, of which the detective story is only the most banal example, the discourse focuses on the bringing to light of a crucial event, identified as a reality which determines significance. Someone killed Laius and the problem is to discover what in fact happened at that fateful moment in the past.

One of millions of enthusiastic readers, Sigmund Freud, describes the play as follows:

> The action of the play consists of nothing other than the process of revealing, with cunning delays and ever-mounting excitement, that Oedipus himself is the murderer of Laius, but further, that he is the son of the murdered man and of Jocasta. Appalled at the abomination he has unwittingly perpetrated, Oedipus blinds himself and forsakes his home.[4]

Freud emphasizes that the logic of signification here is one in which events, conceived as prior to and independent of their discursive representation, determine meanings: the play brings to light an awful deed which is so powerful that it imposes its meaning irrespective of any intention of the actor. The prior event has made Oedipus guilty, and when this is revealed he attains tragic dignity in accepting the meaning imposed by the revealed event.

This way of thinking about the play is essential, but there is a contrary perspective which is also essential to its force and which an apparently marginal element will help us to grasp. When Oedipus first asks whether anyone witnessed Laius's death he is told, 'All died save one, who fled in terror and could tell us only one clear fact. His story was that robbers, not one but many, fell in with the King's party and killed them.'[5] And later when Oedipus begins to wonder whether he might not himself be the murderer he tells Jocasta that everything hangs on the testimony of this witness, whom they await. 'You say he spoke of robbers, that robbers killed him. If he still says robbers, it was not I. One is not the same as many. But if he speaks of one lone traveller, there is no escape, the finger points to me.' To which Jocasta answers, 'Oh, but I assure you, that was what he said. He cannot go back on it now; the whole town heard it, not only I.'

The only witness has publicly told a story that is incompatible with Oedipus's guilt. This possibility of innocence is never eliminated, for when the witness arrives Oedipus is interested in his relation to Laius and asks only about his birth, not about the murder. The witness is never asked whether the murderers were one or many.[6]

I am not, of course, suggesting that Oedipus was really innocent and has been falsely accused for 2,400 years. I am interested in the significance of the fact that the possibility of innocence is never dispelled. The 'whole action of the play' is the revelation of this awful deed, but we are never given the proof, the testimony of the eye-witness. Oedipus himself and all his readers are convinced of his guilt but our conviction does not come from the revelation of the deed. Instead of the revelation of a prior deed determining meaning, we could say that it is meaning, the convergence of meaning in the narrative discourse, that leads us to posit this deed as its appropriate manifestation.

Once we are well into the play, we know that Oedipus must be found guilty, otherwise the play will not work at all; and the logic to which we are responding is not simply an esthetic logic that affects readers of literary works. Oedipus, too, feels the force of this logic. It had been prophesied that Oedipus would kill his father; it had been prophesied that Laius would be killed by his son; Oedipus admits to having killed an old man at what may have been the relevant time and place; so when the shepherd reveals that Oedipus is in fact the son of Laius, Oedipus leaps to the conclusion, and every reader leaps with him, that he is in fact the murderer of Laius. His conclusion is based not on new evidence concerning a past deed but on the force of meaning, the interweaving of prophesies and the demands of narrative coherence. The convergence of discursive forces makes it essential that he become the murderer of Laius, and he yields to this force of meaning. Instead of saying, therefore, that there is a sequence of past events that are given and which the play reveals with certain detours, we can say that the crucial event is the product of demands of signification. Here meaning is not the effect of a prior event but its cause.

Oedipus becomes the murderer of his father not by a violent act that is brought to light but by bowing to the demands of narrative coherence and deeming the act to have taken place. Moreover, it is essential to the force of the play that Oedipus take this leap, that he accede to the demands of narrative coherence and deem himself guilty. If he were to resist the logic of signification, arguing that 'the fact that he's my father doesn't mean that I killed him,' demanding more evidence about the past event, Oedipus would not acquire the necessary tragic stature. In this respect the force of the narrative relies on the contrary logic, in which event is not a cause but an effect of theme. To describe this logic is not to quibble over details but to investigate tragic power.

Moreover, one might note that this contrary logic is in fact necessary to Freud's reading of the play, even though he himself stresses in his account the priority of event to meaning. If we were to follow this logic and say that the prior deed, committed without understanding, is what makes Oedipus guilty of patricide, then Oedipus can scarcely be said to have an Oedipus complex.[7] But suppose we stress instead that as soon as Oedipus learns that Laius is his father he immediately declares what he has hitherto denied: if Laius is my father, he in effect says, then I must have killed him. If we emphasize this point, we can indeed identify an Oedipus complex: that is to say, a structure of signification—a desire to kill the father and a guilt for that desire—which does not result from an act but precedes it.

This logic by which event is a product of discursive forces rather than a given reported by discourse is essential to the force of the narrative, but in describing the play in this way we have certainly not replaced a deluded or incorrect model of narrative by a correct one. On the contrary, it is obvious that much of the play's power depends on the narratological assumption that Oedipus's guilt or innocence has already been determined by a past event that has not yet been revealed or reported. Yet the contrary logic in which Oedipus posits an act in response to demands of signification is essential to the tragic force of the ending. These two logics cannot be brought together in harmonious synthesis; each works by the exclusion of the other; each depends on a hierarchical relation between story and discourse which the other inverts. In so far as both these logics are necessary to the force of the play, they put in question the possibility of a coherent, noncontradictory account of narrative. They stage a confrontation of sorts between a semiotics that aspires to produce a grammar of narrative and deconstructive interpretations, which in showing the work's opposition to its own logic suggest the impossibility of such a grammar. If an analysis of the logic of signification shows that *Oedipus* requires a double reading, a reading according to incompatible principles, this would suggest both the importance of narratological analysis and the impossibility of attaining its goal.

If *Oedipus* seems a special case, in that the analysis turns on a possible uncertainty about the central event in the plot, let us consider an example from a very different period and genre, George Eliot's *Daniel Deronda*, as analyzed in a recent article by Cynthia Chase. Deronda, the adopted son of an English nobleman, is a talented, sensitive young man, moving in good society, who has been unable to decide on a profession. He happens to rescue a poor Jewish girl who was trying to drown herself, and later, in searching for her family, he meets her brother Mordecai, an ailing scholar with whom he begins to study Hebrew. He develops an intense interest in Jewish culture, falls in love with Mirah, the girl he has saved, and is accepted by Mordecai and others as a kindred spirit.

At this point, Deronda receives a summons from his mother, who, obeying her dead father's injunction, reveals to him the secret of his birth: he is a Jew. The novel emphasizes the causal force of this past event: because he was born a Jew he is a Jew. Origin, cause, and identity are linked in an implicit argument that is common to narrative. With the revelation of Deronda's parentage it is implied that his present character and involvement with things Jewish have been caused by his Jewish origin.

But on the other hand, as Chase notes,

> The sequence of events in the plot as a whole presents Deronda's revealed origins in a different perspective. The account of Deronda's situation has made it increasingly obvious to the reader that the progression of the hero's destiny—or, that is to say, the progression of the story—positively requires a revelation that he is of Jewish birth. For Deronda's bildungsroman to proceed, his character must crystallize, and

this must come about through a recognition of his destiny, which has remained obscure to him, according to the narrator's account, largely because of his ignorance of his origins. The suspenseful stress on Deronda's relationship with Mordecai and with Mirah orients his history in their direction, and Mordecai explicitly stresses his faith that Deronda is a Jew. Thus the reader comes upon Deronda's Jewish parentage as an inevitable inference to be drawn not simply from the presentation of Deronda's qualities and his empathy with the Jews but above all from the patent strategy and direction of the narrative. The revelation of Deronda's origins therefore appears as an effect of narrative requirements. The supposed cause of his character and vocation (according to the chapters recounting the disclosure), Deronda's origin presents itself (in the light of the rest of the text) rather as the effect of the account of his vocation: his origin is the effect of its effects. [8]

By one logic Deronda's birth is a past cause of present effects; by another contrary logic, named by Deronda's friend Hans Meyrick in a flippant letter, one should speak rather of 'the present causes of past effects.' [9] It is essential to stress here that, as in the case of Oedipus, there is no question of finding a compromise formulation that would do justice to both presentations of the event by avoiding extremes, for the power of the narrative depends precisely on the alternative use of extremes, the rigorous deployment of two logics, each of which works by excluding the other. It will not do to say, for example, that Deronda's involvement with Judaism is partly but not completely the result of his birth, and that the revelation of his birth is therefore in part an explanation and in part a narrative fulfillment. This sort of formulation is wrong because the power of Eliot's novel depends precisely on the fact that Deronda's commitment to Judaism and idealism, instead of to the frivolous society in which he has been raised, is presented as a free choice. To have exemplary moral value it must be presented as a choice, not as the ineluctable result of the hidden fact of parentage. It must also be presented as wholehearted, not as a dilettantish dabbling which would then be transformed into commitment by revelation of the fact of birth. The novel requires that Deronda's commitment to Judaism be independent of the revelation of his Jewishness—this is thematically and ethically essential—yet its account of Jewishness does not allow for the possibility of conversion and insists on the irreplaceability of origins: to be a Jew is to have been born a Jew. These two logics, one of which insists upon the causal efficacy of origins and the other of which denies their causal efficacy, are in contradiction but they are essential to the way in which the narrative functions. One logic assumes the primacy of events; the other treats the events as the products of meanings.

One could argue that every narrative operates according to this double logic, presenting its plot as a sequence of events which is prior to and independent of the given perspective on these events, and, at the same time, suggesting by its implicit claims to significance that these events are justified by their appropriateness to a thematic structure. As critics we adopt the first perspective when we debate the significance of a character's actions (taking those actions as given). We adopt the second perspective when we discuss the appropriateness or inappropriateness of an ending (when we debate whether these actions are appropriate expressions of the thematic structure which ought to determine them). Theorists of narrative have always, of course, recognized these two perspectives, but they have perhaps been too ready to assume that they can be held together, synthesized in some way without contradiction. Not only is there a contradiction, but it will characteristically manifest itself in narratives, as a moment that seems either superfluous—a loose end, as in *Oedipus Rex*—or too neat, as in *Daniel Deronda*. Recent work on narrative has brought such moments to the fore, stressing their importance to the rhetorical force of narratives.

Though my examples so far have been classics of European literature, this double logic is by no means confined to fictional narrative. Recent discussions of the nature and structure of narrative in Freud enable us to identify a similar situation. In general, Freudian theory makes narrative the preferred mode of explanation. Psychoanalysis does not propose scientific laws of the form 'if X, then Y.' Psychoanalytic understanding involves reconstructing a story, tracing a phenomenon to its origin, seeing how one thing leads to another. Freud's case histories themselves are indeed narratives with a *fabula* and a *sjuzhet*: the *fabula* is the reconstructed plot, the sequence of events in the patient's life, and the *sjuzhet* is the order in which these events are presented, the story of Freud's conduct of the case.[10] Like *Oedipus* and *Daniel Deronda*, Freud's narratives lead to the revelation of a decisive event which, when placed in the true sequence of events, can be seen as the cause of the patient's present situation.

One of Freud's more dramatic cases is that of the Wolfman, in which analysis of key dreams and associations leads Freud to the conclusion that at an age of 1½ years the child woke up to witness his parents copulating. Freud reconstructs a sequence of events that begins with this decisive 'primal scene' and includes the transformation of the memory into a trauma at age 4, a striking example of *Nachträglichkeit*. Though the event has been posited or projected ('constructed' is Freud's term) from the discourse produced by the patient, and thus might seem the product of discursive forces, Freud argues vigorously for the reality and decisive priority of the event. 'It must therefore,' he concludes, 'be left at this (I can see no other possibility): either the analysis based on the neurosis in his childhood is all a piece of nonsense from start to finish, or else everything took place just as I have described it above.'[11] To question the priority of the event is to court absurdity.

At this point Freud is attempting to hold together in a synthesis the two principles of narrative that we have found in opposition elsewhere: the priority of events and the determination of event by structures of signification. Indeed, he cites the fact that his construct makes sense, hangs together nicely, as evidence that the event must have occurred. He rejects the conception of the event as a meaningful, highly determined fiction by refusing to see it as a possibility; he admits only the two alternatives: a real, prior event or a narrative without significance. But later Freud comes to see another possibility, and in what Peter Brooks calls 'one of the most daring moments in Freud's thought and one of his most heroic gestures as a writer,' he allows his first argument to stand and adds a further discussion, by way, he says, 'of supplementation and rectification.'[12] It is possible, Freud says, in supplementation, that this primal event did not occur and that what we are dealing with is in fact a trope, a transference from, say, a scene of copulating animals to his parents to produce at age 4 the fantasy of witnessing at 1½ years of age a scene of parental copulation. To the possible objection that it is implausible for such a scene to have been constructed, Freud replies by citing as evidence for the possibility of this fantasy precisely the structural coherence that had previously been adduced as evidence for the reality of the event itself. For example, if the fantasized event is to work in a plausible narration, it must be imagined as taking place at a time when the child was sleeping in his parents' bedroom. 'The scene which was to be made up had to fulfill certain conditions which, in consequence of the circumstances of the dreamer's life, could only be found in precisely this early period; such, for instance, was the condition that he should be in bed in his parents' bedroom.'[13]

In this second argument, then, Freud separates the two principles of narrative instead of attempting to conflate them as he did previously. One may maintain the primacy of the event: it took place at the appropriate moment and determined subsequent events and their significance. Or one can maintain that the structures of signification, the discursive requirements, work to produce a fictional or tropological event. At this point Freud admits the contradiction between these two perspectives, but he refuses to choose between them, referring the reader to a discussion of the problem of primal scenes versus primal fantasies in another text.

When he does return to the problem in this case history it is with a rich and pertinent formulation: 'I should myself be glad to know whether the primal scene in my present patient's case was a fantasy or a real experience; but, taking other similar cases into account, I must admit that the answer to this question is not in fact a matter of very great importance.'[14] Confronted with the difficulty of deciding whether a putative narrative event should be regarded as a given or a product, Freud notes that it is not decisively important, in that either perspective gives us the same narrative sequence.

But Freud also recognizes that the reader or analyst can never calmly accept this conclusion when he has engaged with a narrative. There is no happy compromise, for the force, the ethical import of a narrative, always impels the reader or analyst toward a decision. Understandably, Freud desires to know whether he has discovered the decisive event of his patient's past—an event which, for example, other parents might on the basis of Freud's discovery be enjoined to avoid—or whether the parents' behavior was in no way decisive, since whatever they did could be transformed by the tropes of fantasy into what the forces of signification in the narrative required. The ethical and referential dimensions of the narrative, that is to say, make such questions of compelling interest, even though the theorist resists this interest with the suggestion that the choice does not matter.

In one sense, however, Freud is right, for the two alternatives give us very similar narratives. If one opts for the production of the event by forces of signification, it becomes clear that the primal fantasy, as we might call it, can be efficacious only if the imagined event functions for the 4-year-old as a real event from his past. And if, on the other hand, we opt for the reality of the primal scene, we can see that this event could not have had the disastrous consequences it did unless the structures of signification which made it a trauma for the Wolfman and gave it irresistible explanatory power were so suited to it as to make it in some sense necessary. The fact that the event supposedly experienced at age 1½ became a trauma only through deferred action at age 4 shows the powerful role of the forces of meaning. But however close these two accounts may be, the fact remains that from the point of view of narratology, and also from the point of view of the engaged reader, the difference between an event of the plot and a imaginary event is irreducible. As Brooks concludes, 'the relationship between *fabula* and *sjuzhet*, between event and its significant rewriting is one of suspicion and conjecture, a structure of undecidability which can offer only a framework of narrative possibilities rather than a clearly specifiable plot.'[15] This undecidability is the effect of the convergence of two narrative logics that do not give rise to a synthesis.

The same pattern of narrative and analysis appears in another text of Freud's which tells not the story of an individual but the story of the race. In *Totem and Taboo* Freud tells of a decisive historical event in primitive times: a jealous and tyrannical father, who kept all the women for himself and drove away the sons as they reached maturity, was killed and devoured by the sons who had banded together. This 'memorable and criminal deed' was the beginning of social organization, religion, and moral restrictions, since the guilt led to the creation of taboos. This historical event, Freud claims, remains efficacious to this day. We inherit and repeat the wish if not the actual deed, and the guilt which arises from this wish keeps the consequences of the deed alive in an unbroken narrative.

But clearly if guilt can be created by desires as well as by acts, it is possible that the originary act never took place. Freud admits that the remorse may have been provoked by the sons' fantasy of killing the father (by the imagination of an event). This is a plausible hypothesis, he says, 'and no damage would thus be done to the causal chain stretching from the beginning to the present day.'[16] Choosing between these alternatives is no easy matter; however, he adds, 'it must be confessed that the distinction which may seem fundamental to other people does not in our judgment affect the heart of the matter.' As in the case of the Wolfman, emphasis on event and emphasis on meaning give the same narrative. But once again, one cannot fail to wish to choose, and Freud does: primitive men were uninhibited; for them thought passed directly into action. 'With them it is rather the deed that is the substitute for thought. And that is why, without laying claim to any finality of judgment, I think that in the case before us it may be assumed that "in the beginning was the Deed."'[17]

A safe assumption, perhaps, but safe because it is so equivocal. Freud here starts with the fantasy and asserts that for primitive men the deed was a substitute for the fantasy. The deed truly took place, he claims, but his formulation prevents one from taking the deed as a given since it is itself but a substitute for the fantasy, a product of this primal fantasy. And in claiming that in the beginning was the Deed, Freud refers us not to an event but to a signifying structure, another text, Goethe's *Faust*, in which 'deed' is but a substitute for 'word.' Faust is translating the opening words of *Genesis*, 'In the beginning was the Word,' and, unhappy with the German *Wort*, decides to substitute for it, in the very gesture Freud repeats, the word for 'deed': *Tat*. Quoting Goethe in asserting an originary deed, Freud cannot but refer us to a prior Word. Freud's text shows that even when one tries to assert the primacy of either word or deed one does not succeed in escaping the alternative one tried to reject.

I emphasize the impossibility of synthesis because what is involved here in narrative is an effect of self-deconstruction. A deconstruction involves the demonstration that a hierarchical opposition, in which one term is said to be dependent upon another conceived as prior, is in fact a rhetorical or metaphysical imposition and that the hierarchy could well be reversed. The narratives discussed here include a moment of self-deconstruction in which the supposed priority of event to discourse is inverted. The most elementary form of this deconstruction, somewhat different but still very relevant to narrative, is Nietzsche's analysis of causation as a trope, a metonymy.

Causation involves a narrative structure in which we posit first the presence of a cause and then the production of an effect. Indeed, the very notion of plot, as E. M. Forster taught us, is based on causation: 'the king died, then the queen died' is not a narrative, although 'the king died, then the queen died of grief' is.[18] This, one might say, is the *fabula* of the causal narrative: first, there is cause; then, there is effect; first a mosquito bites one's arm, then one feels pain. But, says Nietzsche, this sequence is not given; it is constructed by a rhetorical operation. What happens may be, for example, that we feel a pain and then look around for some factor we can treat as the cause. The 'real' causal sequence may be: first pain, then mosquito. It is the effect that causes us to produce a cause; a tropological operation then reorders the sequence pain–mosquito as mosquito–pain. This latter sequence is the product of discursive forces, but we treat it as a given, as the true order.[19]

This account of the production of causation does not imply that we can scrap the notion of causation, any more than the discursive production of events implies that narratives could function without the idea of causation, but there are moments when narratives identify their own tropological production and when the second perspective is indispensable to an account of their force. This is true not only of complex literary or theoretical narratives but also of what the sociolinguist William Labov calls 'natural narrative'—an interesting case for the narratologist.

In his studies of the black English vernacular, Labov became interested in the narrative skills displayed by adolescents and preadolescents. In interviews he would ask, for example, 'Were you ever in a fight with a guy bigger than you?' and if the answer were 'Yes' would pause and then ask, simply, 'What happened?' Labov begins his formal analysis of these stories by assuming the primacy of events: he defines narrative as 'a method of recapitulating past experience by matching a verbal sequence of clauses to the sequence of events.'[20] But, starting from this definition, he discovers that

> there is one important aspect of narrative that has not been discussed—perhaps the most important element in addition to the basic narrative clause. This is what we term the *evaluation* of the narrative: the means used by the narrator to indicate the point of the narrative, its *raison d'être*, why it was told and what the narrator was getting at.[21]

Labov even concludes that the narrator's primary concern may not be to report a sequence of events, as the definition of narrative would suggest, but rather to tell a story that will not be thought pointless: 'Pointless stories are met [in English] with the withering rejoinder, "So what?" Every good narrator is continually warding off this question; when his narrative is over it should be unthinkable for a bystander to say, "So what?"'[22]

Labov's narrators prove skilled at warding off this question. They construct their narratives so that the demands of signification are met and the story perceived as worthy of telling, as narratable. Labov's analysis distinguishes these discursive, evaluative elements from the sequence of actions reported in the narrative clauses; it is thus based on yet another version of the basic narratological distinction between story and discourse.

Labov's analysis works very well as long as he can distinguish story from discourse. If he can separate narrative clauses from evaluative clauses, then he can maintain the view that a narrative is a sequence of clauses reporting events, to which are added clauses evaluating these events, but when he comes to describe the evaluative devices, he discovers that some of the most interesting and powerful are not comments external to the action but actually belong to the sequence of actions. Instead of oneself remarking how exciting or dangerous or what a close call an incident was, one can emphasize the reportability of a story by attributing an evaluative comment to one of the participants and narrating this comment as an event in the story: 'And when we got down there her brother turned to me and whispered, "I think she's dead, John."' Or, as Labov says, the evaluation 'may itself be a narrative clause' in that an action one reports has the primary function of emphasizing the dramatic character of the event, as in 'I never prayed to God so fast and so hard in all my life!'[23]

Labov is certainly correct to claim that many clauses reporting actions are in fact determined by their evaluative function; instead of thinking of them as reports of prior actions, he prefers to see them as in effect producing an action so as to comply with the requirements of significance and make the story one to which no one will say 'So what?' But given this possibility, the analyst finds himself in an awkward position. For every report of an action there is the possibility that it should be thought of as evaluative, determined by the requirements of significance, and not as the narrative representation of a given event. Since the analyst's most basic distinction is between narrative and evaluative clauses, since for him analyzing a tale is first of all a matter of sorting elements into these two classes, he must make this choice, which may be a very dubious one. Of course, in a sense, as Freud said, his choice may not matter, since however he describes a particular event we still have the same tale. But if we are concerned with the force of the story, and those who tell or listen to natural narratives are especially concerned with their force, then we are invited to choose.

In natural narrative the desire to choose, the urgency of choice, is likely to emerge in the form of suspicion: it sounds too neat, too dramatic, too good to be true: did it really happen that way, or is this incident an evaluative device designed to prevent us from saying 'So what?' Is this particular element of the story a product of discursive requirements? In so-called 'natural narrative' the choice usually emerges as a question about fictionality (Is this incident true?), but as soon as the narrative as a whole is placed under the aegis of fiction, as soon as we approach it as a short story rather than a narrative of personal experience, then the question of the relation of story and discourse finds no such simple outlet. We cannot ask simply whether an incident is true or false; it would be very odd to say of Daniel Deronda that we do not believe he was actually born a Jew. We have to ask instead whether this is an event that determines meaning and discourse or whether it is itself determined by various narrative and discursive requirements.

The analysis of narrative is an important branch of semiotics. We still do not appreciate as fully as we ought the importance of narrative schemes and models in all aspects of our lives. Analysis of narrative depends, as I have argued, on the distinction between story and discourse, and this distinction always involves a relation of dependency: either the discourse is seen as a representation of events which must be thought of as independent of that particular representation, or else the so-called events are thought of as the postulates or products of a discourse. Since the distinction between story and discourse can function only if there is a determination of one by the other, the analyst must always choose which will be treated as the given and which as the product. Yet either choice leads to a narratology that misses some of the curious complexity of narratives and fails to account for much of their impact. If one thinks of discourse as the presentation of story, one will find it difficult to account for the sorts of effects, discussed here, which depend upon the determination of story by discourse, a possibility often posed by the narrative itself. If, on the other hand, one were to adopt the view that what we call 'events' are nothing other than products of discourse, a series of predicates attached to agents in the text, then one would be even less able to account for the force of narrative. For even the most radical fictions depend for their effect on the assumption that their puzzling sequences of sentences are presentations of events (though we may not be able to tell what those events are), and that these events in principle have features not reported by the discourse, such that the selection operated by the discourse has meaning. Without that assumption, which makes the discourse a selection and even a suppression of possible information, texts would lack their intriguing and dislocatory power.

Neither perspective, then, is likely to offer a satisfactory narratology, nor can the two fit together in a harmonious synthesis; they stand in irreconcilable opposition, a conflict between two logics which puts in question the possibility of a coherent, non-contradictory 'science' of narrative. But this identification of a certain self-deconstructive force in narrative and the theory of narrative should not lead to rejection of the analytical enterprise that drives one to this discovery. In the absence of the possibility of synthesis, one must be willing to shift from one perspective to the other, from story to discourse and back again.

10

The Turns of Metaphor

What you gain on the swings you lose on the roundabouts.

English proverb

Rhetoric, once rumored to have died in the nineteenth century, is once again a flourishing discipline, or at least a very active field; and much of this activity is focussed on *metaphor*. Recent years have witnessed a proliferation of conferences on the nature of metaphor and special issues of journals devoted to the problem of metaphor.[1] Our illustrious forbears in the field of rhetoric, Quintilian, Puttenham, Dumarsais, and Fontanier, would doubtless be delighted at this revival of interest in rhetoric, but they would be puzzled, I believe, at the extraordinary privilege accorded to metaphor. 'Why metaphor?' they might ask. Why not organize a symposium on simile or synecdoche, on metalepsis or meiosis, or on such complex figures as anadiplosis, alloiosis, or antapodosis? Metaphor is an important figure, they would concede, but by no means the only figure. Why should it usurp the attention of modern students of rhetoric?

It is not easy to explain why the idea of a conference on metaphor seems perfectly natural, while the idea of a conference on simile seems distinctly bizarre and unlikely. It is as though the scope or status of rhetoric has been reduced, while that of metaphor has been amplified. In the days when rhetoric was, as Aristotle called it, a 'counterpart' of dialectic and logic, or when it encompassed, as in Cicero's account, invention, arrangement, style, memory, and delivery, then metaphor was simply one prominent stylistic device, one of the many categories defined by rhetorical theory. Today, however, it is scarcely an exaggeration to say that metaphor is more respectable than rhetoric itself. We all acknowledge the importance of metaphor and therefore are willing to grant a certain status to a discipline that studies metaphor. The primary contemporary meaning of *rhetoric* is doubtless 'insincere or grandiloquent language,' but a second meaning is 'the study of figurative devices such as metaphor.' It is only the connexion with metaphor that gives rhetoric respectability, and it may well be that what is at stake in the privileging of metaphor is rhetoric itself.

I am suggesting, in other words, that today metaphor is no longer one figure among others but the figure of figures, a figure for figurality; and I mean this not figuratively but quite literally: the reason we can devote journals and conferences to metaphor is that metaphor is not just the literal or proper name for a trope based on resemblance but also and especially a figure for figurality in general. Thus the term *metaphor* in discussions of 'the nature of metaphor' or 'the problem of metaphor' already poses some of the central questions at issue: Is it literal or figurative? How can we tell the difference? What is the status of that difference? What happens when *metaphor* operates in this way? We can see that the difficulties of an investigation of metaphor are compounded if we cannot be sure whether our conceptual instruments, terms such as *metaphor, literal, proper,* lie inside or outside the domain we are attempting to study. We need to ask how *metaphor* operates in discussions of metaphor, how and why it becomes metaphorical.

We can begin to understand the metaphorical privileging of metaphor with the help of a passage from Stephen Ullmann's *Language and Style* which makes explicit the argument that is doubtless covertly at work in many discussions of metaphor. In an essay on 'The Nature of Imagery,' which summarizes the conclusions of his *Style in the French Novel* and *The Image in the French Novel*, Ullmann distinguishes two types of imagery: the metaphorical, which is based on a relationship of similarity; and the metonymical, which is based on an external relationship of contiguity. When the narrator of Proust's *Du Côté de chez Swann*

speaks of 'la couleur vive, empourprée et charmante' of the name
Champi (in George Sand's novel *François le Champi*), attaching this
'lively and charming crimson color' to the name may seem a
striking metaphorical gesture, 'yet if we look closely at the context we notice that the connection between the colour and the
name is metonymic, not metaphorical; it is based, not on some
hidden resemblance or analogy, but on a purely external relation:
the accidental fact that the book had a red binding.'[2]

Metonymies, Ullmann argues, generally lack the 'originality
and expressive power of metaphor,' because instead of forging
new links or uncovering new resemblances they are motivated by
relationships of spatial juxtaposition. But occasionally, as in the
example cited, they do give rise to what may be called a genuine
metaphorical effect: in their expressive force they achieve the
metaphorical quality of 'an authentic image.' Metonymies are
interesting, in other words, only when they resemble metaphors;
and moreover, Ullmann continues, 'it should be added at once
that the vast majority of images are metaphorical; the remarks
that follow will therefore be confined to this type.'[3] While
insisting in principle on the distinction between the metaphorical
and metonymical, Ullmann argues that interesting cases of the
latter can be assimilated to the former so that a discussion of
imagery can be a discussion of 'metaphor' alone.

This argument not only shows how the privileging of metaphor might arise and be justified but also will help to indicate, if
we pursue its implications, what is at stake here. We began with a
distinction between two figures: metaphor, based on the perception of an essential similarity; and metonymy, based on a merely
accidental or contingent connexion. Now an analyst might for
various reasons prefer to restrict his study of imagery to figures of
the first kind, but at this point he would have to admit that the
study of imagery ought to cover both cases. But if he argues that
the interesting, expressive, or worthwhile examples of the figure
based on accident do in fact reveal or express essential properties
and therefore deserve to be assimilated to the figures based on
essences, then there are no longer two distinct classes of figures,
both of which should be encompassed by a study of imagery.
Instead, one can regard the existence of figures based on accident

as something of an accident, or at least as not relevant to the essential functions and qualities of figurative language. Setting aside the accidental and focusing on essentials, one can then discuss imagery under the heading of *metaphor*, a term which applies literally to metaphors and figuratively to metonymies, or at least to those metonymies which are worthy of interest.

This setting aside of the accidental is important because of its bearing on the cognitive status of rhetoric and thus ultimately on the value of rhetoric. If rhetoric were assumed to encompass both metaphor and metonymy, both essential resemblances and accidental connexion, it might be difficult to make compelling claims for the value of rhetorical devices. But if the exemplary cases of metonymy can be brought under the heading of 'metaphor' and the other cases set aside as inessential, then the situation is very different. Of all the figures metaphor is the one that can most easily be defended or justified on cognitive grounds: 'the child is father to the man' presents the relation of generations in a new light; 'the foul rag and bone shop of the heart' implies a rather unusual account of human sensibility; 'the slings and arrows of outrageous fortune' presents an attitude toward fortune that one could accept or dispute. Whatever may be true of other figures, metaphors generally make claims that could in principle be restated as propositions, albeit with difficulty and prolixity. Doubtless for this reason, metaphor has long been thought of as the figure *par excellence* through which the writer can display creativity and authenticity: his metaphors are read as artistic inventions grounded in perceptions of relations in the world.

In privileging metaphor and making it the heading under which to discuss figurality in general, one thus asserts the responsibility and authenticity of rhetoric; one grounds it in the perception of resemblances in experience, in intimations of essential qualities. One represses or sets aside rhetoric as a non-referential play of forms by taking as representative of rhetoric or figure in general a figure whose referentiality can be defended: in 'the sessions of sweet silent thought' the legal metaphor of 'sessions' tells us something about the act of rememoration, whereas admirers of the line's alliteration might find it hard to claim that this formal device predicates something of the event. Small wonder, then, that defenses of poetry have always appealed not to ends achieved by assonance, metonymy, hendiadys, etc., but to something very much like the function of metaphor: poetry presents human experience to us in a new way, giving us not scientific truth but a higher imaginative truth, the perception of fundamental connexions and relationships. By taking metaphor as the representative figure one relegates to a problematical limbo the long list of figures with classical names that involve essentially formal processes of ordering, reordering, repetition; and one thereby makes it easier to defend literature as a mode of vision whose language is functional. Modern interest in rhetoric is focussed on metaphor because the value of rhetoric and of literature itself are at stake.

Ullmann's argument is interesting not only because it illustrates and helps to explain how the contemporary focus on metaphor is justified. It also inaugurates an investigation of the relation between metaphor and metonymy which has some revealing results. Roman Jakobson had argued in 'Two Aspects of Language and Two Types of Aphasic Disturbances' that aphasia afflicts either the paradigmatic or the syntagmatic axis of language: 'The relation of similarity is suppressed in the former, the relation of contiguity in the latter type of aphasia.'[4] Even in normal linguistic activity, discourse will develop primarily through similarity or through contiguity: 'The metaphoric way would be the most appropriate term for the first case and the metonymic way for the second, since they find their most condensed expression in metaphor and metonymy respectively.' These two 'poles' of language, Jakobson suggests, are in a relationship of competition such that one or the other will prevail in a given discourse. Metaphor is the mode of poetry, particularly of Romanticism and Symbolism, whereas metonymy is the mode of Realism.

Against Jakobson's claim that these two tropes represent the opposition between the most fundamental aspects of language, Ullmann notes in his discussion of Proust's imagery the potentially intimate relationship between them and the difficulty of separating the metaphorical from the metonymical in synesthetic imagery.[5] Gérard Genette goes a step further, arguing that many of Proust's most characteristic metaphors are generated by metonymy: if the steeples of Saint-André-des-Champs are described in terms appropriate to ears of corn and those of Saint-Mars-le-Vêtu as fish with mossy reddish scales, it is because the first rise out of fields of grain while the second are by the sea.[6] The descriptions function metaphorically—they do not simply designate the contexts from which they emerge, as the metonymy *crown* stands for the monarchy—but they are generated by metonymic transfer, and they thus allow one to speak, as Genette urges, of metaphor supported by metonymy:

> The metonymical sliding is not just 'disguised' but actually transformed into metaphorical predication. Thus, far from being antagonistic and incompatible, metaphor and metonymy support each other and interpenetrate one another; and to do justice to the latter does not consist of drawing up a list of metonymies over and against the list of metaphors but rather of showing the presence and action of relations of 'coexistence' at the very heart of the relation of analogy: the role of metonymy *in metaphor*.[7]

Genette also argues, as Ullmann had before him, that involuntary memory in Proust is based on metonymy: the taste of a madeleine, the feel of uneven paving-stones, the sound of a spoon against a glass, bring back the contexts with which they were contiguously associated. Thus the capture of essences which is said to result from reliving the past in the present through involuntary memory turns out to depend upon a metonymic connexion.[8] But at this point a question arises: can this really be a case of cooperation and harmonious interpenetration of metaphor and metonymy? For the capture and appreciation of essences, if it is to mean anything or carry any value, must be distinguished from the purely fortuitous or accidental relationships brought about by juxtaposition. What are the possible relations between essence and accident? Consider this famous passage from *Le Temps retrouvé* concerning metaphor, truth, and essences:

La vérité ne commencera qu'au moment où l'écrivain prendra deux objets différents, posera leur rapport analogue dans le monde de l'art à celui qu'est le rapport unique de la loi causale dans le monde des sciences, et les enfermera dans les anneaux d'un beau style, ou même, ainsi que la vie, quand en rapprochant une qualité commune à deux sensations, il dégagera leur essence en les réunissant l'une et l'autre pour les soustraire aux contingences du temps, et les enchaînera par les liens indescriptibles d'une alliance des mots.

[Truth will not begin until the moment when the writer takes two different objects, sets down the relation between them that is the analogue in the world of art to the unique relation of the law of causation in the world of the sciences, and locks them together in the rings of a beautiful style, or even, when, like life itself, in bringing together two sensations with a common quality he extracts their essence by uniting them with one another to withdraw them from the contingencies of time and fixes them by the indescribable bonds of a marriage (wedding ring) of words.][9]

The writer produces truth—the artistic analogue of a scientific law—by metaphor, bringing together two objects of sensations and identifying their common quality. In praising metaphor as the instrument of artistic truth, Proust asserts a contrast between the metaphorical presentation of atemporal essences and a different kind of connexion, an accidental juxtaposition of items in time. If metonymies are at work in Proustian metaphors, then, this may be not so happy or innocent a cooperation as Genette claims, for the intermingling of metaphor and metonymy, of essential and contingent connexions, would have implications for the claims made for the metaphors in question. This is a line of argument that Paul de Man has developed in an analysis of a particularly salient passage in Proust, where the narrator explicitly identifies the value of literature and of reading with the metaphorical perception of essences, but the text's powerful and persuasive metaphors, as de Man shows, turn out to depend upon a metonymy, an accidental connexion of precisely the sort to which metaphor has been contrasted.

The passage from *Du Côté de chez Swann* describes Marcel reading in his room during the summer. His grandmother wants him to play rather than to sit reading, to be outside rather than inside; Marcel goes on to defend reading as offering him more genuine adventures, more direct access to people and passions, than he would have gained by venturing outdoors. This familiar if unusually explicit reflection on the value of reading is introduced and given a foundation by the passage which claims that Marcel's withdrawal from the light, heat, and activity of summer to the cool tranquility of his room is not in fact a sacrifice, nor does it involve any cognitive loss. On the contrary, it is claimed that by withdrawing to his room he is able to grasp the essence of summer in a way that he could not if he were outside playing. 'L'obscure fraîcheur de ma chambre,' the narrator claims, '. . . offrait à mon imagination le spectacle total de l'été, dont mes sens, si j'avais été en promenade, n'auraient pu jouir que par morceaux.' [The dark coolness of my room . . . gave my imagination the total spectacle of the summer, whereas my senses, if I had been on a walk, could only have enjoyed it in fragments.][10]

In explaining how it is that the essence of summer can be transfered or transported to him as he sits inside, Marcel insists on the distinction between a transfer of meaning based on the accidental contiguity of sensations, which would be a metonymical transfer of associations, and a transfer of meaning based on necessary connexions, a metaphorical revelation of essence. The 'sensation of light and splendour' is conveyed to him, as he lies inside in the dark,

> par les mouches qui exécutaient devant moi, dans leur petit concert, comme la musique de chambre de l'été: elle ne l'évoque pas à la façon d'un air de musique humaine, qui, entendu *par hasard* à la belle saison, vous la rappelle ensuite; elle est unie à l'été par un *lien plus nécessaire*: née des beaux jours, ne renaissant qu'avec eux, contenant un peu de *leur essence*, elle n'en réveille pas seulement l'image dans notre

mémoire, elle en certifie le retour, la *présence effective*, ambiante, immédiatement accessible (my italics).

[by the flies who were performing before me, in their little concert, the chamber music of summer: evocative not in the manner of a human tune which, heard perchance during the summer, afterwards reminds you of it, but united to summer by a more necessary link: born from beautiful days, resurrecting only when they return, containing something of their essence, it not only awakens their image in our memory; it guarantees their return, their actual, persistent, immediately accessible presence.][11]

The distinction between contingent and necessary connexions is firmly asserted, but in order to persuade us that nothing essential of summer has been lost in this transfer from outside to inside and that Marcel resting indoors does indeed experience the 'total spectacle of summer,' the passage must maneuver in such a way that the notion of heated activity, associated with the scene outside, is transfered to the inside. This transfer is brought about in the next paragraph, which begins with the claim previously quoted that 'l'obscure fraîcheur de ma chambre . . . offrait à mon imagination le spectacle total de l'été,' and which continues with the assertion that this 'obscure fraîcheur . . .

s'accordait bien à mon repos qui (grâce aux aventures racontées par mes livres et qui venaient de l'émouvoir) supportait, pareil au repos d'une main immobile au mileu d'une eau courante, le choc et l'animation d'un torrent d'activité.

[suited my repose which (thanks to the adventures narrated in my books and which had stirred my tranquility) supported, like the quiet of a hand held motionless in the middle of a running brook, the shock and animation of a torrent of activity.]

In the context of a description of summer, the image of a hand feeling the cool sensation of a running brook is seductive, but this image also works, as de Man says, to capture for the cool inside world the property that is essential if Marcel is to experience the full spectacle of summer, the property of warmth.

> The cool repose of the hand must be made compatible with the heat of action. This transfer occurs, still within the space of a single sentence, when it is said that repose supports a 'torrent d'activité.' In French this expression is not—or is no longer—a metaphor but a cliché, a dead or sleeping metaphor which has lost its literal connotations (in this case, the connotations associated with the word 'torrent') and has only kept a proper meaning. 'Torrent d'activité' properly signifies a lot of activity, the quantity of activity likely to agitate someone to the point of making him feel hot. The proper meaning converges with the connotation supplied, on the level of the signifier, by the 'torride' ('hot') that one can choose to hear in 'torrent.' Heat is therefore inscribed in the text in an underhand, secretive manner, thus linking the two antithetical series in one single chain that permits the exchange of incompatible qualities: if repose can be hot and active without however losing its distinctive virtue of tranquility, then the 'real' activity can lose its fragmentary and dispersed quality and become whole without having to be any less real. [12]

This image, which is essential to the overall success of the passage, is, de Man argues, metonymical rather than metaphorical: it is based first of all on the accidental association or linkage of the words *torrent* and *activité* in a cliché or idiom (it is an accidental association in that the essential and literal qualities of 'torrent' are not important to the idiom); and it depends, secondly, on the fact that the juxtaposition of the cliché *torrent d'activité* with the image of the hand in the water reawakens, as an effect of contiguity, the association of *torrent* with water. The power and persuasiveness of this text, which celebrates reading and sequestration as a way of capturing essences after the fashion of metaphorical language, turns out to depend on metonymical effects of contiguity. This structure, de Man concludes, is typical of Proust's language throughout the novel. In a passage that abounds in successful and seductive metaphors and which, moreover, asserts the superior efficacy of metaphor over that of metonymy, persuasion is achieved by a figural play in which contingent figures of chance masquerade deceptively as figures of necessity. A literal and thematic reading that takes the value assertions of the text at their word, would have to favor metaphor over metonymy as a means to satisfy a desire all the more tempting since it is paradoxical: the desire for a secluded reading that satisfies the ethical demands of action more effectively than actual deeds. Such a reading is put in question if one takes the rhetorical structure of the text into account. [13]

De Man does not claim that all metaphorical effects rely on metonymical connexions, but his argument certainly leads one to look again at the sort of cases Ullmann and Genette cite, where metaphor and metonymy are said to support one another in a harmonious way, and to ask whether metaphors that are proposed and celebrated as examples of the revelation of essences and imaginative truth that literary language can achieve do not depend upon accidental connexions, metonymical contiguities that put in question the claims made for the figures. If the plausibility and persuasiveness of striking metaphors, such as the description of steeples as ears of corn, depend upon metonymical connexions, a certain contingency already attaches to the 'essence' thereby revealed.

The privileging of metaphor over metonymy and other figures is an assertion of the cognitive value and respectability of literary language; the accidental play of verbal associations and contingent juxtapositions is given an ancillary status so that it can be ignored. Yet the supremacy of metaphor depends upon metonymy, either because, as in Ullmann's case, one assimilates to metaphor the best metonymies, which justify the valorization, or else because the persuasiveness and excellence of daring metaphors (and thus the excellence claimed for metaphor in general) depend on metonymies. We can see further that the privileging of metaphor is not simply a move made by critics and theorists, who might be expected to celebrate tropes that are cognitively respectable. Jakobson argues that since the relation between the critic's metalanguage and the texts he discusses is metaphorical, he 'possesses a more homogeneous means to handle metaphor, whereas metonymy, based on a different principle, easily defies interpretation.'[14] But literary works themselves, which might be assumed to have freer access to this different principle, emphasize their preference for the mechanisms of metaphor over those of metonymy. Powerful forces are at work to make *metaphor* at once the opposite of tropes based on accident and the authoritative representative of figurative language in general, the figure for figurality.

None the less, there is a further complication here. Ullmann and others who employ *metaphor* for imagery of all kinds assimilate other figures to metaphor on the basis of similarity (the quality they share is that of 'an authentic image'). For de Man, however, who stresses not similarity but contiguity, the privilege of metaphor is an effect of metonymy: metonymies are assimilated to metaphors with which they are contiguously associated. One might even say that de Man's own deconstructive strategy is to reverse the metaphorical privileging of metaphor by assimilating metaphors metonymically to metonymy: emphasizing the relations of contiguity and association between metaphors and metonymies in the text, de Man implies, by metonymy, that metaphors belong to metonymy. This then becomes in turn a kind of metaphor: metonymy, with its exploitation of accidental, arbitrary relations, becomes a metaphor for figurative language in general.

To make *metonymy* rather than *metaphor* one's metaphor of figurality is, of course, to take a very different view of figurative language and of language in general, but it also involves a different analytical perspective, as we can see from an interesting discussion by Umberto Eco, an attempt to deal with 'The Semantics of Metaphor' in a semiotic framework. Asking how it is that a code can make creativity possible, Eco takes metaphor as his example: 'The goal of this discussion is to show that each metaphor can be traced back to a subjacent chain of metonymic connexions which constitute the framework of the code and upon which is based the constitution of any semantic field, whether partial or (in theory) global.'[15] Though Eco's argument is not as clear as one might wish, his project seems to lead him to concentrate on the production of metaphors rather than their effect. One example: in *Finnegans Wake* Shaun is called 'Minucius Mandrake.' Minucius Felix is an apologist father of the Church; Mandrake, Eco argues, is Mandrake the Magician; and the juxtaposition is based on a third term, Felix the Cat.

> Here, then, is the mechanism subjacent to the metaphoric substitution: Minucius refers by contiguity to Felix, Felix refers by contiguity (belonging to the same universe of comic strips) to Mandrake. Once the middle term has fallen, there remains a coupling that does not seem justified by any contiguity and thus appears to be metaphoric. The always possible substitution between Minucius and Mandrake is attributable no longer to the possibility of passing from one to the other through a series of successive choices but to the fact that they seem to possess characteristics which are 'similar' (advocates, rhetoricians, and so on) and thus 'analogous.'[16]

This argument may sound similar to de Man's, but there is one important difference, for while de Man claims that the *effect* or persuasiveness of his metaphorical passage depends upon a metonymical connexion, Eco is reconstructing metonymic connexions that have been abandoned by the text: their role lies in the production of the metaphor, not in its functioning. However, Eco's project makes explicit what is only implicit in de Man: an inclination to identify metonymy with the code, with language itself as a system of arbitrary signs which depend for their identity on their relations with one another. This is a new development in the analysis of figures. For Jakobson, the metaphorical and metonymic axes are equally part of the linguistic system: paradigmatic relations among linguistic items—relations of phonological, semantic, and syntactic similarity—are associated with metaphor, and syntagmatic relations—the possibilities of combining items to form sequences—are associated with metonymy. If anything, Jakobson links metaphor more closely with the linguistic code, since relations of similarity occur primarily in the code or system. Only in the exercise of the poetic function of language are relations of similarity important constituents of the sequence. Metaphor is linked with *la langue* and metonymy with *la parole*, since relations of contiguity are manifested in the actual combinations of speech sequences.[17]

Eco inverts the Jakobsonian relationship, apparently because he thinks of systems and codes as spatial. If the system is spatial, then relations between items in the system may be thought of as relations of contiguity and hence as metonymic. Codes connect Felix the Cat with Mandrake the Magician or the notion of 'a beautiful woman' with the feature 'a long white neck'; they also connect 'swan' with 'a long white neck' and thus make possible, through these two relations of contiguity, the metaphorical substitution of swan for woman (or woman for swan). Eco argues that

> A metaphor can be invented because language, in its process of unlimited semiosis, constitutes a multidimensional network of metonymies, each of which is explained by a cultural convention rather than by an original resemblance. The imagination would be incapable of inventing or recognizing a metaphor if culture, under the form of a possible structure of the Global Semantic System, did not provide it with the subjacent network of arbitrarily stipulated contiguities.[18]

The assumption that relations within the code are relations of contiguity must seem rather dubious, but the general tenor of the argument is defensible: though metaphors are often said to be based on the perception of real similarities, even essences, they are to a large extent based on contingent cultural conventions (there is scant physical basis for comparing women with swans), as becomes apparent when one reads poems from a radically different culture. The argument about the relation between metaphor and metonymy thus involves the question of the relation between thought and language. To maintain the primacy of metaphor is to treat language as a device for the expression of thoughts, perceptions, truth. To posit the dependency of metaphor on metonymy is to treat what language expresses as the effect of contingent, conventional relations and a system of mechanical processes. *Metaphor* and *metonymy* thus become in turn not only figures for figurality but figures for language in general. In Eco's argument, the linguistic system is essentially metonymic; for others, language is essentially metaphorical in that it names objects according to perceived similarities.

The turns of these terms are annoying as well as fascinating, and one frequently wishes, when reading and writing about figures, to put an end to the tropological inflation of tropes. Could we not avoid all these problems if we restricted *metaphor* and *metonymy* to their literal meanings? A certain austerity in their use might indeed avoid some problems, but in fact the issues that have emerged in the swings and reversals of *metaphor* and *metonymy* have an uncanny way of reappearing everywhere in this domain, particularly when one sets about to distinguish the literal from the metaphorical.

There seem to be two ways of thinking about the relation between the literal and the metaphorical, which we might christen the *via philosophica* and the *via rhetorica*. The first locates metaphor in the gap between sense and reference, in the process of thinking of an object, event, or whatever *as* something: thinking of the heart as a foul rag-and-bone shop, of fortune as an enemy wielding slings and arrows, of the beloved as a swan. This is the approach one generally takes when one wishes to emphasize the cognitive respectability of metaphor because one can argue that cognition itself is essentially a process of seeing something as something. Metaphor thus becomes an instance of general cognitive processes at their most creative or speculative.

However, precisely because this approach assimilates metaphor to general cognitive processes, it makes it difficult to establish any firm distinction between the literal and the metaphorical. Since to use language at all is to treat something as a member of a class, to see it as an instance of some category, language itself seems to be metaphorical. A non-metaphorical language would consist of logically proper names only; but, as it turns out, logically proper names are something natural languages do not have. To call something by a name in a natural language is to ascribe to it some properties, to bring it under some loose heading. It would seem, then, that as soon as we speak we engage in metaphor.

If we pursue this line of argument, we reach the paradoxical conclusion that is outlined, for example, by Rousseau in his *Essai sur l'origine des langues* or by Vico in the *Scienza Nuova*: that language originates in metaphor and that figurative language precedes literal language. Though this argument may be coupled with claims about primitive modes of perception—that the first men were poets—this need not be the case, since the act of grouping distinct particulars under a common heading on the basis of perceived or imagined resemblance, which is the central act in any narrative of the origin of language, corresponds to the classical definition of metaphor: substitution on the basis of resemblance.[19] If language originates in figure and is essentially metaphorical, then what we call 'literal meaning' or 'literal language' is nothing but figurative language whose figurality has been forgotten.

The appropriateness of this claim may seem questionable when one focuses on what one thinks of as ordinary terms, such as *chair, book, tree, sleep*; but it is easy to grasp when one considers an appellation where we still have some notion of the act of cognition involved: for example, study of the behavior of bees and the identification of certain resemblances between their communicative behavior and human communication led some writers to extend the term *language* to 'the language of bees.' It may well be that this expression is now regarded as literal rather than figurative, in which case it is an instance of an expression whose literalness consists in the erosion of its initial figurality.

The most famous statement of this position is Nietzsche's in the essay 'Uber Wahrheit und Lüge im aussermoralischen Sinn':

> What is truth? A moving army of metaphors, metonymies and anthropomorphisms, in short a summa of human relationships that are being poetically and rhetorically sublimated, transposed, and beautified until, after long and repeated use, a people considers them as solid, canonical, and unavoidable. Truths are illusions whose illusionary nature has been forgotten, metaphors that have been used up and have lost their

imprint and that now operate as mere metal, no longer as coins. [20]

I noted above that the *via philosophica* gives metaphor considerable cognitive respectability, but, as this passage from Nietzsche makes clear, that respectability is achieved at some cost. If metaphor is identified with truth itself, that may seem to elevate metaphor, but it undermines truth. The line of argument that gives metaphor cognitive respectability ends by abolishing cognitive respectability. In general one might observe that any attempt to ground trope or figure in truth always contains the possibility of reducing truth to trope.

If the *via philosophica* leads to a problematizing of the very distinction between literal and figurative which it set out to explore and if it brings us to a paradoxical assertion of the priority of the figurative over the literal, it might seem wise to try the other road. The *via rhetorica* locates metaphor not in the gap between sense and reference but in the space between what is meant and what is said: between a literal or proper verbal expression and a periphrastic substitute. By thus placing itself on the terrain of language itself, it avoids the consideration of cognition which led the *via philosophica* to find all language fundamentally figurative. Indeed, by assuming that metaphorical language is another way of saying something which could in principle be said literally, the *via rhetorica* makes the potential virtues of metaphor not cognitive but stylistic: a metaphor may be more concise and vivid than the corresponding literal version.

This approach works quite well for expressions such as *John is a fox*, where we can identify *fox* as the metaphorical substitute for a literal formulation such as *devious, crafty, creature*. Indeed, it is under this heading that one should locate traditional definitions of metaphor as a substitution based on resemblance, whether resemblance be defined in terms of common semantic features, membership in a common class, or proportional analogy (Aristotle's A:B::C:D). The difficulties arise in situations where we want to claim that a sequence is metaphorical without being able to compare the figurative detour or substitute with the literal expression which it replaces. Literary critics are often inclined to insist that creative and successful metaphors say something that cannot be said any other way and must not be regarded as simply vivid substitutes for a literal statement. The value of 'foul rag-and-bone shop of the heart,' they might argue, lies in the fact that its full import cannot be approximated by any paraphrase.

The rhetorician may be inclined to regard this attitude as a kind of mystical defensiveness which should not be allowed to obstruct theory. After all, he would argue, if we claim to understand a metaphor, then in principle we ought to be able to say what we understand by it, and it is precisely the contrast between the expression itself and what we understand by it that is the difference between the literal and the metaphorical. It may be difficult to produce a literal statement in some cases, but in principle these cases are no different from *John is a fox*. Certainly the rhetorician would wish to insist that the existence of difficult cases is no grounds for refusing to take simple cases as the norm.

But there is a certain perversity in an account of metaphor which works well for highly uninteresting and even artificial figures of replacement and which breaks down, or at least becomes relatively useless, in the case of the creative, suggestive literary metaphors which interest us most. Indeed, the problems of this approach are nicely summed up by the case of what rhetoricians have called *catachresis*. Catachresis occurs, according to Fontanier, when a sign already assigned to a first idea is assigned to a new idea which had no expression—that is to say, where there is no existing literal expression which the figurative designation is replacing.[21] One example of catachresis would be *head of lettuce*, in which *head*, which is already assigned to one idea, is assigned to another idea which has no other designation. Another example of catachresis, however, would be a truly creative metaphor which names something that previously had no name, which discloses or identifies something that we have no other way of describing. In both cases there is no substitution of a figurative expression for a literal one—which puts into question the claim that it is the contrast between the literal and the figurative which constitutes metaphors. And we cannot adopt the expedient of excluding catachresis from the domain of metaphors (on the grounds that so-called 'dead' metaphors are no longer metaphors), because truly creative metaphors also lack this crucial contrast between the literal paraphrase and the figurative denomination.

Thus, the *via rhetorica* also seems to lead us to a point where the distinction between the literal and the metaphorical becomes problematic. We started with a normal, literal use of language against which was to be set the deviant figurative use, and sought to define the second precisely by its contrast with the first, but we then came upon cases where the first was not something given but at best something to be constructed with difficulty. In both approaches to metaphor, then, it proves difficult to maintain the priority of the literal over the figurative, but since the figurative is defined as a deviation from the literal, on which it is thus said to depend, this reversal of priority creates problems for the distinction itself. In both cases the distinction between the literal and the metaphorical is essential yet thoroughly problematic.

The problem of metaphor, as it has been discussed here, involves two separate problems, two oppositions which are necessary to any account of metaphor but which prove awkward and paradoxical. The distinctions between metaphor and metonymy and between the literal and the figurative turn out to behave in surprisingly similar ways. In both cases we have a binary opposition which is asymmetrical: one of the terms is treated as privileged, as more fundamental; and in both cases the privileged term, seen as cognitively respectable, is set against a certain rhetoricity, a linguistic detour which is primarily ornamental. Metonymy as opposed to metaphor and the metaphorical as opposed to the literal are relegated to a secondary status for reasons that seem fundamental to our culture's way of thinking about language.

In both cases, however, the asymmetry turns out to be unstable, and as one explores the logic of the situation further, one discovers that the term treated as secondary and derivative can be seen as basic. In the case of metaphor and metonymy, not only does the power of certain metaphorical passages or celebrations of metaphor depend upon metonymies, but we can see that the privileging of the category itself can only be accomplished by assimilating interesting metonymies to it. In the case of the literal versus the figurative, the terms in which the figurative is defined so as to be distinguished from the literal lead one, paradoxically, to recognize the primacy of the figurative, either by identifying it with general cognitive processes and seeing the literal as figures whose figurality has been forgotten, or else by focusing on cases of catachresis where the figure seems to work without being contrasted with the literal.

Ideally, a discussion of metaphor and its problems would conclude by offering an elegant and convincing solution, but it may well be that there is no solution, that metaphor is not something we could see clearly if only we could resolve these problems. It may be, rather, that the domain of metaphor is constituted by these problems: the unstable distinction between the literal and the figurative, the crucial yet unmasterable distinction between essential and accidental resemblances, the tension between thought and linguistic processes within the linguistic system and language use. The pressure of these various concepts and forces creates a space, articulated by unmasterable distinctions, that we call *metaphor*. What one can do by way of conclusion, however, is to attempt to see the problem of metaphor in a different perspective.

The philosopher Donald Davidson claims, in an argument that has definite attractions, that discussions of the meaning of metaphorical expressions are fundamentally in error. His argument can be succinctly illustrated. Consider the simile 'a geometrical proof is like a mousetrap.' This sentence asserts that there is a similarity or similarities between a geometrical proof and a mousetrap and enjoins us to think of possible similarities, but it does not tell us which features of the objects we should think of. There is no reason to claim that any particular similarities are part of the meaning of the sentence; the sentence says simply that there is similarity. In the case of a metaphor, however—'a geometrical proof is a mousetrap'—theorists usually insist that to give the meaning of the metaphor is to identify the similarities in question, to define what is being predicated of geometrical proofs. Would it not be preferable to claim, asks Davidson, that in asserting an identity the metaphor leads us to think about possible similarities but does not itself define them and that no particular similarities are part of the meaning of the metaphor, any more than they are part of the meaning of the simile?[22] After all, if I say 'geometrical proofs are horrible,' my assertion will lead people to think about properties that might provoke distaste, but to give the meaning of this sentence one need not produce a list of properties provoking distaste.

Davidson's theory is attractive because of its simplicity, but simplicity is usually purchased at the cost of complexity elsewhere, and that is certainly the case here. By denying that metaphors have any special meaning (they assert literal equivalences which are false) he makes necessary an elaborate account of the *effect* of metaphorical assertions, a complex analysis of the way readers and listeners respond to these false assertions of identity. Generally analysts of metaphor have assumed that metaphors communicate because they have a complex structure that must be described. They treat metaphors as tropes or devices, elements of a system, structures of *la langue* in the largest sense, semiotic units which have effects because of their particular structural features. Davidson's theory claims that from the point of view of *la langue* and of codes generally what we call 'metaphor' is no more than a false assertion of identity, and the question of what is communicated by metaphors is a question about *parole*, about language use, about persuasion. It is not a matter of structure but of effect, and the study of metaphor should be a study of response.

This might well be a fruitful line of inquiry. It would involve treating the notion of metaphor as a description of certain interpretive operations performed by readers when confronted by a textual incongruity, such as the assertion of a patently false identity. When the narrator of Baudelaire's 'Spleen' says 'Je suis un cimetière abhorré de la lune' the reader confronts this enigma with a set of rhetorical categories which is, as Michel Charles has argued, 'a system of possible questions,' a set of possible relations that might be established between the 'I' and the 'cemetery abhorred by the moon.'[23] We can ask about similarities, some of which are outlined in the following lines of the poem, about relations of contiguity or of container and contained. In this case, interpretations are likely to call upon several modes of relation:

cemeteries contain, by lugubrious convention, 'de longs vers', and this relation of contiguity can ground a relation of similarity with a poet whose verses also 's'acharnent toujours sur mes morts les plus chers.' And, of course, other possible relations can be identified.

From the perspective of reading, metaphor is the name of one sort of move in an ongoing process of interpretation, but it would be a mistake to suppose that by adopting this perspective we avoid the problems that arise when we treat metaphor as a device or structure. Since we do not believe that responses to metaphors are purely random or idiosyncratic phenomena, we will attempt to account for responses by positing norms, conventions, codes, structures. Considerable emphasis is likely to fall on cultural codes and clichés (what is conventionally associated with cemeteries that can be exploited in metaphoric interpretation?), and we will repeat at a slightly different level Eco's move in positing a network of conventional associations to account for the production of a metaphor. Instead of explaining the original production of the metaphor by the author, however, we would be describing the production of a metaphorical reading by the reader. But there will still be the problem of distinguishing a metaphorical move from a metonymical move, essential from contingent relations, thought and perception from the mechanical operation of syntactic and phonological processes—with perhaps this difference, that a rhetoric focussed on persuasion rather than tropes will be engaged from the outset in an uncertain calculus, trying to account for effects of force which are never wholly predictable. This is in part because one can never construct a position outside tropology from which to view it; one's own terms are always caught up in the processes they attempt to describe. But it is in part also because the figurative is the name we give to effects of language that exceed, deform, or deviate from the code; codifications of previous excesses, deformations, and deviations only create opportunities for new turns.

11

Literary Theory in the Graduate Program

As the shrinking job market makes graduate study in English less attractive and as real or threatened budget cuts force departments to watch carefully the number of students in their various classes, there has been considerable debate about what should be done with graduate programs in English. Everyone agrees that other universities should cut back their graduate intake or eliminate their programs entirely, but there is little consensus about what should be done in the numerous programs that will remain. Addressing an Association of Departments of English meeting in 1977, William Schaefer urged a broadening and liberalizing of Ph.D. programs. If we teachers of English believe that the study of literature is a central and valuable experience, then we do ourselves and others a disservice by drawing a line between undergraduate and graduate studies, assuming that liberal education is appropriate only in the former and presenting the latter as a specialized activity suitable only for future teachers of English. If we have anything worthwhile to teach, it ought to be made available to those who have already received a B.A. as well as to those who have not. By devoting graduate programs exclusively to professional training, Schaefer argued, we have effectively destroyed the M.A. in most of the humanistic disciplines and have eliminated learning that we ought to be encouraging. 'We have got to liberalize our graduate as well as undergraduate programs and persuade ourselves and others that there is no answer to the question "how high is higher education?,"' making it possible for students to go as high as they can.[1]

Yet at the same time others have claimed that graduate programs should be more professional, should explicitly set out to offer thorough preparation for the teaching profession. John C. Gerber, in a visionary 'Glimpse of English as a Profession,' has reported that the flourishing English departments of the twenty-first century ('English professors are now associated in the public mind with lawyers and physicians,' a participant in an ADE seminar of 2,026 reports[2]) owe their triumph to their new professionalism, part of which is a long and rigorous graduate program 'devised to prepare the student for his or her profession.' Reinhard Kuhn, in an MLA talk entitled 'The Return to Basics in Graduate Studies,' has called for the reintroduction of those professional requirements (systematic coverage of a national literature, Latin, philological training) that have been allowed to lapse. 'The highly competitive market,' he argues, 'does present an ideal opportunity for imposing or reimposing the highest levels of achievement.'[3] This recommendation is seconded by John Algeo in an article called 'After the Fall: Some Observations on Graduate Curricula.' The paradise we have lost turns out to be the 1960s, when grants, graduate students, and jobs were plentiful. We cannot regain this happy state; we must go forward 'with wandering steps and slow,' but, Algeo advises, 'we can increase course requirements to encompass all of English language and literature.' 'Holders of the Ph.D.,' he concludes, 'should be equipped to teach any course in the undergraduate curriculum.'[4]

These two lines of thought are certainly incompatible, both in spirit and in their concrete proposals: liberalization versus rigorous professionalization. But it seems to me that each has a valid concern, to which one might hope to do justice. Neither side in this debate is likely to be satisfied by a compromise solution, but it ought not to lie beyond the wit of man or chair to imagine courses of reading and study that would be both of interest in themselves, as an extension of the liberal education begun at the undergraduate level, and of use in preparing students to teach in universities. The kind of work that would make graduate study an extension of undergraduate education is not necessarily incompatible with the sort of preparation our graduate students need today.

Indeed, it seems to me that the advocates of back to basics' in graduate studies have not given sufficient thought to the situations their students will encounter when they begin, or seek to begin, teaching. They do not discuss whether the situations their students will encounter are the same as the situations for which the traditional Ph.D. program prepared students. If one asks what sort of faculty the departments who hire recent Ph.D.s are likely to need, the most common answer will doubtless be that they need people who can teach reading and writing and who can get undergraduates interested in reading and writing. It is wholly understandable that professors whose own graduate training involved considerable work in Anglo-Saxon and Middle English and who passed through an examination covering all of English literature should feel that this is the ideal preparation for a college teacher, but most departments are already heavily staffed with people who have had such training, and when there is teaching to be done that requires this sort of preparation—in philology, for example, or literary history—there will probably be tenured professors qualified to do it. Most departments have no shortage of faculty trained in 'basics' to which the advocates of professionalism want us to return, and it is not clear that they have a pressing need for more people with the same preparation. Nor is it evident that recent Ph.D.s are in an advantageous position if their education suits them to teach precisely those courses that their senior colleagues want to teach.

On the contrary, in most universities the traditional English courses organized according to periods have suffered a decline in enrollments. Deans, students, and chairmen are often interested in courses organized according to other principles, and a department may be better served by an assistant professor who can develop new courses that are attractive to students than by one who can take over the Elizabethan literature course and offer a Spenser seminar for any upperclassmen who might be interested. But whatever the politics of a particular situation, whatever chairmen, deans, and curriculum committees want or think they want, young teachers will find themselves in institutions where it cannot be taken for granted that any educated person will study the great works of English literature. English depart-

Indeed, it seems to me that the advocates of back to basics' in graduate studies have not given sufficient thought to the situations their students will encounter when they begin, or seek to begin, teaching. They do not discuss whether the situations their students will encounter are the same as the situations for which the traditional Ph.D. program prepared students. If one asks what sort of faculty the departments who hire recent Ph.D.s are likely to need, the most common answer will doubtless be that they need people who can teach reading and writing and who can get undergraduates interested in reading and writing. It is wholly understandable that professors whose own graduate training involved considerable work in Anglo-Saxon and Middle English and who passed through an examination covering all of English literature should feel that this is the ideal preparation for a college teacher, but most departments are already heavily staffed with people who have had such training, and when there is teaching to be done that requires this sort of preparation—in philology, for example, or literary history—there will probably be tenured professors qualified to do it. Most departments have no shortage of faculty trained in 'basics' to which the advocates of professionalism want us to return, and it is not clear that they have a pressing need for more people with the same preparation. Nor is it evident that recent Ph.D.s are in an advantageous position if their education suits them to teach precisely those courses that their senior colleagues want to teach.

On the contrary, in most universities the traditional English courses organized according to periods have suffered a decline in enrollments. Deans, students, and chairmen are often interested in courses organized according to other principles, and a department may be better served by an assistant professor who can develop new courses that are attractive to students than by one who can take over the Elizabethan literature course and offer a Spenser seminar for any upperclassmen who might be interested. But whatever the politics of a particular situation, whatever chairmen, deans, and curriculum committees want or think they want, young teachers will find themselves in institutions where it cannot be taken for granted that any educated person will study the great works of English literature. English depart-

cemeteries contain, by lugubrious convention, 'de longs vers', and this relation of contiguity can ground a relation of similarity with a poet whose verses also 's'acharnent toujours sur mes morts les plus chers.' And, of course, other possible relations can be identified.

From the perspective of reading, metaphor is the name of one sort of move in an ongoing process of interpretation, but it would be a mistake to suppose that by adopting this perspective we avoid the problems that arise when we treat metaphor as a device or structure. Since we do not believe that responses to metaphors are purely random or idiosyncratic phenomena, we will attempt to account for responses by positing norms, conventions, codes, structures. Considerable emphasis is likely to fall on cultural codes and clichés (what is conventionally associated with cemeteries that can be exploited in metaphoric interpretation?), and we will repeat at a slightly different level Eco's move in positing a network of conventional associations to account for the production of a metaphor. Instead of explaining the original production of the metaphor by the author, however, we would be describing the production of a metaphorical reading by the reader. But there will still be the problem of distinguishing a metaphorical move from a metonymical move, essential from contingent relations, thought and perception from the mechanical operation of syntactic and phonological processes—with perhaps this difference, that a rhetoric focussed on persuasion rather than tropes will be engaged from the outset in an uncertain calculus, trying to account for effects of force which are never wholly predictable. This is in part because one can never construct a position outside tropology from which to view it; one's own terms are always caught up in the processes they attempt to describe. But it is in part also because the figurative is the name we give to effects of language that exceed, deform, or deviate from the code; codifications of previous excesses, deformations, and deviations only create opportunities for new turns.

11

Literary Theory in the Graduate Program

As the shrinking job market makes graduate study in English less attractive and as real or threatened budget cuts force departments to watch carefully the number of students in their various classes, there has been considerable debate about what should be done with graduate programs in English. Everyone agrees that other universities should cut back their graduate intake or eliminate their programs entirely, but there is little consensus about what should be done in the numerous programs that will remain. Addressing an Association of Departments of English meeting in 1977, William Schaefer urged a broadening and liberalizing of Ph.D. programs. If we teachers of English believe that the study of literature is a central and valuable experience, then we do ourselves and others a disservice by drawing a line between undergraduate and graduate studies, assuming that liberal education is appropriate only in the former and presenting the latter as a specialized activity suitable only for future teachers of English. If we have anything worthwhile to teach, it ought to be made available to those who have already received a B.A. as well as to those who have not. By devoting graduate programs exclusively to professional training, Schaefer argued, we have effectively destroyed the M.A. in most of the humanistic disciplines and have eliminated learning that we ought to be encouraging. 'We have got to liberalize our graduate as well as undergraduate programs and persuade ourselves and others that there is no answer to the question "how high is higher education?,"' making it possible for students to go as high as they can.[1]

Yet at the same time others have claimed that graduate programs should be more professional, should explicitly set out to offer thorough preparation for the teaching profession. John C. Gerber, in a visionary 'Glimpse of English as a Profession,' has reported that the flourishing English departments of the twenty-first century ('English professors are now associated in the public mind with lawyers and physicians,' a participant in an ADE seminar of 2,026 reports[2]) owe their triumph to their new professionalism, part of which is a long and rigorous graduate program 'devised to prepare the student for his or her profession.' Reinhard Kuhn, in an MLA talk entitled 'The Return to Basics in Graduate Studies,' has called for the reintroduction of those professional requirements (systematic coverage of a national literature, Latin, philological training) that have been allowed to lapse. 'The highly competitive market,' he argues, 'does present an ideal opportunity for imposing or reimposing the highest levels of achievement.'[3] This recommendation is seconded by John Algeo in an article called 'After the Fall: Some Observations on Graduate Curricula.' The paradise we have lost turns out to be the 1960s, when grants, graduate students, and jobs were plentiful. We cannot regain this happy state; we must go forward 'with wandering steps and slow,' but, Algeo advises, 'we can increase course requirements to encompass all of English language and literature.' 'Holders of the Ph.D.,' he concludes, 'should be equipped to teach any course in the undergraduate curriculum.'[4]

These two lines of thought are certainly incompatible, both in spirit and in their concrete proposals: liberalization versus rigorous professionalization. But it seems to me that each has a valid concern, to which one might hope to do justice. Neither side in this debate is likely to be satisfied by a compromise solution, but ought not to lie beyond the wit of man or chair to imagine courses of reading and study that would be both of interest in themselves as an extension of the liberal education begun at the undergraduate level, and of use in preparing students to teach universities. The kind of work that would make graduate study an extension of undergraduate education is not necessarily compatible with the sort of preparation our graduate students need today.

ments cannot take for granted large enrollments in traditional courses.

There are various possible responses to this situation, but most of those that are not simply nostalgic involve attempts to think seriously and creatively about literature in its relation to other kinds of writing and communication. Confronted with students for whom literature is simply one aspect of their culture, and an aspect with which they are relatively unfamiliar, teachers need to be able to discuss literature in its relations to more familiar cultural products and in its relations to other ways of writing about human experience, such as philosophy, psychology, sociology, anthropology, and history. Since students do not take for granted that literature is something they ought to study, teachers have to be able to relate literature to what they do take for granted or to alternative accounts of human experience in order to make apparent the virtues of literature as an object of study and a source of pleasure.

I am not suggesting that English departments should offer courses on other cultural creations—film, comic books, soap operas, science fiction. Such courses may be successful and intellectually respectable or they may not; each department must make its own decisions on such matters. I am not urging the addition of nonliterary courses to a literature program but rather am proposing something more fundamental yet also more obvious: that in planning literature courses teachers think of literature not as a hallowed sequence of works defined by literary history but as a species of writing, a mode of representation, that occupies a very problematic role in the cultures in which our students live. We often complain that students have not read enough when they come to college, but the problem is not a quantitative one that would be solved by more assigned readings. The problem is structural, involving the marginal situation of literature within the students' cultures. In combating or dealing with the cultural formation of today's undergraduates, Ph.D.s whose professional training has consisted of rigorous grounding in philology and a comprehensive chronological survey of English literature may be quite badly equipped for the tasks they face. Proper professional preparation ought perhaps to involve something other than a reimposition of the tough requirements and high standards of yesteryear.

Indeed, I have been suggesting that one thing that might help prepare teachers to find imaginative solutions to the problems that will confront them in the classroom would be extensive work on the relationship between literature and other forms of writing and modes of representation, and it is here that the requirements of professional training might coincide with the continuation of general education that William Schaefer wished to see in graduate programs. A liberal education is supposed to involve not just a knowledge of the great works of literature, though it should involve that, but an ability to see literature in relation to political, ethical, social, and psychological concerns, an ability to see literature in relation to the other forms and forces of one's culture. In *The Liberal Imagination* Lionel Trilling observed of 'our cultural situation' that, 'briefly put, it is that there exists a great gulf between our educated class and the best of our literature.'[5] Eliminating that gulf ought to be the goal both of general literary education as conducted at the undergraduate and graduate levels and of professional training for future teachers. In the time since Trilling wrote, this gulf has doubtless been widened or deepened by the tendency of literary critics to treat literature as a thing apart, something to be studied in and for itself.

I am not suggesting that there is nothing distinctive about literature, only that its distinctiveness, its privileged character, cannot be taken for granted, as some kind of given or inherent quality. If one is interested in the nature of literature, and such an interest seems central to the concerns of both a liberal education and a professional training in English, then the most strategic approach in graduate courses might be one that does not concentrate on literary works to the exclusion of all else but one that adopts a comparative perspective, comparing literature with other forms of discourse and other modes of representation.

One topic, for example, that enables us to focus on the qualities of literature by comparing it with other cultural products is narrative. Considerable work has been done in recent years on narration as a basic mode of intelligibility. W. B. Gallie has argued in *Philosophy and Historical Understanding* that the kind of understanding afforded by history writing involves not grasping causal laws but rather seeing how one thing leads to another as in a story.[6] In other areas as well, it can be shown that the notion of understanding can be explained in terms of following a story, perceiving a narrative pattern. Thus the question of what is a story or what are the basic patterns of narrative becomes the focus of a new and important inquiry, to which literary critics, with their interest in plot, can make important contributions. Indeed, as the domain in which plots are explicitly recognized as fictional constructs and in which authors frequently call attention to the qualities and effects of their plots, literature is the area in which plot structure is most easily and productively studied. Northrop Frye's account of plot structures or *mythoi*, Tzvetan Todorov's description of basic 'narrative transformations,' and Claude Bremond's characterization of plots in terms of essential 'life situations' can take their place with the work of Claude Lévi-Strauss and Hayden White as attempts to describe fundamental structures of experience: categories through which the meaning of events can be grasped.[7]

The study of basic narrative structures is one example of the way in which models and categories that are initially drawn from the study of literary works turn out to have wider implications and make possible productive investigations of the relationship between literature and other modes of ordering and representing experience. A course on narrative, which ought to include diverse narratives from a variety of fields, would doubtless lead to the discovery of complicated patterns of similarity and difference, since some 'literary narratives' are very like historical narratives, others resemble myths, and still others resemble autobiographical narratives. However, it is within such a context—the theory of narrative—that one can pose the question of the distinctiveness of literature while also demonstrating the centrality of literary structures to the organization of experience.

A second topic that could serve as the basis for course work at the graduate level is the revival of rhetoric and rhetorical categories to describe the production of meaning in discourse. Literature has often been thought of as the prime example of figurative language and therefore as the privileged object for rhetorical analysis, but it has become apparent in recent years that not only are other types of discourse inextricably involved with figurative language but rhetorical figures provide models that are applicable to discursive formations of all sorts. That is to say, rhetorical figures can be used to describe not just particular deviations from literal meaning but also basic strategies for producing meaning by establishing connexions and associations. Roman Jakobson's association of metaphor and metonymy with two types of aphasia (contiguity disorder and similarity disorder) and his claim that the development of a discourse may take place essentially through contiguity or through similarity are only the best known of various uses of tropological structures to describe the organization of discourse.[8] David Lodge has extensively explored the distinction between metaphorical and metonymic modes of writing in relation to the twentieth-century English novel.[9] Others, such as Hayden White in his analysis of the tropological moves by which historians construct their objects of study, have preferred a more elaborate scheme of categories, such as Kenneth Burke's 'four master tropes': metaphor, metonymy, synecdoche, and irony.[10] Each of these figures describes an operation that can occur at various levels of organization in a text. Metaphor, a comparison or substitution based on likeness, can be thought of, Burke says, as the use of *X* as a perspective on *Y*. Metonymy moves from one thing to another on the basis of contiguity and thus produces meaning and order by positing spatial or temporal series. Synecdoche, in contrast, is a totalizing figure, the common operation whereby a discourse infers qualities of the whole from the qualities of a part or extracts an essence from an example. Finally, irony produces meaning by the dialectical juxtaposition of opposites.

These basic devices or modes of inference and interpretation are often foregrounded in literature; we are accustomed to looking for them because we think of literary works as imaginative constructions, but we gain an enhanced sense of their power and importance when, having learned to discover them in literary works, we identify them as the constitutive structures of other discourses as well. Burke's success in analyzing the rhetorical structure of a great variety of writings is an indication of the fruitfulness of developing tropological models to describe the basic structures of discourse. One of the most fascinating areas of recent investigation, and one that would strengthen a graduate course on tropological structures, is the investigation of Freud's writings as simultaneously an analysis of tropes and a tropological construct.[11] Freud's own theory is, of course, an account of the tropological mechanisms of the psyche: the way it connects, substitutes, represses. His own writing, however, is itself a process of connecting, substituting, repressing that ought to be described. Even crucial concepts of psychoanalysis can be analyzed as tropological products. Jean Laplanche has argued, for example, that the ambiguity of the concept of the *ego* in Freud can be explained in terms of two different ways of deriving or producing the concept, one metaphorical and one metonymical.[12]

My purpose in citing these two cases is a simple one—to suggest that we can think about literature in its relation to other types of discourse by focusing on a theoretical topic, such as narrative or theory of tropes, that will enable us to do two things: first, to see the importance and pervasiveness of structures that we traditionally regard as 'literary' and thus to justify the importance that we think literary study ought to have; second, to make the distinctiveness of literary works not a quality that must be taken for granted from the outset but a variety of qualities that emerge as we consider basic ways of ordering experience. In other words, literary works will appear not as monuments of a specialized high culture but as powerful, elegant, self-conscious, or perhaps self-indulgent manifestations of common patterns of sense-making.

Focusing on topics that encompass other forms of discourse as well as literature would also enable us to draw on some of the most interesting and powerful work in contemporary criticism, which has been especially concerned with exploring the relations between the literary and nonliterary. Whether one thinks of the linguistically inspired study of sign systems, or of recent critical readings of Freud as a literary text, or of Paul de Man's studies of Rousseau's and Nietzsche's writings as allegories of reading, or of Jacques Derrida's deconstructive readings of a wide range of literary and philosophical texts, or even of critical and historical projects such as Edward Said's *Orientalism*, contemporary work in literary criticism seems to reach its greatest intensity when dealing with a theoretically defined problem that explores the relationship between the literary and the nonliterary. In fact, for those who are inclined to think of contemporary criticism as a battlefield on which advocates of various 'approaches' attempt to destroy one another, it is important to point out that most of these critical projects share this interest in the relationship between literary and nonliterary discourse. Indeed, one could go further and argue that to see contemporary critical theory as essentially a set of approaches or methods of interpretation is to miss the interest and force of these writings. As Irvin Ehrenpreis wrote in a dreary discussion of literary theory, 'when one tries to decide whether or not *The Golden Bowl* condemns Charlotte, at the end, to a terrible punishment, one will probably not reach a decision through an application of some grand analytical technique.'[13] If one's primary interest is in interpretive decisions of this sort, most literary theory will be of little use, though one will have to make certain theoretical decisions, such as whether evidence about authorial intention should count heavily in one's determination of meaning. Even when critical theory takes the form of a reading of particular texts, it is not an attempt to provide techniques to solve these local problems of interpretation. Literary theory is, rather, the study of problems about the nature of literature: its forms, its components, their relations. Literary theory is not a set of competing methods for the analysis of literary works—methods that are to be judged by their relevance to problems such as whether Charlotte is condemned—any more than linguistics is a set of competing models that are to be judged by their success in helping puzzled listeners understand obscure utterances. The relationship between a theory of language and the sentences and utterances of a language is comparable with the relationship between literary theory and literary works, in that the forms of the latter and our dealings with them are the objects of interest for the former.

Indeed, literary theory has an important role in the discipline of literary studies, not because it offers methods for discovering what works really mean, but because it deals with what is involved and what is at stake in literature and literary interpretation. It is striking that disagreement about any important issue in our profession is likely to emerge as a debate in the realm of literary theory involving claims about the nature of literature. For example, pedagogical questions about the relationship in the classroom between teacher, student, and work have been debated in discussions about what has come to be called 'reader-response criticism.' Stanley Fish's presentation of 'Affective Stylistics: Literature in the Reader' involved the claim that the literary work should be regarded not as an object whose properties the student seeks to know but rather as an experience of the reader, so that false starts, errors, changes of mind are to be thought of, not as undesirable experiences of ill-prepared students, but as part of the experience, and thus part of the meaning of the work.[14] What ever else it is, this is clearly an important proposal about the teaching of literature, about the sort of attitude and strategy that a teacher ought to adopt in a classroom. And other versions of reader-response criticism—from Norman Hollland's adaptation of American ego psychology and David Bleich's emphasis on the conversion of students' private feelings into elements of a collective investigation to Wolfgang Iser's emphasis on the normative role of an implied reader and Michael Riffaterre's account of powerful constraints that ought to lead the reader to respond in very precise ways to a text—all make different claims about the appropriate attitude for teachers to adopt in the classroom.[15]

These debates about the relationship between reader and text are not, of course, just arguments about pedagogy; but they are, it seems to me, the principal way in which questions of pedagogy have been argued in recent years. Those who wish to be aware of what is happening in our discipline and how it proposes to engage with students and with other aspects of our culture must at least be in a position to follow these debates. They must, in other words, be conversant with the problems and central concepts of literary theory.

But let me turn to the more practical question of how critical theory might fit into the discipline as it is represented in graduate study. Perhaps the favorite way of relating literary theory to the discipline is to offer some kind of seminar on 'methods' of literary criticism, in which beginning graduate students read a certain amount of theory. I do not want to suggest that such courses may not be extremely valuable to those who take them, and no doubt in departments where they provide the only context for literary theory they may be invaluable. But I do think that courses in which students read theorists as a series of 'approaches' to literary works are predicated on two interconnected but fallacious assumptions: that the function of literary theory is to make possible better interpretations of literary works; and that one cannot become a skilled interpreter without being exposed to the principal writings in literary theory.

Of course, it is true that acquaintance with literary theory will affect the way in which people write about literary works, but so may immersion in history, philosophy, astrology, or a love affair, and that does not mean that the function of these enterprises is to produce new interpretations of literary works. We may be inclined to think that this is the purpose of literary theory because we often assume, in part as the result of the New Criticism, that the goal of literary study in general is to produce interpretations of works; and with so many interpretations around today, the only way to produce a new, yet plausible interpretation may be to translate a work into the terms of a theory that is itself relatively new. But though professional requirements and assumptions about literary study force us to devise a plethora of new interpretations, we should not allow ourselves to forget that theories are not ways of solving interpretive problems, for problems always arise within the framework of a set of assumptions, and a new theory can only challenge or explain those assumptions, not add a supplementary tool to an interpreter's toolbox.

Instead of being presented as sampler courses preliminary to the real work of interpreting texts, courses in literary theory ought to be regarded as substantive courses on a topic or problem—on the nature of literary language or representation, or genre, or narrative, or tropes. In a small graduate program, where it is difficult to justify a number of courses of this kind, one ought to consider the possibility of arranging, in cooperation with other departments, courses to be taken by students in a number of fields. The English department could collaborate with other literature departments to produce a group of theory courses available to all students in literature, and, depending on the interests of colleagues in other disciplines, it might hope to work out cooperative arrangements with such departments as philosophy, linguistics, anthropology, sociology, and perhaps even psychology or history. The kind of course I envision is impossible so long as 'theory' is assumed to mean 'method'; it becomes conceivable, and practicable, if theory is treated as a series of substantive topics, such as the nature of narrative, myth, symbolic exchange, and speech acts.

But it would also be possible, instead of addressing unified topics, each of which straddles several disciplines, to adopt the comparative approach I suggested earlier, considering literature in relation to other forms of discourse. This is especially important, it seems to me, in universities where philosophy departments fail to teach traditional philosophy and psychology departments reject psychoanalysis, producing a situation in which central texts of the humanist tradition—Plato, Descartes, Hegel, Nietzsche, Freud—are neglected, unless they are taught in literature courses.

I recognize that this may seem a peculiar suggestion—to have English departments go 'outside the field' to teach what other departments neglect—but I want to argue that there can be a particular virtue in having psychoanalytic and philosophical texts taught in relation to literary texts. I say this not just because one should be alert to the literary elements in the texts of philosophy or psychoanalysis, for that presupposes the possibility of an authoritative distinction between literary and nonliterary elements. I want to suggest that the benefit of teaching psychoanalytic, literary, and philosophical texts in a comparative relationship is the discovery of certain qualities and operations of language, 'textuality' for short—a discovery facilitated by one's continual attempt, in a comparative perspective, to distinguish between literary and nonliterary discourse.

First, why philosophical and literary texts? In an important sense they belong together. Philosophy and literature exist only by distinguishing themselves one from the other. One could argue that philosophy has always depended for its existence on a notion of literary discourse and that the move which represses or ignores the signifier and sets aside certain kinds of language as fictional or rhetorical, with an oblique and problematic relationship to truth, is the gesture by which philosophy, since Plato, has exorcized certain problems and defined itself. This positing of an opposition between the philosophical and the literary has been philosophy's way of recognizing (and containing) the threat that language poses to its activities. Philosophy conjures that threat by conceiving of another realm where language can be as linguistic as it likes and then treating that realm as derivative, problematical, nonserious. Philosophy has often dreamed of pure, logical means of expression that would protect it from the machinations and metaphoricity of words.

But it is always possible to read a philosophical text not as truth but as act—as act of persuasion, narrative, trope, rhetoric. Because language can always be read referentially or rhetorically, philosophy needs to constitute itself in opposition to the literary, but it can never avoid the possibility of being read as rhetoric. Indeed, one could argue that reading a philosophical text as rhetoric is *the authentic* philosophical move: to read a philosophical text as rhetoric is to put in question its concepts, to treat them as textual strategies or tropes.

This is, for example, what logical positivists did in analyzing the discourse of metaphysics and attempting to show that it was ungrounded, fictional, metaphorical, a kind of literature. It is also the strategy Nietzsche employed in his analyses of cause and effect as a metonymy, of truth as metaphor whose metaphoricity has been forgotten, and of the identity principle as a rhetorical imposition, a synecdoche.[16]

I am claiming that the authentic philosophical move, the move that may affect the history of philosophy, is an attempt at a literary or rhetorical reading of philosophical discourse; conversely, one can maintain that literature, though it identifies itself as fiction, as rhetoric, nevertheless elicits a reading that seeks to make it meaningful, true. Conventions of literary reading, such as our ways of interpreting metaphors, are a repertoire of techniques for naturalizing literary discourse at the appropriate level, a level at which the language can be significant and explore important truths about man and the world.

Both philosophy and literature, which exist through the tension between them, are inescapably dependent on the undecidable rhetorical status of language, the possibility of moving between the performative and the constative modes. The exploration of textual activity is best carried out, I am arguing, when one encounters the dialectic between the literary and the philosophical. The most important contemporary example of this encounter is, of course, the work of Jacques Derrida, whose readings suggest that so-called philosophical texts are most acute and precise when their figures and their rhetorical strategies are given close attention and, conversely, that texts usually identified as 'literary' reveal powerful philosophical deconstructions once the functioning of their special logics, such as the logic of *supplementarity* or *marginality*, is identified.[17]

If this is the nature of the interplay between literature and philosophy, what of the relationship between literature and psychoanalysis. I can make my point most clearly, I believe, by saying that there are two views of psychoanalysis. According to the first, the analyst gathers information about the patient's dreams, memories, and feelings, and then, armed with the metalanguage of psychoanalytic theory, produces an interpretation of this material, an interpretation that reveals the truth of the patient's condition. This view of psychoanalysis as an authoritative interpretive metalanguage is the one usually at work in psychoanalytic criticism: the theory is applied either to the work as a symptomatic biographical document or to the language and behavior of the characters in order to produce an interpretation.

This is certainly the common conception of psychoanalysis. But, as Freud observes, when the analyst armed with his theoretical knowledge encounters the patient, a remarkable thing happens. The analyst asks the patient to provide the material for interpretation, to reveal even details that seem to him completely trivial and nonsensical:

But it is far from being the case that his ego is content to play the part of passively and obediently bringing us the material we require and of believing and accepting our translation of it. A number of other things happen, a few of which we might have foreseen but others of which are bound to surprise us. The most remarkable thing is this. The patient is not satisfied with regarding the analyst in the light of reality as a helper and adviser who, moreover, is remunerated for the trouble he takes and who would himself be content with some such role as that of a guide on a difficult mountain climb. On the contrary, the patient sees in him the return, the reincarnation, of some important figure out of his childhood or past, and consequently transfers on to him feelings and reactions which undoubtedly applied to this prototype. This fact of transference soon proves to be a factor of undreamt-of importance, on the one hand an instrument of irreplaceable value on the other hand a source of serious dangers. [18]

Transference is important, as Freud says, because the patient in repeating with the analyst a crucial relationship from his past reveals the truth of his past; it is dangerous because the analyst finds himself in a position of special authority and is tempted to exercise that authority to advance the cure, but it is essential, Freud insists, that the analyst resist this temptation lest he repeat the mistakes of the parent whose position of authority he now occupies.

Now if, as Freud's discussion suggests, the truth of the unconscious is revealed not by the metalanguage of the analyst but by the position in which he finds himself placed during interaction with the patient, then we have a strange reversal: a relationship (analyst to patient) that was thought to be cognitive turns out to be performative. The interpreter who was expected to master the text from a position of detachment and scientific authority discovers that he has become involved in such a way that his authority is of a very different kind; a relationship has been produced that he has not sought or controlled, but it is precisely this relationship in which he finds himself involved that reveals the most important aspects of the cause by enacting or reenacting them.

If we now think about psychoanalysis, thus understood, and its relationship to literature, we can see that transference might also be central here. Rather than suggest that psychoanalysis is a body of theory whose scientific authority enables it to reveal the truth of literature, we might note that much of its authority derives precisely from its repetition of powerful literary narratives and relations—the oedipal drama, the Narcissus myth. The relationship between *Oedipus the King* and Freud's *Interpretation of Dreams*, for example, can be studied as an act of transference, in which Freud's quest for meanings and origins repeats in uncanny ways the oedipal quest he seeks to interpret. [19] Awareness of the centrality of transference, recognition that the truth of a text may lie not in what an authoritative interpreter says about it but in the interpreter's unexpected relationship to it, makes possible a subtle and fruitful investigation of the problems of interpretation posed by the conjuncture of literature and psychoanalysis:

There is another point on which literature can inform psychoanalytical discourse in such a way as to deconstruct the temptation of the master's position and the master–slave pattern. There is one crucial feature which is constitutive of literature but is essentially lacking in psychoanalytical theory, and indeed in theory as such: irony. Since irony precisely consists in dragging authority as such into a scene which it cannot master, of which it is *not aware* and which, for that very reason, is the scene of its own self-destruction, literature, by virtue of its ironic force, fundamentally deconstructs the fantasy of authority in the same way, and for the same reasons, that psychoanalysis deconstructs the authority of the fantasy—its claim to belief and to power as the sole window through which we behold and perceive reality, as the sole window through which reality can indeed reach our grasp, enter into our consciousness. Psychoanalysis tells us that the fantasy is a fiction, and that consciousness is itself, in a sense, a fantasy-effect. In the same way, literature tells us that authority is a *language effect*, the product or the creation of its own *rhetorical power*: that authority is the *power of fiction*. [20]

I am suggesting that there is a lot to be learned from the interaction of these two types of discourse. Psychoanalysis is not a way of solving literary problems, since to every claim that psychoanalysis can master literature one can reply that literature, with its manipulation of irony, can comprehend and master psychoanalysis. Let me emphasize this point, since the work of theorists often seems to imply that a chosen discipline—philosophy, psychoanalysis, linguistics—has the power and authority to account for literature. I am claiming, on the contrary, that literature can illuminate and situate the problems addressed by these disciplines by offering a perspective that consists primarily of awareness of rhetorical structures and forces, awareness of textuality.

What emerges through this reading of literary and nonliterary texts is *literary theory*. By posing through this kind of reading the problem of the relationship between the concrete and exemplary dramas of literature and the more abstract claims of philosophical and psychoanalytic discourse, we can both give literary theory its appropriate place in the discipline of literary studies and offer courses that embody the central concerns of humanistic education. Such courses might also help to make graduate study in English the exciting activity that it ought to be.

References

Preface

1 Barbara Johnson, 'The Critical Difference', *Diacritics*, 8:2 (1978) p. 3.

1 Beyond Interpretation

1 R. S. Crane, *The Languages of Criticism and the Structure of Poetry*, University of Toronto Press, 1953, pp. 123–4.
2 Northrop Frye, *Anatomy of Criticism*, New York, Atheneum, 1965, p. 16.
3 Ibid., p. 11.
4 Ibid., pp. 17–18.
5 Frederick Crews, *The Sins of the Fathers*, New York, Oxford University Press, p. 263.
6 See Shoshana Felman, 'Turning the Screw of Interpretation,' *Yale French Studies*, 55/56 (1977) pp. 94–207, and Cynthia Chase, 'Oedipal Textuality: Reading Freud's Reading of *Oedipus*,' *Diacritics*, 9:1 (Spring 1979) pp. 54–71, for excellent discussions and applications.
7 Leo Bersani, *Baudelaire and Freud*, Berkeley, University of California Press, 1977.
8 W. K. Wimsatt, *The Verbal Icon*, Lexington, Kentucky, University of Kentucky Press, 1954, p. 21.
9 Stanley Fish, *Self-Consuming Artifacts*, Berkeley, University of California Press, 1972, pp. 387–8.
10 Fish's later book, *The Living Temple: George Herbert and Catechizing*, Berkeley, University of California Press, 1978, combines a description of readers' responses to Herbert's poems with a historical thesis about Herbert's model of organization. The redescription of response alone would not suffice to produce a new and valuable interpretation.

11 Fredric Jameson, *Marxism and Form*, Princeton University Press, 1971, p. 341.
12 Ibid., p. 374.
13 See Hans Robert Jauss, *Literaturgeschichte als Provokation*, Frankfurt, Suhrkamp, 1970, and in English, 'Literary History as a Challenge to Literary Theory,' *New Directions in Literary History*, ed. Ralph Cohen, Baltimore, Johns Hopkins University Press, 1974, pp. 11–41.
14 Geoffrey Hartman, 'History-writing as Answerable Style,' in ibid., p. 100.
15 Paul de Man, *Blindness and Insight*, New York, Oxford University Press, 1971, p. 165.
16 Harold Bloom, *The Anxiety of Influence*, New York, Oxford University Press, 1973, p. 70.
17 Jacques Derrida, *Of Grammatology*, Baltimore, Johns Hopkins University Press, 1976, part II, ch. 2. For further discussion, see Jonathan Culler, *On Deconstruction: Literary Theory in the 1970s*, Ithaca, Cornell University Press/London, Routledge & Kegan Paul, forthcoming.
18 Paul de Man, *Blindness and Insight*, ch. 7, pp. 102–41.
19 J. Hillis Miller, 'Deconstructing the Deconstructors,' *Diacritics*, 5:2 (Summer 1975) pp. 30–1.
20 See Paul de Man, *Allegories of Reading*, New Haven, Yale University Press, 1979; and Barbara Johnson, *Défigurations du langage poétique*, Paris, Flammarion, 1979.
21 E. D. Hirsch, 'Carnal Knowledge,' *New York Review of Books*, 26:10 (14 June 1979) p. 20.

2   In Pursuit of Signs

1 Ferdinand de Saussure, *Cours de linguistique générale*, 3rd edn, Paris, Payot, 1967, p. 33.
2 Charles Sanders Peirce, *Collected Papers*, 8 vols, Cambridge, Mass., Harvard University Press, 1931–58, vol. V, p. 448.
3 Ibid., vol. II, p. 276. See Thomas Sebeok, 'Iconicity,' *MLN*, 91:6 (December 1976) pp. 1457–72; and Michael McCanles, 'Conventions of the Natural and the Naturalness of Conventions,' *Diacritics*, 7:3 (Fall 1977) pp. 54–63.
4 Ernst Cassirer, 'Structuralism in Modern Linguistics,' *Word*, 1:1 (1945) p. 99.
5 Peirce, *Collected Papers*, vol. VII, p. 570.
6 Claude Lévi-Strauss, *Tristes Tropiques*, Paris, Union générale d'éditions, 1962, p. 43.
7 Ibid., p. 44.
8 Claude Lévi-Strauss, *Anthropologie structurale*, Paris, Plon, 1958, p. 40. The article first appeared in *Word* in 1945.

9 Claude Lévi-Strauss, *Le Totémisme aujourd'hui*, Paris, Presses Universitaires de France, 1962, p. 44.

10 Claude Lévi-Strauss, *Le Cru et le cuit*, Paris, Plon, 1966, p. 18.

11 Ibid., p. 20.

12 Michel Foucault, *Les Mots et les choses*, Paris, Gallimard, 1966, p. 15.

13 Claude Lévi-Strauss, *La Pensée sauvage*, Paris, Plon, 1962, p. 326.

14 Michel Foucault, *L'Archéologie du savoir*, Paris, Gallimard, 1969, p. 22.

15 Jean-Marie Benoist, *La Révolution structurale*, Paris, Grasset, 1975, p. 16.

16 Umberto Eco, *A Theory of Semiotics*, Bloomington, Indiana University Press, 1976, pp. 9–13.

17 Julia Kristeva, *Semiotiké*, Paris, Seuil, 1969, p. 30.

18 Gérard Genette, 'Discours du récit,' *Figures*, vol. III, Paris, Seuil, 1972.

19 See Jonathan Culler, *Saussure*, London, Fontana, 1976/New York, Penguin, 1977, ch. 2.

20 See Jonathan Culler, *On Deconstruction*, Ithaca, Cornell University Press, forthcoming.

21 Jacques Derrida, 'La Mythologie blanche,' *Marges de la philosophie*, Paris, Minuit, 1972.

22 This program for literary criticism is announced in different tones by Paul de Man, 'Semiology and Rhetoric,' *Diacritics*, 3:3 (Fall 1973) p. 32; and J. Hillis Miller, 'Stevens' Rock and Criticism as Cure,' part II, *Georgia Review*, 30:2 (Summer 1976) p. 405.

3 Semiotics as a Theory of Reading

1 Norman H. Holland, *Five Readers Reading*, New Haven, Yale University Press, 1975, p. 44.

2 Frederick C. Crews, 'Reductionism and its Discontents,' *Critical Inquiry*, 1:3 (March 1975) p. 554.

3 Hans Robert Jauss, 'Literary History as a Challenge to Literary Theory,' in *New Directions in Literary History*, ed. Ralph Cohen, Baltimore, Johns Hopkins University Press, 1974, p. 13.

4 Karl Popper, 'Naturgezetze und theoretische Systeme,' in *Theorie und Realität*, ed. Hans Albert, Tubingen, Mohn, 1972, p. 49.

5 Jauss, 'Literary History as a Challenge to Literary Theory,' p. 16.

6 Ibid., pp. 38–41.

7 Hans Robert Jauss, 'Racines und Goethes Iphigenie—Mit einem Nachwort über die Partialität der rezeptionsästhetischen Methode,' in *Rezeptionsästhetik*, ed. Rainer Warning, Munich, Fink, 1975, p. 355.

8 Hans Robert Jauss, 'La Douceur du foyer: The Lyric of the Year 1857 as a Pattern for the Communication of Social Norms,' *Romanic Review*, 65:3 (May 1974) pp. 207, 210.

9 Jauss, 'Racines und Goethes Iphigenie,' p. 385.
10 See Hans Robert Jauss, *Asthetische Erfahrung und literarische Hermeneutik*, vol. I, Munich, Fink, 1977.
11 Tzvetan Todorov, *Introduction à la littérature fantastique*, Paris, Seuil, 1970.
12 See Jonathan Culler, *Flaubert: The Uses of Uncertainty*, Ithaca, Cornell University Press/London, Elek, 1974, pp. 212–25; and Veronica Forrest-Thomson, 'The Ritual of Reading *Salammbô*,' *Modern Language Review*, 67:4 (October 1972).
13 Sir Walter Scott, 'The Novels of Ernest Theodore Hoffmann,' *Miscellaneous Works*, Edinburgh, Black, 1870, vol. 18, p. 292.
14 Scott, 'Remarks on Frankenstein,' *Miscellaneous Works*, vol. 18, p. 254.
15 Ivor Indyk, 'Reading Conventions: An Examination of the Problem of Interpretative Relevance, with Special Reference to Richardson's *Pamela* and Fielding's *Tom Jones*,' Unpublished PhD thesis, University College, London, 1980, pp. 270–426.
16 Hayden White, *Metahistory: The Historical Imagination in Nineteenth-Century Europe*, Baltimore, Johns Hopkins University Press, 1973. See also Hayden White, *Tropics of Discourse*, Baltimore, Johns Hopkins University Press, 1978.
17 See Jonathan Culler, 'Literary History, Allegory, and Semiology,' *New Literary History* 7 (Winter 1976) p. 283.
18 See, for example, Paul de Man, *Allegories of Reading*, New Haven, Yale University Press, 1979, part II, for Rousseau; and Cynthia Chase, 'The Accidents of Disfiguration: Limits to Literal and Rhetorical Reading in Book V of *The Prelude*,' *Studies in Romanticism*, 18:4 (Winter 1979) pp. 547–66.
19 White, *Metahistory*, p. 317. See Hans Kellner, 'The Inflatable Trope as Narrative Theory: Structure or Allegory,' *Diacritics* 10:4 (Winter 1980).
20 Kellner, 'The Inflatable Trope.'
21 See also de Man, *Allegories of Reading*, ch. 4.
22 Susan R. Horton, *Interpreting Interpreting: Interpreting Dickens' 'Dombey'*, Baltimore, Johns Hopkins University Press, 1979, pp. 68–72.
23 Ibid., p. 17.
24 Stephen Mailloux, '*The Red Badge of Courage* and Interpretive Conventions: Critical Response to a Maimed Text,' *Studies in the Novel*, 10 (1978) p. 49.
25 Stanley Fish, *Surprised by Sin: The Reader in Paradise Lost*, 2nd edn, Berkeley, University of California Press, 1971. For discussion see Chapter 6.
26 William Blake, *Complete Writings*, ed. Geoffrey Keynes, London, Oxford University Press, 1966, p. 216.
27 S. Foster Damon, *William Blake: His Philosophy and Symbols*, London, Dawsons, 1969, p. 283.

28 Geoffrey Keynes (ed.), *Songs of Innocence and Experience*, London, Rupert Hart-Davis, 1967, plate 46.
29 Mark Schorer, *William Blake: The Politics of Vision*, New York, Vintage, 1959, p. 212.
30 Heather Glen, 'The Poet in Society: Blake and Wordsworth on London,' *Literature and History*, 2 (May 1976) p. 10.
31 E. D. Hirsch, *Innocence and Experience*, New Haven, Yale University Press, 1964, p. 94.
32 Keynes (ed.), *Songs of Innocence and Experience*, plate 46.
33 D. G. Gillham, *Blake's Contrary States*, Cambridge University Press, 1966, p. 12.
34 Bernard Blackstone, *English Blake*, Hamden, Connecticut, Archon Books, 1966, p. 314.
35 Hazard Adams, *William Blake: A Reading of the Shorter Poems*, Seattle, University of Washington Press, 1963, p. 282.
36 Harold Bloom, *The Visionary Company*, New York, Doubleday, 1961, p. 42.
37 Martin Price, *To the Palace of Wisdom*, Carbondale, Southern Illinois University Press, 1964, p. 401.
38 Thomas Edwards, *Imagination and Power*, London, Chatto & Windus, 1971, p. 143.
39 See Barbara H. Smith's excellent *Poetic Closure: A Study of How Poems End*, University of Chicago Press, 1968.
40 Edwards, *Imagination and Power*, p. 132.
41 Hirsch, *Innocence and Experience*, p. 265.
42 Adams, *William Blake*, p. 285.
43 Kenneth R. Johnson, 'Blake's Cities: Romantic Forms of Urban Renewal,' in *Blake's Visionary Forms Dramatic*, ed. D. Erdman and John Grant, Princeton University Press, 1970, p. 417; Hirsch, *Innocence and Experience*, pp. 93–4; Damon, *William Blake*, p. 283.
44 Price, *To the Palace of Wisdom*, p. 401.

4 Riffaterre and the Semiotics of Poetry

1 Michael Riffaterre, *Semiotics of Poetry*, Bloomington, Indiana University Press, 1978. References for all quotations from this book will be identified by page numbers in the text.
2 Riffaterre, *Essais de stylistique structurale*, Paris, Flammarion, 1971. For discussion see my review in the *Journal of Linguistics*, 8:1 (February 1972) pp. 177–83.
3 Arthur Rimbaud, *Oeuvres*, ed. Antoine Adam, Paris, Gallimard, 1972, pp. 83–4.
4 Charles Baudelaire, *Les Fleurs du Mal*, ed. Antoine Adam, Paris, Garnier, 1961, p. 78.

5 See Michael Riffaterre, 'The Self-sufficient Text,' *Diacritics*, 3 (Fall 1973) pp. 39–45.

5 Presupposition and Intertextuality

1 Roland Barthes, *S/Z*, Paris, Seuil, 1970, p. 16.
2 Roland Barthes, 'De l'oeuvre au texte,' *Revue d'esthétique* (1971) p. 229.
3 Julia Kristeva, *Semiotiké*, Paris, Seuil, 1969, p. 146.
4 Laurent Jenny, 'La Stratégie de la forme,' *Poétique*, 27 (1976) p. 257.
5 Ibid., p. 262.
6 Ibid., p. 263.
7 Julia Kristeva, *La Révolution du langage poétique*, Paris, Seuil, 1974, pp. 388–9.
8 Kristeva, *Semiotiké*, p. 225.
9 Ibid., p. 194.
10 Kristeva, *La Révolution du langage poétique*, pp. 337–58.
11 Ibid., p. 343.
12 Kristeva, *Semiotiké*, p. 257.
13 Harold Bloom, *Poetry and Repression*, New Haven, Yale University Press, 1976, pp. 2–3.
14 Harold Bloom, *A Map of Misreading*, New York, Oxford University Press, 1975, p. 32.
15 Bloom, *Poetry and Repression*, p. 2.
16 Harold Bloom, *The Anxiety of Influence*, New York, Oxford University Press, 1973, pp. 86, 85, 30.
17 Neil Hertz, 'The Notion of Blockage in the Literature of the Sublime,' in *Psychoanalysis and the Question of the Text*, ed. G. Hartman, Baltimore, Johns Hopkins University Press, 1978, p. 76.
18 Edward L. Keenan, 'Two Types of Presupposition in Natural Language,' in *Studies in Linguistic Semantics*, ed. Charles Filmore and D. Terence Langendoen, New York, Holt, Rinehart & Winston, 1971, p. 45.
19 See ibid., pp. 46–8, for discussion and examples.
20 Charles Baudelaire, *Oeuvres complètes*, ed. Y. Le Dantec and C. Pichois, Paris, Gallimard, p. 70.
21 Ibid., p. 7.
22 Ted Hughes, *Selected Poems*, London, Faber, 1972, p. 25.
23 William Blake, *Complete Writings*, ed. Geoffrey Keynes, Oxford University Press, 1966, p. 214.
24 Baudelaire, *Oeuvres complètes*, p. 112.
25 Keenan, 'Two types of Presupposition in Natural Language,' p. 49.
26 For discussion of the relevance of speech-act theory, see Stanley Fish, 'How to Do Things with Austin and Searle,' *MLN*, 91 (1976); and Mary

Louise Pratt, *Toward a Speech Act Theory of Literature*, Bloomington, Indiana University Press, 1977.
27 Paul Valéry, *Oeuvres*, ed. J. Hytier, Paris, Gallimard, 1957, vol. I, p. 1439.

6 Stanley Fish and the Righting of the Reader

1 Stanley Fish, *Self-Consuming Artifacts: The Experience of Seventeenth-century Literature*, Berkeley, University of California Press, 1972, pp. 387–8.
2 Stanley Fish, 'What is Stylistics and Why are They Saying Such Terrible Things About It?,' *Approaches to Poetics*, ed. Seymour Chatman, New York, Columbia University Press, 1973, p. 148.
3 Ibid., p. 149.
4 Ibid., p. 151.
5 Fish, *Self-Consuming Artifacts*, p. 406.
6 Ibid., p. 1.
7 Stanley Fish, *Surprised by Sin: The Reader in Paradise Lost*, 2nd edn, Berkeley, University of California Press, 1971, p. 1.

7 Apostrophe

1 Quintilian, *Institutio Oratoria*, IV, i, 63.
2 M. H. Abrams, 'Structure and Style in the Greater Romantic Lyric,' in *Romanticism and Consciousness*, ed. H. Bloom, New York, Norton, 1970, pp. 201–29; Earl Wasserman, *The Subtler Language*, Baltimore, Johns Hopkins University Press, 1959.
3 George N. Shuster, *The English Ode from Milton to Keats*, New York, Columbia University Press, 1940, pp. 11–12.
4 Ibid., p. 255.
5 Northrop Frye, *Anatomy of Criticism*, Princeton University Press, 1957, pp. 249–50.
6 Pierre Fontanier, *Les Figures du discours* (1830), Paris, Flammarion, 1968, p. 372.
7 William Blake, *Complete Writings*, ed. Geoffrey Keynes, Oxford University Press, 1966, p. 1.
8 Geoffrey Hartman, *Beyond Formalism*, New Haven, Yale University Press, 1959, p. 193.
9 Harold Bloom, *Shelley's Mythmaking*, New Haven, Yale University Press, 1959, p. 75.
10 John Keats, 'Sleep and Poetry,' *The Poems of John Keats*, ed. Jack Stillinger, Cambridge, Mass., Harvard University Press, 1978, p. 72, lines 136–8.

11 W. H. Auden, 'In Memory of W. B. Yeats,' *Selected Poems*, London, Faber, 1979, p. 82.

12 Alphonse de Lamartine, *Oeuvres poétiques*, Paris, Gallimard, 1963, p. 392.

13 Charles Baudelaire, 'Spleen,' *Les Fleurs du Mal*, ed. Antoine Adam, Paris, Garnier, 1961, p. 79.

14 Jean-Jacques Rousseau, 'Monuments de l'histoire de ma vie,' *Oeuvres autobiographiques*, Paris, Seuil, 1967, p. 74.

15 Bloom, *Shelley's Mythmaking*, p. 84.

16 Walt Whitman, *Works*, New York, Funk & Wagnalls, 1968, vol. II, p. 293.

17 John Keats, 'Ode to a Nightingale,' *The Poems of John Keats*, p. 372.

18 Baudelaire, 'Le Cygne,' *Les Fleurs du Mal*, pp. 95–6.

19 R. M. Rilke, *Duino Elegies*, trans. J. B. Leishman and Stephen Spender, New York, Norton, 1939, p. 77.

20 Rilke, *Selected Works*, trans. J. B. Leishman, London, Faber, 1960, p. 38.

21 Paul de Man, *Allegories of Reading*, New Haven, Yale University Press, 1979, p. 29.

22 Percy Bysshe Shelley, 'On Life,' *Shelley's Prose*, ed. D. L. Clark, Albuquerque, University of New Mexico Press, 1954, p. 174.

23 Shelley, 'A Defense of Poetry,' ibid., p. 281.

24 Percy Bysshe Shelley, 'Adonais,' *Complete Poetical Works*, ed. T. Hutchinson, Oxford University Press, 1904, pp. 432–41.

25 W. B. Yeats, 'Among School Children,' *Variorum Edition of the Poems of W. B.Yeats*, London, Macmillan, 1940, pp. 445–6.

26 William Wordsworth, 'Elegiac Stanzas, Suggested by a Picture of Peele Castle,' *The Poems*, ed. John Haydon, Harmondsworth, Penguin, 1977, vol. I, p. 641.

27 Paul de Man, 'Autobiography as Defacement,' *MLN*, 94 (1979) p. 928.

28 Keats, 'This Living Hand,' *The Poems of John Keats*, p. 503.

8 The Mirror Stage

1 M. H. Abrams, *The Mirror and the Lamp*, New York, Oxford University Press, 1953. Quotations from this work will be identified by page numbers in the text.

2 For discussion see Jacques Lacan, 'Le stade du miroir comme formateur de la fonction du Je,' *Ecrits*, Paris, Seuil, 1966, pp. 93–100.

3 Jacques Derrida, *Positions*, Paris, Minuit, 1972, p. 15. For deconstructive readings of romantic theory, see Jacques Derrida, 'Economimesis,' *Mimesis des articulations*, ed. Sylviane Agacinski *et al.*, Paris, Aubier-Flammarion, 1975, pp. 55–93. Among deconstructive readings of romantic literature are Paul de Man, *Allegories of Reading*, New

Haven, Yale University Press, 1979, part II; Cynthia Chase, 'The Accidents of Disfiguration: Limits to Literal and Rhetorical Reading in Book V of *The Prelude*,' *Studies in Romanticism*, 18 (Winter 1979), pp. 547–65; and Richard Rand, 'Geraldine,' *Glyph*, 3 (1978).

4 S. T. Coleridge, *Biographia Literaria*, London, Dent, 1956, p. 167.
5 S. T. Coleridge, *Shakespeare Criticism*, ed. T. M. Raysor, London, Constable, 1930, vol. I, p. 223.
6 M. H. Abrams, *Natural Supernaturalism*, Oxford University Press, 1971, pp. 65–6.
7 For an acute analysis of the theological nature of the freedom that is at stake in 'purposive wholes without purpose,' see Derrida, 'Econo-mimesis.'
8 Ernst Cassirer, *The Philosophy of the Enlightenment*, Boston, Beacon, 1966, p. 124.
9 W. B. Yeats, 'Introduction,' *Oxford Book of Modern Verse*, Oxford University Press, 1936, p. xxxiii.
10 Ibid., pp. xxvii–xxx.
11 Abrams, *Natural Supernaturalism*, pp. 19–32.
12 W. B. Yeats, 'The Statues,' *Collected Poems of W. B. Yeats*, New York, Macmillan, 1956, p. 322.
13 See Lacan, 'Le stade du miroir'.
14 William Wordsworth, 'Essay on Epitaphs III,' *Wordsworth's Literary Criticism*, ed. W. J. B. Owen, London, Routledge & Kegan Paul, 1974, p. 154.
15 For further discussion see Derrida, 'Economimesis,' and Jonathan Culler, *On Deconstruction: Literary Theory in the 1970s*, Ithaca, Cornell University Press/Routlege & Kegan Paul, forthcoming, ch. 2.

9 Story and Discourse in the Analysis of Narrative

1 For a bibliography and useful synthesis, see Seymour Chatman, *Story and Discourse: Narrative Structure in Fiction and Film*, Ithaca, Cornell University Press, 1978. For more recent discussions and further bibliography, see the three issues of *Poetics Today* devoted to narrative: 1:3 (1980), 1:4 (1980) and 2:2 (1981).
2 Mieke Bal, *Narratologie: essai sur la signification narrative dans quatre romans moderns*, Paris, Klincksieck, 1977, p. 6.
3 Ibid., p. 4.
4 Sigmund Freud, *The Interpretation of Dreams*, New York, Avon, 1965, p. 295.
5 Sophocles, *Oedipus the King*, translated with a commentary by Thomas Gould, Englewood Cliffs, N.J., Prentice-Hall, 1970, lines 842–7.
6 See Sandor Goodhart, 'Oedipus and Laius's Many Murderers,' *Diacritics*, 8:1 (Spring 1978) pp. 55–71.

7 See Cynthia Chase, 'Oedipal Textuality: Reading Freud's Reading of *Oedipus,'* *Diacritics*, 9:1 (Spring 1979) p. 58.

8 Cynthia Chase, 'The Decomposition of the Elephants: Double-Reading *Daniel Deronda,'* *PMLA*, 93:2 (March 1978) p. 218.

9 Ibid., p. 215.

10 This is a simplification of a more complex account in Peter Brooks, 'Fictions of the Wolfman,' *Diacritics*, 9:1 (Spring 1979), pp. 75–6.

11 Sigmund Freud, *The Wolfman and Sigmund Freud*, Harmondsworth, Penguin, 1973, p. 220.

12 Brooks, 'Fictions of the Wolfman,' p. 78; Freud, *The Wolfman*, p. 221.

13 Freud, *The Wolfman*, p. 223.

14 Ibid., p. 260.

15 Brooks, 'Fictions of the Wolfman,' p. 77. See also Brooks, 'Freud's Masterplot: Questions of Narrative,' *Yale French Studies*, 55/56 (1977) pp. 280–300.

16 Freud, *Totem and Taboo*, New York, Norton, 1950, p. 16.

17 Ibid., p. 161.

18 E. M. Forster, *Aspects of the Novel*, Harmondsworth, Penguin, 1962, p. 93.

19 Friedrich Nietzsche, *Werke*, ed. Karl Schlechta, Munich, Hanser Verlag, 1956, vol. 3, pp. 804–5. For discussion see Jonathan Culler, *On Deconstruction: Literary Theory in the 1970s*, Ithaca, Cornell University Press/Routledge & Kegan Paul, forthcoming, ch. 2.

20 William Labov, *Language in the Inner City*, University of Pennsylvania Press, 1972, p. 360.

21 Ibid., p. 366.

22 Ibid.

23 William Labov, 'Narrative Analysis: Oral Versions of Personal Experience,' *Essays on the Verbal and Visual Arts: Proceedings of the American Ethnological Society* (1966) pp. 37–9.

10   The Turns of Metaphor

1 Several recent examples, and there are doubtless others, are: Conference on Metaphor and Thought, University of Illinois, September 1977; Symposium on Metaphor, University of Chicago, February 1978; Interdisciplinary Conference on Metaphor, University of California at Davis, April 1978; Conference on Philosophy and Metaphor, University of Geneva, June 1978. *New Literary History*, 6:1 (1974) and *Critical Inquiry*, 5:1 (1978) are devoted to metaphor.

2 Stephen Ullmann, *Language and Style*, Oxford, Blackwell, 1964, p. 178.

3 Ibid., pp. 177–8.

4 Roman Jakobson, *Fundamentals of Language*, The Hague, Mouton, 1956, p. 76.

5 Stephen Ullmann, *Style in the French Novel*, Oxford, Blackwell, 1964, pp. 196–207.
6 Gérard Genette, 'Métonymie chez Proust,' *Figures III*, Paris, Seuil, 1972, pp. 42–3.
7 Ibid., p. 42.
8 Ibid., pp. 55–8.
9 Marcel Proust, *A la recherche du temps perdu*, Paris, Gallimard, 1954, vol. 3, p. 889.
10 Ibid., vol. 1, p. 83.
11 Ibid.
12 Paul de Man, *Allegories of Reading*, New Haven, Yale University Press, 1979, pp. 65–6.
13 Ibid., p. 67.
14 Jakobson, *Fundamentals of Language*, p. 81.
15 Umberto Eco, *The Role of the Reader*, Bloomington, Indiana University Press, 1979, p. 68.
16 Ibid., p. 72.
17 For discussion see David Lodge, *The Modes of Modern Writing*, Ithaca, Cornell University Press, 1977, pp. 73–124.
18 Eco, *The Role of the Reader*, p. 78.
19 See de Man, *Allegories of Reading*, ch. 7.
20 Friedrich Nietzsche, *Werke*, ed. Karl Schlechta, Munich, Hanser Verlag, 1956, vol. 3, p. 311.
21 Pierre Fontanier, *Les Figures du discours* (1821), Paris, Flammarion, 1968, pp. 213–14.
22 Donald Davidson, 'What Metaphors Mean,' *Critical Inquiry*, 5:1 (Autumn 1978) p. 39.
23 Michel Charles, *Rhétorique de la lecture*, Paris, Seuil, 1977, p. 118.

11 Literary Theory in the Graduate Program

1 William Schaefer, 'Still Crazy After All These Years,' *Profession 78*, New York, MLA, 1978, p. 6.
2 John C. Gerber, 'A Glimpse of English as a Profession,' *Profession 77*, New York, MLA, 1977, p. 27.
3 Reinhard Kuhn, 'The Return to Basics in Graduate Studies,' *Modern Language Studies*, 9:1 (Winter 1978–9) p. 9.
4 John Algeo, 'After the Fall: Some Observations on Graduate Curricula,' *Profession 78*, New York, MLA, 1978, p. 20.
5 Lionel Trilling, *The Liberal Imagination*, New York, Doubleday, 1953, p. 97.
6 W. B. Gallie, *Philosophy and Historical Understanding*, London, Chatto & Windus, 1964, pp. 22–50.
7 Northrop Frye, *Anatomy of Criticism*, New York, Atheneum, 1966, pp.

158–239; Tzvetan Todorov, 'Narrative Transformations,' in *The Poetics of Prose*, Ithaca, Cornell University Press, 1977; Claude Bremond, *Logique du récit*, Paris, Seuil, 1973; Claude Lévi-Strauss, 'L'analyse morphologique de contes russes,' *International Journal of Slavic Linguistics and Poetics*, 3 (1960) pp. 122–49; Hayden White, *Metahistory*, Baltimore, Johns Hopkins University Press, 1973, and *Tropics of Discourse*, Baltimore, Johns Hopkins University Press, 1978.

 8 Roman Jakobson, 'Two Aspects of Language and Two Types of Aphasic Disturbances,' in *Fundamentals of Language*, The Hague, Mouton, 1956.

 9 David Lodge, *The Modes of Modern Writing*, Ithaca, Cornell University Press, 1977.

10 Kenneth Burke, 'Four Master Tropes,' in *A Grammar of Motives*, Berkeley, University of California Press, 1969, pp. 503–17.

11 See the special issue of *Diacritics* entitled 'Freud's Tropology,' 9:1 (Spring 1979).

12 Jean Laplanche, *Life and Death in Psychoanalysis*, Baltimore, Johns Hopkins University Press, 1976, pp. 127–39.

13 Irvin Ehrenpreis, 'Lit in Trouble,' *New York Review of Books* (28 June 1979) p. 40.

14 Stanley Fish, *Self-Consuming Artifacts*, Berkeley, University of California Press, 1972.

15 Norman H. Holland, *Five Readers Reading*, New Haven, Yale University Press, 1975; David Bleich, *Subjective Criticism*, Baltimore, Johns Hopkins University Press, 1978; Wolfgang Iser, *The Implied Reader*, Baltimore, Johns Hopkins University Press, 1974; Michael Riffaterre, *Semiotics of Poetry*, Bloomington, Indiana University Press, 1978.

16 See Paul de Man, *Allegories of Reading*, New Haven, Yale University Press, 1979, chs 5 and 6.

17 See Jonathan Culler, *On Deconstruction*, Ithaca, Cornell University Press, forthcoming, ch. 2.

18 Sigmund Freud, *An Outline of Psychoanalysis*, New York, Norton, 1949, pp. 31–2.

19 See Cynthia Chase, 'Oedipal Textuality: Reading Freud's Reading of Oedipus,' *Diacritics*, 9:1 (Spring 1979) pp. 54–68.

20 Shoshana Felman, 'Introduction,' *Yale French Studies*, 55/56 (1977) p. 8.

Index

Abrams, M. H., 136, 155–68
Adams, Hazard, 71
Algeo, John, 211
allegory, 64
Althusser, Louis, 33
ambiguity, 61–2
Aristotle, 188, 204
Auden, W. H., 140

Bal, Mieke, 169–71
Balzac, Honoré de, 62
Barthes, Roland, 33, 37–8, 102–3,
    108, 169, 170
Baudelaire, Charles, 10, 56, 64,
    87–91, 112–13, 115–16, 141,
    144–6, 208–9
Beardsley, Monroe, 10–11
Benoist, Jean-Marie, 33–4
Bersani, Leo, 10
Blackstone, Bernard, 71
Blake, William, 36, 57, 59, 68–79,
    114, 138–9
Bleich, David, 219
Bloom, Harold, 13–14, 72, 107–11,
    118, 139–40, 142, 166
Booth, Wayne, 169
Bremond, Claude, 169–70, 215
Breton, Andre, 60
Brooks, Cleanth, 122
Brooks, Peter, 179–81
Browne, Sir Thomas, 128
Burke, Kenneth, 216

Carroll, Lewis, 37
Cassirer, Ernst, 24–5, 162
catachresis, 205–6
causation, deconstruction of,
    183–4
Charles, Michel, 208

Chase, Cynthia, 176–7
Chatman, Seymour, 169
Cicero, Marcus Tullius, 188
codes: discursive, 102–7; literary,
    5, 35–7, 55–8, 64–79, 88–91,
    95–8; mythological, 29–30;
    rhetorical, 41, 199–201, 209;
    semantic, 199–202
cognition and tropes, 202–4, 206–7
Coleridge, Samuel Taylor, 156–60,
    163–4
competence, literary, 50–1, 53
conventions: of discourse, 100–3;
    of interpretation, 4–5, 49, 63,
    68–79, 90–7, 125–7, 129–30; of
    literature, 117, 125–7, 129–30; see
    also codes
Crane, R. S., 5
Crane, Stephen, 66–7
Crews, Frederick, 9–10, 53
criticism: marxist, 12–13, 16;
    psychoanalytic, 9–10, 221,
    223–6; reader-response, 10–11,
    38–9, 50–3, 66–8, 119–31, 219;
    romantic sources of, 156–68;
    tasks of, 6; thematic, 4; and
    theology, 160–2
Cummings, E. E., 37

Damon, S. Foster, 69
Davidson, Donald, 207–8
deconstruction, 14–16, 39–43, 65,
    158–60, 165–8, 183, 186–7, 199,
    217
Derrida, Jacques, 14–16, 40–3, 158,
    217, 223
descriptive system, 88–90
Dickens, Charles, 66

différance, 41
Donne, John, 60, 155
Dumarsais, C. C., 188
Durkheim, Emile, 25–6

Eco, Umberto, 34, 199–202, 209
Edwards, Thomas, 72, 74
ego psychology, 52, 219
Ehrenpreis, Irving, 218
elegy, 150–1
Eliot, George, 176–8, 186

fabula, 170–1, 181, 183
fantastic, genre of the, 58–9
fantasy, 10, 59–63
Felix, Minucius, 200
Felix the Cat, 200–1
Ferguson, Frances, 167
Feydeau, Ernest, 55
figurative language, 59–60, 64–5,
    70–9, 83–7, 95–7, 113, 135–9,
    142–4, 157–8, 188–209, 215–17,
    222
Fish, Stanley, 10–11, 68–9, 119–31,
    219, 225
Flaubert, Gustave, 36, 55, 61, 64
Fontanier, Pierre, 138, 188, 205
Forster, E. M., 183
Foucault, Michel, 33
Freud, Sigmund, 6, 25–6, 173–6,
    178–83, 217, 223–5
Frye, Northrop, 7–9, 137, 215

Gallie, W. B., 214–15
Gautier, Théophile, 93
Genette, Gérard, 33, 37–8, 169,
    170, 193–4, 198
genre, 56, 58–9, 66–7, 95–6, 123
Gerber, John C., 211
Gillham, D. G., 71
Glen, Heather, 69
Goethe, J. W. von, 55, 57, 65,
    182–3
graduate study, 210–26
Greimas, A. J., 169

Hartman, Geoffrey, 6, 13, 139
Hawthorne, Nathaniel, 9–10
hermeneutic circle, 66
Hertz, Neil, 110
Hirsch, E. D., 16–17, 71, 75
history, the writing of, 18, 63–5,
    215
Holland, Norman, 52–4, 219
horizon of expectations, 54–8
Horton, Susan, 66
Hrushovski, Benjamin, 169
Hughes, Ted, 133
hypogram, 83, 89, 91

ideal reader, 51–2
influence, poetic, 104–11
interpretation: dominance of,
    4–17, 124, 126–9, 220; relation to
    theory, 218–20; study of, 49, 57,
    63–79, 127–8; variations in,
    48–51, 78, 124–5
interpretive ladder, 66
intertextuality, 38, 83, 86–90, 93–5,
    101–18, 166
Iser, Wolfgang, 219

Jakobson, Roman, 60, 122, 192,
    199–201, 216
James, Henry, 59, 169, 218
Jameson, Fredric, 12–13
Jauss, H. R., 13, 54–8
Jenny, Laurent, 104
Johnson, Barbara, 13, 16
Joyce, James, 37, 200

Kayser, Wolfgang, 169
Keats, John, 140, 143, 152–4
Kellner, Hans, 65
Kermode, Frank, 6
Keynes, Sir Geoffrey, 69, 71
Kristeva, Julia, 31, 104–7
Kuhn, Reinhard, 211

Labov, William, 184–6
Lacan, Jacques, 10, 33, 165

Lamartine, Alphonse de, 141
Lämmert, Eberhard, 169
Langer, Susanne, 25
Laplanche, Jean, 217
Lautréamont, 104–6
Lawrence, D. H., 60
Lévi-Strauss, Claude, 26–31, 33, 215
liberal education, 210–11, 214
linguistics, as model, 27–8, 30–4, 37, 104, 111–12, 116, 118, 200–2
literal and figurative, 202–7
literary history, 13–14, 63–5, 103–10, 161–6
literature: as institution, 6, 48, 54–8, 65–6, 125; and the non-literary, 214–26
Lodge, David, 216
logical positivism, 222
logocentrism, 40
Lubbock, Percy, 169

Mailloux, Stephen, 66–7
Man, Paul de, 13–16, 148, 194–9, 217
Mandrake the Magician, 200–1
Marx, Karl, 25–7, 65
marxist criticism, 16, 25–7
meaning: Bloom's account of, 14, 107–8; Fish's account of, 120–3, 129–30; issue of, 50; presupposition and, 111–16; Riffaterre's account of, 80–92; *see also* signification
metaphor, 39, 60–2, 187–209, 215–17
metonymy, 60–2, 189–202, 206, 209, 215–17
Mill, J. S., 137
Miller, J. Hillis, 15–16
Milton, John, 127–8
mimesis, 161–6
Musset, Alfred de, 104
myth, 29–31
myth criticism, 8–9

Nachträglichkeit, 179–83
narcissism, 156, 225
narrative: complexity of, 186–7; resistance to, 148–50; study of, 38, 169–87, 214–15
natural narrative, 184–6
New Criticism, 3–8, 10–12, 52, 109–10, 122, 155, 157, 161, 220
Nietzsche, Friedrich, 203–4, 222

ode, 136–7
Oedipus, 172–6, 178, 225
origins, in narrative, 177–83

Pavel, Thomas, 169
Peake, Mervyn, 61
Peirce, C. S., 22–5
Perry, Menakhem, 169
philosophy, and literature, 221–3
Plato, 157, 222
poetics, 7–9, 11–12, 37–8, 117–18, 125
poetry, 68–79, 80–99, 107–10, 112–16, 126, 135–4
point of view, 168–71
Popper, Karl, 54
presupposition, 102–18
Price, Martin, 72, 74
Prince, Gerald, 169
primal scene, 179–81
professionalism, 210–14
Propp, Vladimir, 169
Proust, Marcel, 189–90, 192–8
psychoanalysis, and literature, 9–10, 221, 223–6
Puttenham, George, 188

Quintilian, 135, 188

Racine, Jean, 5
reader-response criticism, 10–11, 38–9, 50–3, 66–8, 119–31, 219
reading: importance of, 38–9; study of, 50–79; *see also* interpretation

referentiality, of literary language, 78–9, 81–3, 105, 191–2, 222–3
Rezeptionsästhetik, 54–8, 139
rhetoric, 12, 39–42, 178–9, 188–92, 215–17, 222–3
Riffaterre, Michael, 73, 79–99, 105, 109, 111, 219
Rilke, Maria Rainer, 145–8
Rimbaud, Arthur, 84
Robbe-Grillet, Alain, 172
Romanticism, 13, 64, 155–68, 192
Rousseau, Jean-Jacques, 15, 64, 141, 203
Russian Formalism, 170

Said, Edward, 218
Sand, George, 190
Saussure, Ferdinand de, 22–4, 40, 103
Schaefer, William, 210, 214
Schlovsky, Victor, 169
Schmid, Wolf, 169
Schoenberg, Arnold, 47
Schorer, Mark, 69
Scott, Walter, 61
self-destruction, 15–16, 158–66, 183
semiotics: assumptions of, 48–50; of culture, 28–32; and deconstruction, 39–43; history of, 18–43; and intertextuality, 102–11; of literature, 12, 35–43, 80–99; and metaphor, 199–209; and narrative, 173–87; and presupposition, 111–16; of reading, 48–79, 81–94
Shelley, Mary, 61
Shelley, Percy Bysshe, 140, 142–3, 148–50
Shuster, George, 136–7
sign, 24, 40
signification: Lévi-Strauss on, 26–32; in literature, 13–14, 35–8, 59–62, 69–79, 80–1, 86–93, 100–4, 120–2, 135–54; logic of,

15, 173–8; and narrative, 214–15; and presupposition, 111–16; and rhetoric, 39–42, 215–17; semiotic analysis of, 22–5, 48–51, 100–7
simile, 207–8
sjuzhet, 170, 181
Sophocles, 172–6
Stanzl, Franz, 169
Stendhal, 162–3
Sternberg, Meir, 169
structural explanation, 30–4, 40
structuralism, 16, 33–5
structure, and event, 39–42, 159–60, 208–9
subject, 32–4, 102

teaching, of literature, 212–14, 219
theory and criticism, 160–2
Todorov, Tzvetan, 37, 58–9, 63, 169, 215
Tolkein, J. R. R., 60, 62
transference, 10, 224–5
Trilling, Lionel, 24

Ullmann, Stephen, 189–90, 192–3, 198–9
unity, in literature, 68–70, 81–2

Valéry, Paul, 117
Van Dijk, Teun, 169
Vico, Giambattista, 203
vraisemblance, 60

Wasserman, Earl, 136
White, Hayden, 63–5, 215–16
Whitehead, A. N., 25
Wimsatt, W. K., 11
Wolfman, the, 179–82
Wordsworth, William, 64, 136, 148–9, 151–2, 163–4, 166–7
worlds, literary, 60–2

Yeats, W. B., 150–1, 162–3, 165